German Shepherds For Dummies®

Standard in Brief

The following list briefly summarizes the AKC German Shepherd Dog breed standard. See Appendix C for the complete standard.

- Overall strong, agile, well-muscled, and full of life
- Longer than tall, deep-bodied, with an outline of smooth curves
- Males 24 to 26 inches; females 22 to 24 inches at the shoulders
- Noble, strong, chiseled head; long muzzle parallel to back of skull
- Almond-shaped eyes
- Moderately pointed ears facing forward and set parallel to one another
- Black nose
- Scissors bite
- Shoulders are higher than back, which is level and straight
- Sternum reaches to elbows; moderately tucked-up loin
- Tail is bushy, set low, and hanging in slight curve
- Shoulder blades obliquely angled with well-angulated wrists
- Broad thigh with a right angle between upper and lower thigh
- Double coat of medium length, with dense, straight, harsh outer coat
- Most colors are permitted (except for white); rich colors preferred
- Gait is ground-covering and effortless
- Temperament is confident, fearless but aloof; eager, alert, and willing to work

D0565839

Five-Minute Health Check

You need to spend only a few minutes to ensure a lifetime of good health for your Shepherd. Keep an eye out for the following danger signs:

- **General:** Lameness, lack of coordination, asymmetry of muscles, weight change, bloated abdomen, swelling, coughing, gagging, lethargy, increased aggression, appetite, or water consumption
- **Mouth:** Red, bleeding, swollen, or discolored gums; loose or dirty teeth; sores of the tongue or gums; bad breath
- **Eyes:** Squinting, discharge, cloudiness, discolored whites, unequal or unresponsive pupils
- **Ears:** Bad odor, redness, debris, crusted tips, head shaking or tilting, ear scratching
- **Nose:** Thick or colored discharge, crusted top
- **Feet:** Abrasions, split nails, swollen or misaligned toes
- **Anal region:** Redness, swelling, discharge, tracts; also scooting or licking of the area, black or bloody stool
- **Genitals:** Mammary or testicular changes, discharge from penis or vulva, changes in urine or urination
- **Skin:** Parasites, hair loss, crusts, red spots, lumps, sores

Emergency First Aid

In each of the following cases of emergency, transport your Shepherd as quickly as possible to an emergency veterinarian. (See Chapter 13 for more information about emergency situations and how to handle them.)

Abdominal bloating, restlessness, and attempts to vomit: Go to the emergency vet immediately. The problem could be gastric dilatation volvulus.

Airway obstructions: Wrap your hands around the dog's abdomen behind the rib cage and compress once briskly; doing so should dislodge the obstruction. If the dog is unconscious, pull his tongue forward and explore his throat, removing any obstruction you find.

Bleeding: Cover the wound with clean dressing, apply pressure, elevate the wound site, and apply a cold pack.

Burns: Cool burned areas with cold packs or towels soaked in water. Cover the area with a clean bandage or towel and monitor the dog for shock.

Drowning: Hold the dog upside down so that water can run out of his mouth, and then give artificial respiration or take him to the emergency vet.

Heatstroke: Wet the dog and place him in front of a fan, or immerse him in *cool* (not icy) water. Offer small amounts of water for drinking.

Hypothermia: Warm the dog gradually by wrapping him in a warm blanket and placing plastic bottles filled with hot water outside the blanket, not touching the dog.

Insect stings: Remove any visible stingers as quickly as possible. Administer baking soda and water paste to bee stings and vinegar to wasp stings. Call the vet immediately if your dog has an allergic reaction, including swelling that could interfere with breathing or any change in consciousness.

Poisoning: Call the vet or poison control hotline and give as much information as possible; they can advise whether you need to induce vomiting or bring your dog in to be examined.

Important Phone Numbers

Veterinarian's phone number: _____

After-hours or emergency clinic phone number: _____

National Animal Poison Control Center:

800-548-2423 or 888-4ANIHELP
(888-426-4435), $30 per case — credit card
900-680-0000, $30 per case — phone bill

Hungry Minds™

For Dummies: Bestselling Book Series for Beginners

™

References for the Rest of Us!®

BESTSELLING BOOK SERIES

Do you find that traditional reference books are overloaded with technical details and advice you'll never use? Do you postpone important life decisions because you just don't want to deal with them? Then our *For Dummies*® business and general reference book series is for you.

For Dummies business and general reference books are written for those frustrated and hard-working souls who know they aren't dumb, but find that the myriad of personal and business issues and the accompanying horror stories make them feel helpless. *For Dummies* books use a lighthearted approach, a down-to-earth style, and even cartoons and humorous icons to dispel fears and build confidence. Lighthearted but not lightweight, these books are perfect survival guides to solve your everyday personal and business problems.

"More than a publishing phenomenon, 'Dummies' is a sign of the times."

— The New York Times

"A world of detailed and authoritative information is packed into them..."

— U.S. News and World Report

"...you won't go wrong buying them."

— Walter Mossberg, Wall Street Journal, on For Dummies books

Already, millions of satisfied readers agree. They have made For Dummies the #1 introductory level computer book series and a best-selling business book series. They have written asking for more. So, if you're looking for the best and easiest way to learn about business and other general reference topics, look to *For Dummies* to give you a helping hand.

Hungry Minds™

1/01

German Shepherds

FOR

DUMMIES®

by D. Caroline Coile

Hungry Minds™

Best-Selling Books • Digital Downloads • e-Books • Answer Networks • e-Newsletters • Branded Web Sites • e-Learning

New York, NY ◆ Cleveland, OH ◆ Indianapolis, IN

German Shepherds For Dummies®

Published by
Hungry Minds, Inc.
909 Third Avenue
New York, NY 10022
www.hungryminds.com
www.dummies.com

Library of Congress Control Number: 00-104221

ISBN: 0-7645-5280-5

Printed in the United States of America

10 9 8 7 6 5 4

IB/RQ/QV/QS/IN

Distributed in the United States by Hungry Minds, Inc.

Distributed by CDG Books Canada Inc. for Canada; by Transworld Publishers Limited in the United Kingdom; by IDG Norge Books for Norway; by IDG Sweden Books for Sweden; by IDG Books Australia Publishing Corporation Pty. Ltd. for Australia and New Zealand; by TransQuest Publishers Pte Ltd. for Singapore, Malaysia, Thailand, Indonesia, and Hong Kong; by Gotop Information Inc. for Taiwan; by ICG Muse, Inc. for Japan; by Intersoft for South Africa; by Eyrolles for France; by International Thomson Publishing for Germany, Austria and Switzerland; by Distribuidora Cuspide for Argentina; by LR International for Brazil; by Galileo Libros for Chile; by Ediciones ZETA S.C.R. Ltda. for Peru; by WS Computer Publishing Corporation, Inc., for the Philippines; by Contemporanea de Ediciones for Venezuela; by Express Computer Distributors for the Caribbean and West Indies; by Micronesia Media Distributor, Inc. for Micronesia; by Chips Computadoras S.A. de C.V. for Mexico; by Editorial Norma de Panama S.A. for Panama; by American Bookshops for Finland.

For general information on Hungry Minds' products and services please contact our Customer Care Department within the U.S. at 800-762-2974, outside the U.S. at 317-572-3993 or fax 317-572-4002.

For sales inquiries and reseller information, including discounts, premium and bulk quantity sales, and foreign-language translations, please contact our Customer Care Department at 800-434-3422, fax 317-572-4002, or write to Hungry Minds, Inc., Attn: Customer Care Department, 10475 Crosspoint Boulevard, Indianapolis, IN 46256.

For information on licensing foreign or domestic rights, please contact our Sub-Rights Customer Care Department at 212-884-5000.

For information on using Hungry Minds' products and services in the classroom or for ordering examination copies, please contact our Educational Sales Department at 800-434-2086 or fax 317-572-4005.

Please contact our Public Relations Department at 212-884-5163 for press review copies or 212-884-5000 for author interviews and other publicity information or fax 212-884-5400.

For authorization to photocopy items for corporate, personal, or educational use, please contact Copyright Clearance Center, 222 Rosewood Drive, Danvers, MA 01923, or fax 978-750-4470.

About the Author

Caroline Coile has owned, trained, studied, and competed with dogs for most of her life and still finds them fascinating, frustrating, and fun. Never content to accept the established dogma of the dog world, her interest in getting to the real truth led her to research the behavior, physiology, and genetics of dogs, earning a Ph.D. along the way. She has shared her findings in over 100 scientific journal and dog magazine articles and in 17 books about dogs. Her dog writing awards include the Dog Writer's Association of America Maxwell Award, the Denlinger Award, and the Eukanuba Canine Health Award.

Her own dogs include Best in Show, Best in Specialty Show, and Pedigree Award winners, as well as a #1 ranked obedience dog. Others have never set foot in any ring but are still Best in Yard winners and #1 in various vital categories, including puking on manuscripts, digging holes in chairs, pushing people off beds, and grabbing food off counters. This book is dedicated to them: Baha, Kara, Khyber, Bobby, Khyzi, Junior, Sissy, Dixie, Hypatia, Savannah, Kitty, Beany, Jeepers, Wolfman, Stinky, Oman, Minka, Isis, Luna, and Honey.

Author's Acknowledgments

The author is grateful to Dr. Zoë Backman for her invaluable review of the manuscript and her helpful suggestions. Special thanks are due to Chendra Conklin, along with Zoë, for the immense compilation of titles in Appendix D. Finally, a heartfelt thank you to Pam Mourouzis for whipping it all into shape!

About Howell Book House

Committed to the Human/Companion Animal Bond

Thank you for choosing a book brought to you by the pet experts at Howell Book House, a division of Hungry Minds. And welcome to the family of pet owners who've put their trust in Howell books for nearly 40 years!

Pet ownership is about relationships — the bonds people form with their dogs, cats, horses, birds, fish, small mammals, reptiles, and other animals. Howell Book House/Hungry Minds understands that these are some of the most important relationships in life, and that it's vital to nurture them through enjoyment and education. The happiest pet owners are those who know they're taking the best care of their pets — and with Howell books owners have this satisfaction. They're happy, educated owners, and as a result, they have happy pets, and that enriches the bond they share.

Howell Book House was established in 1961 by Mr. Elsworth S. Howell, an active and proactive dog fancier who showed English Setters and judged at the prestigious Westminster Kennel Club show in New York. Mr. Howell based his publishing program on strength of content, and his passion for books written by experienced and knowledgeable owners defined Howell Book House and has remained true over the years. Howell's reputation as the premier pet book publisher is supported by the distinction of having won more awards from the Dog Writers Association of America than any other publisher. Howell Book House/Hungry Minds has over 400 titles in publication, including such classics as The American Kennel Club's *Complete Dog Book*, the *Dog Owner's Home Veterinary Handbook, Blessed Are the Brood Mares,* and *Mother Knows Best: The Natural Way to Train Your Dog.*

When you need answers to questions you have about any aspect of raising or training your companion animals, trust that Howell Book House/Hungry Minds has the answers. We welcome your comments and suggestions, and we look forward to helping you maximize your relationships with your pets throughout the years.

The Howell Book House Staff

Publisher's Acknowledgments

We're proud of this book; please send us your comments through our Online Registration Form located at www.dummies.com.

Some of the people who helped bring this book to market include the following:

Acquisitions, Editorial, and Media Development

Project Editor: Pamela Mourouzis

Senior Editor: Scott Prentzas

Technical Editor: Dr. Zoë Backman

Editorial Administrator: Michelle Hacker

Cover Photo: FPG, © Adolf Schmidecker

Production

Project Coordinator: Maridee Ennis

Layout and Graphics: Amy Adrian, Jason Guy, Angie Hunckler, Clint Lahnen, Heather Pope, Brent Savage, Rashell Smith, Julie Trippetti, Erin Zeltner

Special Art: Barbara Frake

Proofreaders: Laura Albert, Sally Burton, John Greenough, Susan Moritz

Indexer: Richard T. Evans

Hungry Minds Consumer Reference Group

Business: Kathleen A. Welton, Vice President and Publisher; Kevin Thornton, Acquisitions Manager

Cooking/Gardening: Jennifer Feldman, Associate Vice President and Publisher

Education/Reference: Diane Graves Steele, Vice President and Publisher

Lifestyles/Pets: Kathleen Nebenhaus, Vice President and Publisher; Tracy Boggier, Managing Editor

Travel: Michael Spring, Vice President and Publisher; Suzanne Jannetta, Editorial Director; Brice Gosnell, Publishing Director

Hungry Minds Consumer Editorial Services: Kathleen Nebenhaus, Vice President and Publisher; Kristin A. Cocks, Editorial Director; Cindy Kitchel, Editorial Director

Hungry Minds Consumer Production: Debbie Stailey, Production Director

Contents at a Glance

Table of Contents

Introduction

. . . .

*E*verybody thinks that they know the German Shepherd Dog (commonly referred to as the German Shepherd). Many of us grew up with Rin Tin Tin, or we saw German Shepherds in nightly news reports breaking up riots, or we saw them in neighbors' backyards protecting children. But that only scratches the surface of one of the most fascinating and confusing breeds on Earth. And if you're thinking of adding a German Shepherd to your family, or you already have one, you need to know this breed in depth.

It takes only a little investigation to discover that the German Shepherd is a complex breed. All you need to do is flip through the ads of a dog magazine to be inundated with terms and abbreviations like Grand Victrix, SV, VA, and *Bundesleistungshueten.* It's hard to know whether you're buying a dog with a sought-after title or a dreaded disease! And although health-conscious conversations among owners of most other breeds might center around flea control and worming schedules, German Shepherd owners throw around terms such as *degenerative myelopathy, pannus,* and *perianal fistula.* Breeding decisions in other breeds may be based on coat color or length; in German Shepherds, a breeder must be ready to recite an OFA number or a PennHip rating. In most breeds, the biggest training decisions that owners face is whether they want to use a choke or a buckle collar; in German Shepherds, it's whether you want to include Schutzhund or search-and-rescue. Whether it's selection, nutrition, routine health care, training, competing, or just having fun, there's more to it with a German Shepherd than with other breeds. That's because there's more to German Shepherds in general.

Can you own a German Shepherd and remain oblivious to its finer points and intricacies? Sure. But why would you want to miss out?

This book explains not only the basics of the German Shepherd, but also the details that make this breed unique. Even if your shelves are lined with dog books, I wrote this book to be the one book you wear out. It's not a generic dog care book, but instead a German Shepherd Dog care book. It's not filled with unrealistic scare tactics about dog care or with hand-me-down dog lore that has no basis in fact. It's filled with breed-specific information that can help you get the most out of life with a new best friend.

About This Book

This book is a reference book, not a textbook; you're not required to read it from cover to cover to get the information you need. You choose how to read it — go to the table of contents and select an individual chapter that interests you, go to the index to find information about a specific problem you and your dog are having, or curl up in front of the fireplace with your Shepherd and read it from beginning to end if you like. The point is to *empower* you to be a good dog owner, not to lecture you or guilt you into doing so.

How This Book Is Organized

I want you to be able to find what you're looking for quickly and easily, especially if you're in an emergency situation, so I've organized this book as logically as possible. Here's a rundown of what you'll find in each part of the book.

Part I: Getting to Know German Shepherds

Of course I think that the German Shepherd is among the best breeds out there, but I want to convince you of that as well. This part traces the breed's origins so that you can come to appreciate the tremendous care that went into the development of the German Shepherd. Here you can familiarize yourself with the essentials of the German Shepherd physique and mystique, and also do some soul searching to decide whether you are right for this breed.

Part II: Finding the German Shepherd for You

Once you've decided that the German Shepherd is the breed for you, make sure that you get the best dog for you. This part warns you about the red flags and rip-offs and steers you toward the reliable sources of good-quality dogs. And when you're facing a litter of adorable pups, you can find advice on choosing the one who best matches your lifestyle and your expectations.

Part III: Bringing Up Baby

This part of the book deals with everyday life with a German Shepherd, and life with a German Shepherd every day. Here you can find tips to get yourself and your new dog through those difficult first days, hopefully saving your sanity, your carpets, and maybe even your pup's life. I also give you advice on what stuff you really need to buy for your dog and what you can do without, from toys to foods to grooming tools.

Without training, even the best dogs aren't likely to be very well behaved. That's why this part also gives you information about the latest training methods. Nonetheless, no matter how good a job you do, your dog is bound to develop a few bothersome behaviors — look here for the best ways of dealing with them.

Part IV: Keeping Your Dog Healthy

Trying to decide what's normal, what's abnormal, and what's an emergency in an animal with a body so different from your own is a little scary at first — especially when that animal can't even tell you where it hurts. Few dogs make it through life without getting sick or injured. You're the front line of defense when it comes to your dog's health, so this part supplies you with formidable ammunition. I explain how to find and work with a good veterinarian and also tell you about the special needs that an older dog has.

Part V: Having Fun with Your German Shepherd

German Shepherds are smart — channeling their intelligence into productive activities is critical for this breed. In case you can't think of productive activities for a dog, this part includes enough ideas to keep you exhausted. Your Adonis can strut in the show ring, your Einstein can shine in the obedience ring, your Carl Lewis can run marathons with you, or your Mother Theresa can assist people in need — you can find an activity for just about every German Shepherd!

Part VI: The Part of Tens

Every *For Dummies* book includes a Part of Tens — quick and easy chapters that list ten points on various topics. In this book's Part of Tens, you can find ten tips on traveling safely with your dog and ten fun games to play with your GSD.

Appendixes

Dog fanciers toss around a lot of lingo that may be Greek to you — that's why I've included a complete glossary that covers dog parts, dog maladies, and more. I also list resources for more information about GSDs and the complete AKC breed standard. Finally, if you're interested in showing your dog, look to the appendixes for information about titles, awards, and rankings.

Icons Used in This Book

To help you navigate your way through this book and to highlight important information, I've placed icons next to certain paragraphs. Following are the icons and what they mean:

This icon points out ways to do something easier, faster, or better.

This icon draws your attention to information that's worth remembering or referencing again.

This icon highlights dangers to your dog's health or well-being.

This icon marks products or services that earn "two paws up" for their usefulness.

When you need the help of a veterinary professional, this icon alerts you to that fact.

Where to Go from Here

You can use this book in many different ways. If you don't have a German Shepherd yet but want to find out what the breed is like, start with Part I. If you want to know what you need to do to get the very best GSD out there (as if they're not all wonderful!), turn to Part II. If you're already the proud owner of a Shepherd, simply find the information that applies to your situation today, whether you need to begin training, want to bone up on doggy nutrition, or want to show off how great your dog is by entering him in conformation shows. Whatever you do, please use this book to make your German Shepherd's life — and thus your own — happier and healthier.

Part I
Getting to Know German Shepherds

The 5th Wave   By Rich Tennant

"Okay, before I let the new puppy out, let's remember to be real still so we don't startle him."

In this part . . .

The German Shepherd enjoys a universal admiration that few other breeds share. This hero worship is not undeserved; no breed of dog has helped so many people in so many ways. It's only natural that many families considering a new dog think of adding a German Shepherd to the family. But adding even such an intelligent and noble animal to your household is not without pitfalls, and hard though it may be to believe, the German Shepherd is not for everyone. Make sure that you know what you're getting into before you take the plunge into German Shepherd guardianship.

The chapters in this part introduce you to the German Shepherd, give you insights into its reason for being, and trace the story of how these dogs came to be like they are today.

Chapter 1

Making the Decision of a Lifetime

In This Chapter

▶ Deciding whether you're ready for any dog, much less a German Shepherd

▶ Understanding the time, energy, and money involved in dog ownership

▶ Looking at the pitfalls of living with a big, smart, active dog

*W*hoever said, "You can choose your friends, but you can't choose your family," obviously never picked out a dog. With a dog, you can choose both your friend *and* your family!

Despite this great opportunity, most people devote about as much time to choosing a new dog as they do to ordering lunch from a drive-thru window. Not surprisingly, in the United States, even more people divorce their dogs than their spouses. The problem is, unlike divorcees, spurned dogs don't end up in singles bars — they end up in animal shelters. For most of them, it's a one-way trip. So my first mission in this section is to talk you out of getting a dog and to try even harder to talk you out of getting a German Shepherd. If you're still not convinced that this is the mistake of a lifetime, you just might be ready to choose the friend of a lifetime.

The first point to consider is whether you're ready to care for *any* type of dog. Take this quiz to help you assess your dog-readiness:

   ✔ Can you share several hours a day with a dog?

   ✔ Can you devote at least one hour each day to exercising a dog?

   ✔ Can you devote at least 30 minutes each day to training a dog?

   ✔ Can you feed a dog on a regular schedule?

   ✔ Can you provide safe and comfortable sleeping and living accommodations for a dog?

   ✔ Can you afford the food and veterinary bills for a dog?

   ✔ Can you keep a dog for his entire life?

Obviously, you're supposed to answer "yes" to each of these questions. If you did, great! Before heading out to get a dog, however, you need to think about the specifics of dog ownership. The following sections walk you through each major component of owning a dog in general, and a German Shepherd Dog in particular.

Sharing Your Time

Can you picture yourself in this scenario?

> You're late to work again, so you push the dog outside, hustle the kids out the door, and spend a grueling day making a buck. You come home dead tired but determined to spend quality time with your kids. The dog keeps butting in and dancing on top of the Monopoly board on the floor, so back outside he goes. A little while later, your dinner guests arrive, and the dog is sniffing them in embarrassing places — how'd he get back inside, anyway? After the guests are gone, you remember that it's time to feed the dog (patting yourself on the back for being such a responsible dog owner). You go in the yard to fetch the dog and fall into a hole, angrily noticing that all the plants have been dug up.

Is that dog incorrigible? No, that dog is neglected. A dog is an active, intelligent animal who can't be subjected to a life sentence in solitary confinement. Nor is he a toy that you can put away until you feel like playing with it again, or breathing furniture that's there to provide an all-American backdrop for your family picture. If you plan to get a family dog, you must treat him as a member of the family.

A German Shepherd in particular is smarter than the average dog. He needs companionship and activity — even more than most other breeds do. You don't have to quit your job to get a German Shepherd, but you do have to make time for your dog just as though he were a second job, with no time off.

Exercising

For some perverse reason, dogs love to exercise. This trait is incredibly irritating to many dog owners (although a major appeal to the health-crazed minority). German Shepherds *really* love to exercise. They were bred to cover miles of territory every day and to keep on the move for hours. A stroll around the block is not going to cut it.

You have a few choices if you decide to bring a GSD into your family:

- ✔ You can buy 20 acres of land and fence it securely so that your Shepherd can patrol the perimeter.

- ✔ You can buy a doggy treadmill and run up your electric bill.

- ✔ You can get up off the couch and become healthy yourself. Walk, or even jog, your dog a couple of miles every day.

You can cheat by shortening the walk but adding a play session. This way, you get to stand relatively still while throwing sticks and balls that your dog can retrieve. (For more on playing and exercising with your dog, see Chapters 15 and 19.)

If physical exertion is out of the question for you, strongly reconsider getting a German Shepherd.

Training

Most people think that they want canny canines, but very few people are prepared to deal with and nurture that intelligence. An intelligent child who is given no direction or stimulation is on the way to becoming a problem child; the same is true for an intelligent dog. If you plan to keep your dog in a cage for a good part of the day, or locked in the house alone while you work, you don't want a dog whose mind is racing with ideas and who needs entertainment. A dog can't read a book or watch TV when things are slow — he needs activities to do. A smart dog will look for ways to entertain himself, and he will find them.

The problem is that even the most intelligent dog is not smart enough to think of helpful things to do for entertainment. True, he may decide to redecorate your house, but chances are that ripped drapes and chewed paneling are not your thing. A bored dog will dig, bark, get into the garbage, and chew. Then what happens? His owner tries to remove all the items with which the dog could entertain himself or locks the dog in a cage or run.

A dog will always find a way to do something, even if it's only barking or biting himself — and when he finally gets a chance to do something, he will be so crazed with relief and ecstasy that his owners may consider him uncontrollable. They conclude that this supposedly intelligent dog is actually stupid and wild and take him on a one-way trip to the dog pound.

You need to exercise your German Shepherd's mind as well as its body. Training your dog not only tires out his little brain but, he being a German Shepherd, actually results in learning on the dog's part! You have in your power the ability to create a being (perhaps the only one in the world) who will pay attention to what you say and even mind you.

For some breeds, training is a nice option; for German Shepherds, it is a necessity. They are too smart, too powerful, and too active to remain without a leader. If you don't plan to lead, get out of their way, because the dogs will gladly take over. And although GSDs may be smart for dogs, they really aren't leadership material.

Despite (or perhaps because of) their being the near equivalent of canine Einsteins, German Shepherds require you to have plenty of patience. Can you calmly say, "Now give me my wallet — oh, I see you've eaten a $50 bill" and then walk away without contemplating murder? Can you return to your car to find your dog's face poking up from a sea of upholstery foam and simply get in and sit on the springs for the drive home? German Shepherds are ingenious, and like gifted children they're prone to occasional experimentation. If you're thinking of owning a GSD, keep this inevitability in mind.

Calculating the Cost of Loving Index

"All you add is love," the ads claim — and a lot of work and a mound of money. Dogs are the best love money can buy, but they don't come cheap. Besides the initial cost of a German Shepherd (which can range from $100 to $10,000), you need to feed the dog, house the dog, and fix the dog — not to mention all the fun stuff you can spend money on, such as toys, accessories, classes, and competitions, and all the not-fun stuff, such as replacing your carpets, doors, and plants.

Use the following expense calculator to estimate the cost of dog ownership.

One-Time Expenses

Dog: _____

Puppy vaccinations: _____

Fence: _____

Cage: _____

Bedding: _____

Collar and tags: _____

Leash: _____

Grooming tools: _____

First-aid kit: _____

Neuter/spay:	_____
Toys:	_____
Total one-time expenses:	_____

Yearly Expenses

Food:	_____
Checkup/vaccinations:	_____
Heartworm preventive:	_____
More toys:	_____
Total yearly expenses:	_____

When-You-Least-Expect-It Expenses

Replace carpeting:	_____
Replace interior of car:	_____
Emergency trip to vet to remove carpeting and auto upholstery from the dog's stomach:	_____
Total when-you-least-expect-it expenses:	_____

Optional Expenses

Classes:	_____
More classes:	_____
New home with a bigger yard:	_____
Total optional expenses:	_____

Grand Estimated Total Over the Next 12 Years: _____

Were you shocked at that 12-year total? You're not alone. But remember that you get what you give. Owning a dog brings you many benefits, including the possibility of a longer life!

You may think that you can scrimp a little on some of these things, but you can't scrimp on the most important things: feeding, housing, and caring for your dog.

Feeding the dog

Dogs not only like to eat, but they *have* to eat. German Shepherds are good-sized dogs who need to eat 3 to 6 cups of food each day. Feeding a dog does not require the combined efforts of the great chefs of Europe, but it does require consistency and an outlay of money to buy a decent-quality food. You can't just throw your leftovers in a vat and slop the dog, or you will spend all the money you think you're saving at the vet's office. A typical food bill for an adult GSD is $300 to $500 per year.

Some dog owners think that if they have to stay late at work or even spend the night away from home, the dog can just go without. This approach is not right, and it's not healthy. Then there's the child who promises to feed the dog but fails to keep the promise. Too often, the parents resolve to teach the child a lesson by not giving in and feeding the dog. Huh? A dog needs nourishment just like you do, and neglecting to feed him is cruel.

For information about what to feed, how much to feed, and how often to feed a German Shepherd, see Chapter 7.

Housing the dog

Where will your new family member live? In the basement? The garage? A pen? What a lovely welcome! You can modify these places to serve as temporary quarters, but if you want your German Shepherd to be a part of your family, you must make some compromises so that he can share your household. Some people who want their dogs to function as guard dogs reason that sleeping inside will spoil them for their duties, but you'll find that your dog is far more likely to guard his family if he actually knows who his family is.

This doesn't mean that you have to give your dog the run of the house and first rights to all your furniture, however. A dog needs his own place, so wherever you want your dog to sleep, make him a special spot all his own, complete with soft bedding. A cage (or "crate") fulfills this role; I suggest that you purchase one. See Chapter 5 for what to look for in a good cage.

If you plan for your dog to spend a good deal of his time outside, you must provide a warm shelter for winter, shade for summer, and a fence year-round. A German Shepherd's intelligence is both his greatest asset and perhaps his greatest undoing. Owners convinced of their dog's high IQ figure that Rin Tin Twin is too smart to need supervision and allow him to roam at will. The smartest dog is nonetheless dumb by (most) human standards, and a loose dog is likely to be a dead dog eventually.

Keep in mind too that, like all dogs, German Shepherds shed. In fact, German Shepherds shed a lot. If you can't tolerate hair in any part of your home, a GSD is *not* the dog for you. Also consider that GSDs are large dogs. If you live in tight quarters, adding a dog to step over every time you cross the room may not be a good idea.

Fixing the dog and keeping him healthy

Your German Shepherd will have to go the veterinarian, and although vets may be nice folks, they don't work for free. Your dog will need vaccinations, worming, neutering, and heartworm checks and preventives. Add a couple of visits for when your dog is puking on your couch and other assorted pleasantries, and you have a normal year's vet expenses of about $150 to $400.

As with people, the threat of catastrophic illness looms. German Shepherds are predisposed to several serious health problems, including hip and elbow dysplasia, osteochondrosis dessicans, cauda equina, gastric torsion, and perianal fistulas, all of which can be very expensive to treat (see Chapter 12 for details). Cancer, trauma, and all sorts of weird ailments can cost thousands of dollars to treat as well. Chances are they won't happen, and you can't be expected to spend your children's college fund on your dog, but be aware of the possibility of such a problem. Veterinary bills are usually highest in the first and last years of a dog's life.

Having a Friend of a Lifetime for a Lifetime

How does a dog fit into your long-term plans? Do you know where you'll be living a year from now? Can you say with assurance that you'll live somewhere that allows you to have a dog and that you will not allow your circumstances to change to the point where you can no longer keep a dog? If you add a baby to the household, does the dog go?

Plan on having your Shepherd for the next 12 years or so and on caring for him every single day of those 12 years. Shepherds make great dogs in part because of their loyalty to their families. Don't get a Shepherd on a trial-run basis. They are sentient beings who do not understand why they have been banished to the backyard or abandoned to a dog shelter. After you use up your dog's irresistibly cute puppy months, few people will line up to offer him a new home. If the old standby line "We found him a home in the country" were true, country roads would be impassable with the millions of these former city-slicker dogs. That home in the country was most likely the city pound, and most dogs don't leave there alive.

The number-one pet problem is lack of responsibility and commitment. The human half is always the unfaithful one — your dog will remain loyal to you no matter how big a jerk you are. Can you be as responsible as your dog? Before you get a dog, can you vow to care for him "in sickness and in health, for richer or poorer, 'til death do us part?"

Now's the time to sit down for a serious reality check with your entire family. If your reality check bounces, fish make great pets!

Chapter 2

Setting the Standard for the Breed

• •

• •

og fanciers know that having a defined standard for each breed is vital to the breed's success. The folks who control that standard, and thus the breed, work to eliminate or reduce health problems, develop a sound temperament in the dogs, and so on. This chapter explains how the German Shepherd Dog came into being and was developed into the dog that we know and love today — the most incredibly versatile breed ever known. To understand this amazing dog, you must understand its roots.

Understanding How the Breed Was Developed

A low growl warns of an intruder's presence . . . A steady pull guides a blind person away from danger . . . A hurtling form brings down a fleeing criminal . . . A lithe shape searches a pile of rubble for buried victims . . . A warm body huddles close to keep a lost person alive . . . The best dog in the world joins his special boy on a grand adventure every day and guards the foot of his bed every night.

Intelligent, loyal, noble, sensitive, courageous — the German Shepherd is what we wish humans were like. It is the dog not only of movie action adventures, but also of real-life heroism. But this wasn't always so. The GSD of today arose from humble beginnings, an unassuming dog with a great work ethic. Many such dogs existed in the late 19th century; what eventually made the German Shepherd different was in large part the life work of a single man. Max von Stephanitz shaped the German Shepherd into the breed that would become the most popular and versatile dog in the world.

Creating the breed

Dogs have shared a relationship with people throughout recorded history — a relationship originally based on function. Some dogs were better at sounding alarms due to intruders, for example, and some were better at chasing down game. Eventually, as breeders mated the best guards to the best guards and the best hunters to the best hunters, breeds were born. As other animal species became domesticated, dogs who could guard and control them became especially important. The German Shepherd claims these early stock-tending dogs as its forefathers.

In time, the strains of dogs became more and more specialized so that by the 19th century, the German countryside was home to a group of adept but diverse sheepherding dogs. Many of the dogs were not large or tough enough to handle some of the larger, stubborn sheep found in Germany.

Enter Captain Max Emil Frederick von Stephanitz, a cavalry officer who had some knowledge of functional animal anatomy. He admired the German sheepdogs but envisioned a dog who consistently combined all their best traits. Although he experimented (somewhat unsuccessfully) with breeding dogs in the 1890s, his luck changed in 1899, when he found the dog who embodied his ideal. He bought the dog and immediately changed the dog's name to Horand von Grafhath. Having found the dog who would found the breed, von Stephanitz founded a club devoted to the breed, the *Verein fur Deutsche Schaferhunde* (SV), with Horand the first dog registered.

The SV immediately began holding annual shows, in which von Stephanitz judged and chose the best male (the *Sieger*) and female (the *Siegerin*). He based his awards not only on the dogs' merits but also on their pedigrees and their ability to counteract prevalent faults in the breed. Because breeders usually flocked to the *Sieger* of the year, von Stephanitz was able to steer the breed's development.

As the SV grew, local branch clubs arose. Local Breed Wardens were appointed who inspected litters and evaluated breedings. This iron-fisted policy may have seemed tough, but it was largely responsible for the breed's rapid rise in quality. The policy is still in place today.

Proving the dogs' usefulness

von Stephanitz demanded that the dogs be useful. Beauty, though appreciated, was not a top priority. Sound temperament and body, as well as a zest for life and work, were paramount, and he devised herding and obedience trials to test them. Yet even as the ultimate German sheepherding breed was growing in popularity, German sheepherding was on the decline. Now that von Stephanitz had created the sheepdog of his dreams, it was threatened with large-scale unemployment!

Leave it to von Stephanitz to reinvent his precious breed, promoting German Shepherds as police and military dogs. Although the military scoffed at the notion at first, he demonstrated the dogs' courage and ability to deter and apprehend criminals by placing several dogs with the police force. As the dogs' reputation for police work grew, the military adopted a few. Those few were so good at their mission that when German troops entered into World War I, they did so with German Shepherds at their sides. Whether searching for wounded soldiers, laying phone lines, or serving as messengers, sentries, or guards, German Shepherds introduced a new element into warfare.

Taking the dogs worldwide

In the early 1900s, purebred dog mania swept across Europe and America. Anything that looked like a pure breed and could be trotted around a show ring was fair game. The German Shepherd was no exception, and the first GSD (then called the German Sheepdog) was registered by the American Kennel Club in 1908. Perhaps because it didn't have the eccentric looks or foo-foo ways of some of the more popular breeds, it wasn't much of a hit, and those early imports had little impact on present GSDs in the United States.

With WWI, all things German became unsavory, and the breed lost much of the favor it had found in America. The American Kennel Club changed the breed's name to Shepherd Dog in an attempt to protect the breed from patriotic zealots. When the war ended in 1918, the American public was quick to forgive the breed its German heritage and, coupled with the tales of the dogs' incredible feats of war service, was even faster to welcome them into its homes. In fact, wherever soldiers came from, German Shepherds followed them home.

Suffering from growing pains

In short order, the German Shepherd became the most popular breed in the world. It seemed that the only limit to the dogs' abilities was the imagination of the people who trained them. During WWII, they were the first dogs to be trained to locate buried victims in British air-raids, the pioneers of today's search-and-rescue dogs. After the war, they were trained to guide the blind, beginning a legacy of helping disabled people to live independently. Their presence on police forces throughout the world grew to unsurpassed levels. Just as important, they proved to be dependable and loyal family members. As more and more German Shepherds gained fame through heroic deeds, often literally saving the lives of family members, more and more families chose GSDs.

Serious dog fanciers continued to breed, compete, and win with GSDs, excelling at obedience, trailing, and conformation competitions. German Shepherds became invincible in the obedience ring and dominated the Working Group, and later the Herding Group, at AKC shows. The German club, the SV, grew to become the largest and most powerful breed club in the world.

Howlywood stars: Famous German Shepherds

Amid the influx of Shepherds from Germany following WWI came a dog that never distinguished himself in the show ring but became the most famous dog in America. Etzel von Oeringen was born in 1917, trained for police work in Germany, and brought to America in 1921, where he eventually became the property of an actor/writer and dog trainer team. Retrained and renamed for the movies, "Strongheart" was an instant screen sensation, the first truly famous animal star.

Such was Strongheart's fame that it seemed it would never be eclipsed. Yet the greatest canine star of all-time had already been born and would become a household name in a very short time. The story began during WWI in a bombed German dog kennel. An American army patrol discovered the lone survivors, a mother and her five newborns, and took them back to base. After the war, one of the patrols, Lee Duncan, returned home with two of the pups, a brother and sister named Rin Tin Tin and Nannette (named after good-luck dolls that children gave to returning soldiers in Europe).

Nannette's luck didn't hold, as she soon died of distemper, but Rin Tin Tin (or Rinty to his friends) went with Duncan to Los Angeles. In 1922, Rinty was entered in a dog show, which he lost, and a jumping competition, which he won with a jump of nearly 12 feet. The jumping event was filmed, and Rinty was a natural on the big screen. He appeared in several film shorts doing various stunts, until his big break came when he was able to step in and play the part of a wolf, completing in 20 minutes what the studio had not accomplished with a real wolf in days. The grateful studio was a small one named Warner Bothers, and it decided to feature Rinty in first one film and then film after film. Rin Tin Tin is credited as the dog who made Warner Brothers.

Whenever something gets popular, people try to make a buck off of it. German Shepherds have been very popular for a long time, and a lot of people have tried to make money at their expense. Even by 1920, opportunists had stepped in and begun breeding GSDs as fast as they could. Not every German Shepherd has the temperament, health, or physical qualities that exemplify the breed, so not every dog should be bred. Yet bad dog after bad dog was bred repeatedly, with no regard for the quality of the dogs produced or the lives they would live. Dogs with poor temperaments were sold to unsuspecting families, and the German Shepherd gained a reputation as a biter.

Breeders also sold dogs in poor health, with their loving families agonizing over diseases that seemed to plague the breed. The German Shepherd became the poster child for hip dysplasia (see Chapter 12), and with the public's growing awareness of hereditary problems in purebred dogs, GSD show breeders got the blame. More German Shepherds fell into the wrong hands, often owned by people who thought that the meaner they could make them, the better protectors they would be. It doesn't work that way, and German Shepherds were blamed unjustly for the bad habits they had been taught. As numbers grew, prices fell, sometimes to nothing, and more people got GSD pups on a whim only to abandon them at the slightest problem.

The German Shepherd has always had staunch and devoted supporters, however. Many breeders refused to sacrifice quality for quantity, and many owners remained who demanded and understood the best this breed could be. Between them, they raised the German Shepherd to even greater heights. The German Shepherd of today remains the most versatile of all breeds, sound of body and mind and adhering as closely as possible to the ideal vision of the breed. It is constantly tested in family homes, working jobs, and performance trials, and by the breed standard of perfection.

Defining the Modern Standard for the Breed

German Shepherds look the way they do for a reason: They're built to do a certain job. But looks aren't everything. A good-looking GSD should also be able to move in an efficient, sound manner and have the good sense to be able to direct its good-looking, good-moving self to do good work. The good Shepherd of today is the result of generations of breeding to an exacting blueprint, a standard of perfection of the idealized German Shepherd.

The breed standard is a comparison by which every individual GSD can be evaluated against the idealized perfect German Shepherd. It ensures that breeders will continue to strive to improve the breed without straying from its original type. In the United States, the accepted standard for German Shepherds is the one that the German Shepherd Dog Club of America submits to the American Kennel Club. Other German Shepherd organizations that are members of the World Union of SV Clubs (WUSV) abide by the SV standard. Few substantial differences exist between the AKC and SV standards, however. A good German Shepherd is a good German Shepherd, no matter by what standard he is judged.

The official AKC standard is printed in Appendix C; I present a summary here. To help you understand the points that the standard mentions, Figure 2-1 highlights the key parts of a German Shepherd.

First of all, a German Shepherd should give the overall impression of agile strength, being well-muscled, alert, noble, and full of life. He is fearless, self-confident, and somewhat aloof, at the same time not hostile or shy.

Males are distinctly masculine, and females distinctly feminine. Males are 24 to 26 inches in height at the *withers* (the highest point of shoulder blades), and females 22 to 24 inches. Both sexes are longer than they are tall, ideally in the proportion of 10 to 8½.

The dog's head is noble, cleanly chiseled, and strong without coarseness. The expression is keen and intelligent, with dark, almond-shaped eyes, erect ears, and a black nose. The muzzle is long and parallel to the top of the skull when viewed from the side, without an abrupt stop at the forehead. The jaws are strong, with full dentition and a scissors bite.

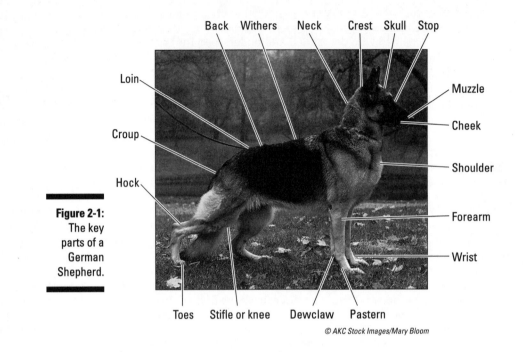

Back Withers Neck Crest Skull Stop

Loin

Croup

Hock

Muzzle

Cheek

Shoulder

Forearm

Wrist

Toes Stifle or knee Dewclaw Pastern

Figure 2-1:
The key
parts of a
German
Shepherd.

© AKC Stock Images/Mary Bloom

The withers are relatively high and slope downward onto the level back. The chest is deep, with the *prosternum,* or forechest, positioned ahead of the shoulder when seen in profile. The abdomen is neither paunchy nor extremely tucked up. The loin is strong and of moderate length, and the croup is relatively long and gradually sloping. The tail is set on low and carried fairly low in a saberlike curve. It is bushy and long, with the last vertebra reaching at least to the hock.

The shoulder blades are long and obliquely angled, meeting the upper arm at an approximate right angle. The forelegs are straight, with oval bone. The strong, springy pasterns slope at about 25 degrees from the vertical. The feet are short, compact, and well arched. The upper and lower thighs are well muscled and articulate at an approximate right angle. The hock is short.

The body is covered with a double coat of medium length. The outer coat is coarse, straight, or slightly wavy and lies close to the body. Most colors are permissible, with rich, strong colors preferred.

Certain faults are considered so untypical of or undesirable for the breed that they are disqualifying faults. Although they don't in any way detract from a dog's ability to function as a companion or worker (except, perhaps, the one about trying to bite the judge), they do render a dog ineligible for conformation competition. As such, dogs with disqualifying faults, as well as other serious faults, should not be bred except under exceptional circumstances.

> ✔ Cropped or hanging ears
>
> ✔ Noses not predominantly black
>
> ✔ Undershot jaw
>
> ✔ Docked tail
>
> ✔ A white coat
>
> ✔ Attempts to bite a judge

The possession of a disqualifying trait doesn't necessarily make a dog unsuitable as a pet. For example, white GSDs are just as healthy as the black-and-tan ones and make beautiful pets and wonderful companions.

Appreciating How a GSD Moves

The German Shepherd standard of perfection involves more than just arbitrary beauty marks. In theory, a dog who is built right moves right — but that doesn't always happen in practice. That's why a big part of evaluating a German Shepherd is watching him move from every angle.

The German Shepherd Dog was developed to trot tirelessly for a full day's work, acting as a moving fence while performing its duties as a herding dog. Subsequent roles also require tireless athleticism, whether the dog is a patrol dog, a service dog, or just a companion.

The German Shepherd standard describes the most efficient trot in dogdom. The hallmark of the GSD's trotting gait is its great elasticity, strength, and fluidity, covering the ground in long, ground-eating strides. The GSD invented the so-called *flying trot,* in which all four feet are off the ground at full extension so that the dog actually floats forward with every stride. (See Figure 2-2, in which the dog is almost to that point.) No other dog breed can approach the GSD's trotting ability.

Figure 2-2: A GSD's gait is known as the *flying trot.*

Good trotters have to be sound when viewed from the front or the rear. In general, this means that the legs converge in a straight line toward the center line of gravity without interfering with one another. Any deviation from a straight line of support (such as cowhocks, turned pasterns, or bow legs) weakens a dog's stride and detracts from its strength.

Evaluating the German Shepherd's Character

The best-looking, best-moving German Shepherd in the world is nothing without character. This is a working breed, and no matter how well built a dog is, you can't force the desire and temperament to do the job on him. If those traits aren't there, you may have a lovely pet, but you won't have a real German Shepherd.

The German Shepherd Dog standard emphasizes temperament perhaps more than any other breed standard. Look at what the SV standard says about temperament:

> "With an effervescent temperament, the dog must also be cooperative, adapting to every situation, and take to work willingly and joyfully. He must show courage and hardness as the situation requires to defend his handler and his property. He must readily attack on his owner's command but otherwise be a fully attentive, obedient and pleasant household companion. He should be devoted to his familiar surroundings, above all to other animals and children, and composed in his contact with people. All in all, he gives a harmonious picture of natural nobility and self-confidence."

The German Shepherd has remained one of the most popular breeds in the world not because of its looks, and not because of its movement, but because of its character. It is the dog at its best, the true companion you wish your best human friends could be: noble, courageous, and loyal, but in private moments saved for you alone, a bit of a clown and a puppy at heart — a real character!

The perfect German Shepherd would conform to every point of the standard and trot with great, sound strides. Beyond that, he would be of strong and noble temperament and of robust health. There is no perfect German Shepherd, but I hope that yours comes close. I'm sure that he will be your perfect friend.

Part II
Finding the German Shepherd for You

The 5th Wave   By Rich Tennant

"Right now I've got a lot of Cybil Shepherds and Alan Shepherds, but no German Shepherds."

In this part . . .

Where do you look for a friend of a lifetime? What do you look for in a new family member? All German Shepherds have the potential to be great dogs, but some German Shepherds have greater potential than others. If you have great plans for your dog, you need a great dog, and no matter what plans you have for your dog, you need a healthy dog with a stable temperament.

This part helps you choose your dog wisely and carefully. You need to know what your choices are and what the danger signals are in order to make the best of finding your new best friend.

Chapter 3

Looking for Love in All the Right Places: Breeders and Shelters

In This Chapter

▶ Knowing where to look for a good German Shepherd
▶ Distinguishing good breeders from bad breeders
▶ Telling the difference between American and European Shepherds
▶ Understanding the meaning of pet, show, and breeding quality

*W*hy should you care if you get a good German Shepherd if you want a dog only as a pet? To a certain degree, you're right: You don't have to be as meticulously choosy as someone in search of a show or working Shepherd. But consider what traits draw you to the GSD in the first place: probably its renowned temperament and its striking appearance. You want to make sure that the GSD you get acts and looks like a GSD. Equally important, you want to make sure that the dog you get will live a long and healthy life. If you want a GSD as a working or competition dog, you want all these traits — and more.

Some things in life should not be easy. Buying a dog is one of them. Impulse puppy buying too often ends in impulse puppy dumping. Nonetheless, it's hard to resist big puppy dog eyes pleading to go home with you. I suggest that you don't go to look at puppies until you have decided that you're ready to get a dog and have narrowed down your sources ahead of time. If you shop before you've done your research, you will likely leave with a very cute puppy whom you will love dearly but who may not be the wisest choice. You've already chosen the best breed in the world — take your time to find a breeder and a pup who can do the breed justice.

Finding Reliable Sources of GSDs

Where you get your dog can make a huge difference in the quality of the dog you end up with. Good breeders raise their dogs with loving care, nurturing each pup and the mother to ensure good health and socialization. Some breeders, though, breed dogs merely to make money — and when they find that breeding is more expensive than they realized, they take shortcuts that can detract from the puppies' health. Or maybe you have a more charitable act in mind: You want to take in a dog who has been abandoned and might otherwise be euthanized. The following sections discuss a few of the common places to find sources of dogs and the pros and cons of each.

Newspaper classified ads

One way to find a new dog is to look in the local paper. Consider these ads to be about as reliable as those in the personals section, however: You never know what you're getting.

Most newspaper ads are placed by what are known as *backyard breeders* — novice breeders who usually breed their pets out of naivete or false hopes of making money. Some backyard breeders breed their dogs as often as possible to bring in a little extra income, which is very hard on the *dams,* or mothers.

Others breed their dogs so that the family can experience the miracle of birth, without having considered the miracle of death that the resulting pups may face because they didn't find homes for them in advance. Still others breed so that they can get a dog just like their beloved mother dog, again without considering that they may get ten dogs (none of which, incidentally, is like the dam).

Some breeders who advertise in the classifieds are quite reputable and knowledgeable, however. Just because their pups are bounding around the backyard doesn't put them in the category of backyard breeder. Here's where your knowledge of what questions to ask and what danger signs to look for come into play. See the section "Telling the Good Breeders from the Bad" for more information.

Be just as careful in evaluating your friends, coworkers, and neighbors as you would any stranger you contact through the classifieds. They may be nice folks, but they aren't necessarily qualified to breed your next family member!

Ads in dog magazines and on the Internet

Breeders who place advertisements in all-breed dog magazines or who have Web sites may or may not be reliable sources. GSD magazines such as *The German Shepherd Dog Review, The German Shepherd Times, The German*

Shepherd Quarterly, and *The German Shepherd Today* are better choices for finding reliable breeders. For German dogs, try the USA (United Schutzhund Club of America) magazine; *Shepherd Sports* covers Schutzhund. You can find contact information for these and other organizations in Appendix B.

Even with magazine advertisements and Web sites, not all GSD breeders have the best interests of the breed at heart. Once again, look to the section "Telling the Good Breeders from the Bad" for information that can help you evaluate breeders.

Deciphering the ads

Reading advertisements for German Shepherds can be like reading a foreign language. That's because a lot of the information is *in* a foreign language: German. Much of the text is filled with a jumble of letters that seem impressive, but what exactly they mean is not obvious. Most of the letters denote titles, with the ones you'd see most often in ads including the following:

- **"a" normal:** German certification of normal hips.

- **AD:** German endurance test.

- **CACIB:** Award toward an International Championship offered by the *Federation Cynologique Internacionale* (the world's largest dog governing organization).

- **CD, CDX, UD, UDX, OTCH:** Increasing levels of AKC obedience degrees.

- **Ch:** Champion, usually indicating an American (Am Ch, or AKC) or sometimes Canadian (Can Ch, or CKC) conformation championship.

- **FH, TD, TDX, VST:** Tracking degrees.

- **G, SG, V, VA:** German (SV) ratings of conformation, from good to best. These titles are often followed by a number, indicating placement in a particular class of competition.

- **Grand Victor, Grand Victrix:** Best male and female at the German Shepherd Dog Club of America National Specialty Show each year.

- **KKL-II, KKL-I:** Dogs recommended for breeding by the SV, with KKL-I being better than KKL-II.

- **OFA:** Orthopedic Foundation for Animals rating, most often for hip or elbow dysplasia. Hips can also be rated by PennHip.

- **OV:** Obedience Victor (male) or Victrix (female) — the top obedience dog at the National Specialty Show. The dog must have no disqualifying faults and must earn the top combined score in the trial.

- **ROM, ROMC:** Register of merit awarded to sires and dams based on achievements of offspring (ROM is based on AKC; ROMC is based on CKC).

- **SchH1, SchH2, SchH3:** Increasing levels of Schutzhund degrees combining protection, obedience, and tracking. (See Chapter 16 for more on Schutzhund.)

- **Seiger, Seigerin:** Best male and female at the SV Seiger show each year.

- **vWD normal:** Rating of test for von Willebrand's disease.

Join an Internet discussion list on German Shepherds, such as GSD-L or showgsd-l, for more information and leads.

Dog-care professionals and dog clubs

Dog-care professionals such as veterinarians, groomers, and boarding kennel personnel often know the reputable breeders in town and can be good sources for puppy leads. They are not infallible, however, so you must approach even the breeders they recommend with the same caution that you would a breeder from a newspaper ad.

Serious GSD fanciers have local clubs throughout the country. The American Kennel Club (AKC) and national clubs such as the German Shepherd Dog Club of America (GSDCA) can give you the name of the GSD or all-breed club contact closest to you. Club members can, in turn, steer you toward local breeders. Appendix B lists contact information for both of these organizations. The AKC Web site (www.akc.org) also lists breed contacts.

A good place to meet a lot of breeders and their dogs in one place is at a dog show or other competitive event, such as obedience, herding, or Schutzhund trials. (See Chapter 16 for more about these events.) These people tend to be serious about their dogs, and they're there to prove their dogs' merits; as such, they may be too nervous biting their nails or too busy cutting their dogs' nails to talk before going into the ring. If you ask to talk after they're through, you'll probably get more coherent information about their dogs and the puppies they have available.

Shelters and rescue homes

Some of the happiest relationships have sprouted because an unclaimed, bedraggled dog showed up on the doorstep or was abandoned by his former owner. Sometimes these dogs end up in animal shelters or in German Shepherd rescue foster homes, where they wait for homes to call their own. Although you can't bring each and every dog home with you, you do have the power to save a life. If you can find room in your home and heart, consider adopting a rescue GSD.

Take heed of a few warnings first, however. Most German Shepherds in rescue are there through no fault of their own, except allowing themselves to have been owned by irresponsible people. Some, however, have been through such bad experiences that they may have special needs that a first-time Shepherd owner is not prepared to provide. Others may have traits that make them unsuitable for all but the most experienced GSD owner, which is probably why their former owners gave up on them.

Coming to the rescue

Please support German Shepherd rescue. Even if you can't add a new permanent member, by volunteering as a foster home you can help nurse a homeless GSD back to physical or emotional health while he awaits a new permanent family. If you've reached your dog or emotional limit, you can still do your part with financial contributions or by joining the network of hard-working people who match dogs and people or who canvass animal shelters for German Shepherds. Even if you're not up to a full-fledged commitment, you can at least register with your local animal shelter and ask to be contacted whenever a GSD comes through its door.

Before adopting a rescue dog, find out as much as you can about his background; the reason he was given up; how he relates to men, women, children, and other pets; and any temperament or health problems he may have. You may feel guilty looking at a dog in need with a critical eye, but you're doing that dog no favors by adopting him if you can't cope with him any better than his former owners could. Good rescue groups carefully match prospective adoptees with new homes, increasing their chances of finding homes for life.

Contact the German Shepherd Dog Club of America at 916-791-5642 or on the Web at www.gsdca.org for information about rescue dogs. You can also try www.userhome.com/shwogsd, which has a large rescue page of links to local rescues.

Telling the Good Breeders from the Bad

The best way to get a good GSD is to find a good breeder. The problem is that virtually everyone who lets two dogs of the same breed mate considers himself or herself to be an expert dog breeder. Your job is to separate these backyard breeders from committed breeders. Beware of breeders who

- ✔ Sell cheap puppies. Good German Shepherds are not cheap. You can expect to pay from $600 to $1,500 for a good pet-quality GSD and $1,000 and up for a competition-quality dog. Raising healthy puppies takes a lot of resources, and cheap pups probably are cheap because the breeder has cut corners by neglecting proper nutrition and health care, as well as by getting the cheapest possible breeding stock.

In general, you should also be wary of a breeder whose dogs are priced well *over* the average price. Some breeders charge outlandish prices for pups because they claim that their dogs are the salvation of the breed. The "chance of a lifetime" litter, puppy, or dog doesn't exist — although chances are, whatever dog you choose will be a once-in-a-lifetime friend.

✔ Use incorrect terms such as *thoroughbred, full-blooded* (instead of *pure-bred*), *spaded* (instead of *spayed*), or *papered* (instead of *registered*) or boast of a "long pedigree" (the length of the pedigree depends only on how large a sheet of paper you have). These terms tip you off that this breeder is no dog expert!

✔ Can't compare their dogs to the German Shepherd standard (see Appendix C), don't know the standard, or scoff at the standard.

✔ Are unfamiliar with GSD health concerns, contend that hip and elbow ratings are meaningless, or insist that they don't have to screen because their dogs are free from problems. (See Chapter 12 for details about common health problems in German Shepherds.)

✔ Have no photos or videotapes of both parents and other relatives. Good breeders know every dog in their pedigrees and will have you running for the door as they go to retrieve yet another album or videotape.

✔ Have no pedigree on hand, or have unregistered stock. Good breeders will have these documents ready for your inspection.

✔ Breed several different breeds of dogs. Most dedicated breeders spend years studying one breed and could never have the resources to do justice to several breeds. Multibreed breeders too often are small-scale puppy mills.

✔ Breed their bitches at every season. Such breeders are demonstrating that they put puppy production over the welfare of their adults. Most breeders will not breed a bitch more than three or four times in her life, and no more often than once a year.

✔ Ask you no questions. Good breeders consider placing a puppy no less a responsibility than arranging adoption for a baby.

✔ Think that German Shepherds are ideal for everyone. They're not! But breeders in search of a buck would have you think so. Good breeders will discuss the good and bad points of the breed.

✔ Tell you that you can make your money back by breeding your German Shepherd. Does the breeder look rich? Good breeders breed for love of the breed, and most of them lose money with every litter.

✔ Will not take the dog back at any time in his life if you're not able to keep him. Good breeders care about the welfare of every dog for his entire life, not just until he walks out the door. They often include a contract stating that you must contact them first if you can't keep the dog.

Expect more of good breeders. Their dogs should boast titles in conformation, obedience, or working competitions. They should have extensive health certifications and even more extensive knowledge of health problems in the breed. They do so because they take pride in their dogs and in the breed. These are the breeders who have the best chance of producing a puppy whom you all can be proud of.

WARNING!

Why you shouldn't breed dogs yourself

Most dog breed books contain a chapter about breeding. This one does not, and for a very good reason. In 1999, 19,005 German Shepherd litters, resulting in 57,256 GSDs, were registered with the AKC. Do you really think that 57,256 good new homes were waiting for these puppies? How many do you think are still in whatever homes they found? How many do you think are still alive? This doesn't even count the German Shepherds who were registered with other organizations or not registered at all.

Unfortunately, people seem to take the term *litter* seriously and treat breeding with about as much thought as producing any other household litter. Keep the following in mind if you're thinking of breeding dogs:

✔ Being a popular breed does not mean that good homes are waiting for every puppy. Many more good German Shepherds are born than there are good homes available. The puppy you sell to a less-than-perfect home may end up neglected, abused, discarded, or returned.

✔ Unless your dog has proven himself by earning titles and awards in competitions, or by being an outstanding working dog, you may have a difficult time finding buyers.

✔ The average litter size for German Shepherds is seven puppies. Breeding so

that you can keep one pup ignores the fact that six others may not get good homes — or may be ransacking your home for the next 12 years.

✔ Selling puppies will not come close to reimbursing you for the stud fee, prenatal care, whelping complications, caesarian sections, supplemental feeding, puppy food, vaccinations, advertising, and a staggering investment of time and energy.

✔ Whelping a litter causes the bitch definite discomfort and some danger. Watching a litter being born is not a good way to teach children the miracle of life; too many things can go wrong.

✔ Responsible breeders spend years researching genetics and the breed, breed only the best specimens, and screen for hereditary defects to obtain superior puppies. Unless you have done the same, you are doing yourself, your dog, the puppies, any buyers, and the breed a great disservice.

If you must breed your German Shepherd, please invest in a book about the mechanics of breeding. Too many uninformed breeders allow their dogs to suffer and even die because they don't have proper information.

Telling the Difference between an American GSD and a German GSD

A great way to start an argument among German Shepherd breeders is to ask them whether American or European (usually German) GSDs are better. As a potential GSD buyer, you may be wondering the same thing.

The pages of popular dog magazines are crowded with more ads for European German Shepherds than for dogs from American lines. Part of the reason is the implied prestige that comes with owning a dog who either was imported directly or traces immediately back to his country of origin. The appeal of foreign GSDs obviously involves more than that, however, because you don't see a similar flood of people importing other breeds.

Many people feel that the continued control of the SV, the organization that created this incredible breed, continues to ensure that the best GSDs come from Europe. With its system of Breed Wardens and surveys, it's unlikely that some of the poor and unhealthy dogs routinely bred in America would pass muster there. In fact, though, most of the poor specimens bred in the U.S. do not pass muster here, either; they seldom have earned Championship titles or other awards.

Unfortunately, the average GSD pet buyer is unaware of the meanings of titles, awards, and health clearances. One advantage of the German system is that the breed wardens and surveys do much of the work for you. German GSDs are not approved for breeding unless they have passed certain confor- mation, temperament, training, and health requirements — meaning that SV registration, unlike AKC registration, carries with it a seal of approval.

Even the best American and German GSDs differ, however, and your choice of lines will depend on just what your want your GSD to do. Each type has its admirers, but keep in mind that they're all German Shepherds, members of one of the best breeds around, no matter where they're from.

If you have your heart set on showing in AKC shows, by all means get an American-bred GSD. American GSDs have been selected for generations for exquisite type, showy attitude, and the most fluid, powerful movement known in the world of dogs. They tend to have more refined heads, yet be a bit larger overall. Perhaps the most noticeable difference is the more extreme *angulation* (bend) of the hind legs, accompanied by a greater slope of the torso from front to rear.

Detractors of American GSDs claim that they are exaggerated, have lost their working ability, and tend to lack courage. Admirers strongly disagree!

European GSDs tend to act and look a bit different. Because of the emphasis on working ability, you'll have a better chance with a GSD from German lines if you want a GSD for protection. These dogs tend to have thicker, stronger heads; less angulation of the hind legs; and less slope from front to rear. Their bodies tend to be slightly shorter and thicker, and their *topline* (the line of the back between the withers and the croup) often has a noticeable arch, often referred to as a *roached back*.

Detractors of European GSDs claim that they are bred with little regard for looks and may be overactive with too high a prey drive for the average owner. They agree that they're great for protection work but claim that they are impractical for people who need quieter, more easygoing companions.

A disadvantage of buying a dog directly from Europe is that you aren't able to visit the kennel or meet the dog beforehand (although it does give you a good excuse to fly off to Europe!). You should be able to see pictures and a video of the dog, however, and also be able to check the importer's references. Make sure that you have a signed contract before you part with your money.

Many American breeders have GSDs from European lines, so if you decide on a German GSD, you need not get a dog directly from overseas. You can find their advertisements in dog magazines and on Web sites. Start your search at USA Schutzhund (www.germanshepherddog.com).

Remember that the differences in conformation between the European and American dogs means that a big winner in SV shows will not necessarily be any kind of a winner in AKC shows (and vice versa). If you plan to show your dog, decide up front which type of shows you want to compete in.

Quality Quandaries: Deciding among Pet Quality, Competition Quality, and Breeding Quality

Experienced breeders rate their dogs as pet quality, competition quality, or breeding quality.

- **Pet quality:** A pet-quality dog is generally the least costly because he has a trait that would prevent him from winning in conformation (or sometimes other) competitions. This trait could be one of those listed as faults in the standard, such as an ear that doesn't stand up, faded coloration, or missing teeth. It should not be a flaw in temperament or health; dogs with these types of flaws are obviously not ideal pets and usually are not available for sale. Being a pet is one of the most important roles a dog can fulfill, and pet quality is an essential trait of every good GSD.

- **Competition quality:** Competition-quality dogs (usually Schutzhund or show, but also obedience or herding prospects) should have good temperament and health. Those dogs destined for the show ring also should possess the attributes that the breed standard calls for. The GSDCA distinguishes between showable and show quality, such that a showable dog is one who is free of disqualifying faults and embodies the basic breed standard, with acceptable temperament and structure. He is of sufficient quality to compete in the show ring but may not win. A show-quality dog goes beyond that; he could reasonably be expected to win in the ring. Dogs destined for Schutzhund or obedience competition or for working should have especially stable temperaments.

Be cautious if a breeder contends that he or she never has anything less than competition-quality dogs. Even the best breeders produce many pet-quality dogs; denying this fact suggests that the breeder has an unrealistic idea of his or her dogs' quality.

✓ **Breeding quality:** Breeding-quality dogs come from impeccable backgrounds and should be of even higher quality than competition-quality dogs. These dogs must pass a battery of health clearances and be of sound temperament and excellent conformation. Being of breeding quality means more than being able to impregnate or conceive, but far too often these are the only criteria that owners apply to prospective parents.

Be extremely wary if a breeder claims that all the pups in a litter are of breeding quality. Picking a competition-quality puppy at an early age is difficult; picking a breeding-quality puppy is impossible. If your goal is to have a breeding-quality dog, you're better off buying an adult.

Decide well ahead of time what your intentions are for your new dog. A lot of hard feelings have arisen because of misunderstandings regarding quality. Don't get a pet-quality dog with plans of showing or breeding him. A reputable breeder has reasons for labeling a pup as pet quality; if you showed up in the ring with that pup, the breeder may be very embarrassed because other breeders might assume that you were duped into thinking that a pet-quality dog was of show quality. Don't get a pet-quality pup with plans of breeding him, either — again, the breeder has good reasons to believe that this dog should not be bred.

To keep their pet-quality dogs from being bred, many ethical breeders sell the dogs with Limited Registration privileges. *Limited Registration* is a type of AKC registration that certifies a dog to be purebred but does not allow him to be shown in conformation, and also prohibits his progeny from being AKC registered. Only the breeder can apply to change a Limited Registration to regular registration status if the dog later turns out to be of exceptional quality. Other breeders will give you the full ownership of the dog only upon proof that you have had the dog spayed or neutered as a means of discouraging breeding. Some buyers accuse these breeders of making these demands so that they won't have competition in the puppy market, and although this claim may be true occasionally, such non-breeding clauses are more often signs of a responsible breeder.

By the same token, don't get a show-quality German Shepherd and then never show him unless you clear this plan ahead of time with the breeder. Good breeders lose money with every pup they sell. Their compensation comes in part with the pride of seeing the dogs they so carefully produced represent them in the show ring. When you promise to show that dog and then never do so, you cheat the breeder.

If you want a competition-quality dog, or especially if you want a breeding-quality dog, paying someone who's knowledgeable in the breed to go with you to the breeder and give you an educated opinion is worthwhile.

The better quality you demand, the longer your search will take. A couple of months is a reasonable amount of time to look for a pet puppy; a couple of years is realistic for a breeding-quality dog. Begin your search for a high-quality GSD by seeing as many GSDs as possible, talking to GSD breeders, attending GSD competitions, reading every available GSD publication, and joining GSD discussion groups on the Internet. (See Appendix B for a host of German Shepherd resources.)

Chapter 4

Picking the Perfect Puppy

. . . .

In This Chapter

▶ Choosing what kind of coat you want your dog to have

▶ Deciding what age and sex of dog are best for you

▶ Knowing that health problems come with guarantees

▶ Knowing what to look for in a German Shepherd puppy or adult

▶ Securing papers for your new pal

. . . .

*I*f you want a cookie-cutter breed in which all the dogs look and act alike, don't look at German Shepherds. They come in different coat lengths and colors (although not all are equally acceptable in accordance with the standard), and they're bred with different emphases: Some are bred as show dogs, some as obedience dogs, some as protection dogs, some as service dogs, and some simply as healthy companions. This breed has a lot to offer — not only as far its incredible abilities, but also in its variety. One size may not fit all.

This chapter can help you narrow down what type of dog you're looking for and then help you evaluate the litter so that you get the very best dog in it (as if they're not all wonderful!).

Letting the Fur Fly

A German Shepherd's coat is one of his most prominent features, so you want to choose the coat you like best. The GSD breed standard calls for a double coat of medium length, with rich coloration. Soft, silky, wooly, curly, and long coats are considered faulty, as are washed-out colors, blues, and livers. Whites are considered so faulty in terms of the standard that they are disqualified. Despite what the standard says, many people prefer dogs with certain "faulty" traits, most notably those with long or white coats.

Long-coated GSDs

Long-coated German Shepherds (see Figure 4-1) occasionally arise in litters from parents with shorter coats. Because the AKC standard calls for a shorter coat, long-coated dogs do not typically compete in conformation shows, and the SV and the FCI — international organizations — also disqualify them for showing and breeding. Many people prefer the look of these dogs, however, and several (usually non-show oriented) kennels even specialize in longer-coated dogs, despite the fact that they're considered faulty according to the standard. Most serious GSD breeders frown on intentionally breeding for these dogs.

Figure 4-1:
A
long-coated
GSD.

The long coat results from a recessive gene, so both parents must carry the gene for it. Telling whether a pup may develop a long coat can be difficult at an early age; the first signs are usually somewhat longer tufts of hair in the ears and between the toes. By the time most puppies are offered for sale at 10 weeks of age, the longer coats should be noticeable.

White GSDs

White German Shepherds (called American-Canadian White Shepherds in Europe) have been around for decades, probably since the inception of the breed. They also have been considered faulty for all that time — that is, except by the people who love them.

Perhaps because certain types of white coats have been associated with health problems in some breeds, early GSD breeders thought it best to discourage them. Or perhaps the white dogs were considered to be less capable of doing their work because they stood out too much. The truth is that the white coloration of the GSD is not associated with health defects and has not been shown to be detrimental to working ability. Still, every breed club has the right to decide what traits are and are not acceptable for its breed, and the German Shepherd clubs have exercised this right by not allowing whites to be shown in conformation.

You may have heard that white German Shepherds are rare and costly. Wrong! True, because of concerted efforts of serious GSD breeders to eliminate the fault from the breed, finding a white GSD from colored parents is rare. However, a large group of dedicated breeders specialize in breeding white German Shepherds intentionally.

Because they have been separated from the mainstream conformation GSDs for many generations, these white dogs tend to differ from other GSDs not only in color but also in conformation. They're usually not as long or as angulated, they often lack a double coat, and they often have a different croup angle and gait as compared to AKC conformation GSDs. Some breeders advocate establishing the White Shepherd as a separate breed. (The color section of this book shows a photo of white GSDs.) And as of January 1, 1999, the United Kennel Club has recognized the White Shepherd as an independent breed, offering registration as White Shepherds to all AKC-, CKC-, and UKC-registered white German Shepherds.

Although white GSDs are less desirable from a show standpoint, they're no less desirable as pets, so if you prefer their look, go for it!

For more information about White Shepherds, contact the White German Shepherd Dog Club International, Inc., at www.aros.net/~wgsdcii or the American White Shepherd Association at www.onewaits.com/awsa.

Engaging in the Battle of the Sexes: Male or Female?

Many people have strong ideas about whether a male or female German Shepherd is better. These ideas are usually wrong, but a few differences do exist.

GSD males are larger (about 25 inches tall at the shoulder and weighing from 75 to 95 pounds) and have heavier bone and larger heads than females. They tend to be somewhat prouder and more territorial, and some people contend that they're more courageous; the drawback is that they don't always get along well with other males. Many people find the males to be more dependent and affectionate. Intact (unneutered) males are apt to go off in search of females (of course, any dog should be securely fenced) and often think nothing of repeatedly lifting their legs on furniture to mark a house as their territory.

Females are smaller — about 22 to 24 inches tall and weighing from 60 to 70 pounds. They may be a bit more level-headed, and they fight less with each other, but when they do fight, the battle can be ferocious — even to the death. Many people contend that the females are the ones they would want to protect them, and that females are more intelligent. Their main drawback is that intact females come in *estrus* ("season" or "heat") twice or three times a year; this period lasts for three weeks, during which time you must keep them away from amorous neighborhood males who may consider your house a singles bar. You must also contend with her bloody discharge and her possible attempts to elope with her suitors. The solution for both sexes is neutering (see Chapter 11).

Figure 4-2 shows a male and a female GSD.

Figure 4-2:
Males
should look
like males,
and females
like females.

Deciding Whether to Get a Puppy or an Adult Dog

Most people consider only a puppy when they set out to get a dog, but choosing a pup isn't always the best idea. No one can deny that a puppy is cute and fun, but a puppy is much like a baby; you can't be too busy to walk, feed, supervise, or clean (and clean and clean). If you work outside your home, have limited patience or heirloom rugs, or demand a competition- or breeding-quality dog, an older puppy or an adult may be a better choice.

GSDs are an exception among breeds in the ready availability of high-quality and highly trained adults. European-titled adults seem to be easier to find than American ones. A dog shown in the conformation ring in Germany will have a *Koer report* (a breed survey) that supplies a detailed analysis of the dog's conformation and temperament, as well as a recommendation of whether it should be used for breeding. If you intend to breed your GSD, a titled adult from any country will give you a good head start.

Buying an adult that is already Schutzhund- or obedience-trained can save you countless hours of hard work and provide you with a well-trained partner, but as always, be forewarned that not all trainers are created equal. Of course, the more training, titles, and accolades a dog has, the more you can expect to pay — several thousand dollars is common. As an aside, if you plan to get such a dog for breeding, you may want to have some assurance that the dog is fertile. With a female, getting this assurance can be difficult, but with a male, a veterinarian can supply a certificate that the dog has an adequate sperm count.

If you simply want a mature companion, contact an established breeder. Breeders may have adult dogs available that would relish the chance to live as pampered pets. They may have adults who simply didn't win as often in the ring as anticipated or who have not proved to be good producers. Several rescue groups are devoted to finding homes for GSDs in need of loving homes, too.

Keep in mind that an adult GSD may take longer to adjust than a puppy. If the dog has been properly socialized (that is, treated gently and exposed to a variety of situations, people, and dogs), your GSD will soon blend into your family and love you as though he's always owned you, no matter what his age.

Getting the Pick of the Litter

Knowing where to look for a dog (see Chapter 3) and what kind you want is half the battle. Now it's time to narrow the field and get the dog of your dreams. Getting to see the parents and even the grandparents of your prospective puppy is the best indicator of how your pup will turn out. Remember the essentials: looks, temperament, and health.

As you look upon this undulating mass of fur balls nipping at your feet, you may find yourself with a bad case of "I'll take that one!" as you point to every little wiggle worm in sight. How will you choose? One way is to let the breeder pick. The breeder knows the pups' personalities and traits better than you will in the short time you evaluate them, so listen carefully to any suggestions the breeder has.

Many people who can't decide let the puppy pick them. It's hard to say no to a little tyke who comes over to say hello and ends up falling asleep in your lap!

If you're looking for an adult, spend some time alone with the dog and see how your personalities mesh. If the dog is being placed by a GSD rescue group, they can give you an idea of whether that particular dog is best for you.

Looks

For looks, consider the essentials of the German Shepherd Dog standard (see Chapter 2 and Appendix C). The GSD has an outline of smooth curves on a body that is longer than it is tall, somewhat higher at the shoulders than at the rear. He is strong, agile, and substantial. He has a strong, chiseled head with medium-sized, almond-shaped eyes and erect, moderately pointed ears. He has a double coat, with the outer coat consisting of dense, straight or slightly wavy, coarse, close-lying hair of medium length, and a bushy tail. His trot covers the ground in great strides. His color is typically either tan with a black saddle or entirely black or sable.

If the parents and grandparents of the puppy you're considering (or the dog himself, if you're buying an adult) conform to this standard, you've found a good one.

Temperament

For temperament, look first to the puppy's parents. They should neither try to attack you nor slink away from you. If the pups are quite young, you may have to make allowances for the dam, as she may be somewhat protective of them. This is one reason it's best to meet the dam of your prospective litter before she is even bred. Pups raised with minimal (or negative) human contact during their critical period of development — from about 6 to 10 weeks of age — may have lifetime personality problems. Notice how the breeder interacts with the adults and pups and whether the puppies are being raised underfoot (good) or out of sight (bad).

Most people are drawn to extremes — either the most outgoing or the most introverted pups in a litter. Your best bet, however, is to go with the middle pup — one who's neither shy nor overconfident. An overconfident pup may be somewhat better as a working dog; a shy one, unfortunately, is not better suited for any role.

You may be drawn to a dog because of his looks, but you will fall in love with a dog because of his personality.

Health

To estimate a pup's health, ask the breeder how long the dogs in the first two generations of the pedigree lived. Ask to see health clearances, especially the certifications concerning clearances for hip dysplasia and elbow dysplasia. Hip certification can be an Orthopedic Foundation for Animals (OFA), PennHip, Ontario Veterinary College (OVC), "a" stamp (Germany), or FCI (international) certification. In America, OFA certification is most common. OFA rates hips as Normal (with Excellent rated better than Good), Transitional (with Fair rated better than Borderline), and Dysplastic (with Mild rated better than Moderate and both rated better than Severe). Elbow certification is either Normal or Dysplastic.

Also ask the breeder about health problems in the line, and look at the parents and puppies to see whether they appear healthy (see Chapter 12). Is the puppy being raised in sanitary conditions? Does he have his puppy vaccinations? Has he been checked or treated for internal parasites?

Puppy temperament testing

Many people put great stock in puppy temperament testing, although little evidence exists of its predictive value. A common test is to place the pup on its back. Ideally, the pup will struggle for a few seconds and then allow you to hold him there without struggling. Another test is to see whether the puppy is inclined to follow you. For a complete description, check out www.golden-retriever.com/pat1.html.

No matter how much research you do into a puppy's background, there's no guarantee that your dog will live a long and healthy life. But why not go with the odds and choose a dog from the healthiest background possible?

You want to look at the individual pups you're considering as well. Extra vet bills will come as part of the package with pups who

- Are dirty or soiled with feces
- Are covered with fleas or ticks
- Are missing hair
- Have crusted or reddened skin
- Are coughing, sneezing, or vomiting
- Have discharge from the eyes, ears, or nose
- Are red or irritated around the anus
- Have diarrhea
- Are thin or pot-bellied
- Have pale gums
- Are dehydrated (Test for dehydration by picking up a fold of skin and releasing it. The skin should "pop" back into place.)
- Are apathetic, lethargic, shy, or hostile

If any of the pups exhibit these signs, you should probably scratch that litter and that breeder off your list.

Many breeders supply health guarantees with their puppies. Unfortunately, a guarantee is of little value if it requires you to return or euthanize a dog you have grown to love in order to be compensated. At the same time, a breeder never has total control over the future health problems of a puppy and generally can't afford to offer you your money back for every problem, especially without a veterinary certification. A good compromise is a guarantee that covers certain problems that can be well documented (most commonly hip and elbow dysplasia — see Chapter 12) and that will compensate you with a

What to look for in a GSD for breeding

If you want a GSD male for conformation (or breeding), make sure that both his testicles are descended into the scrotum by the time you take him home. Both should be down by 8 weeks of age, although some may be as late as 16 weeks (or in very rare cases, longer). The breeder should be able to help you make this determination.

replacement pup and let you keep your original pup as long as you supply documentation of the condition, return the original pup's registration, and supply proof that the dog has been neutered or spayed.

Good looks attracts you to a dog, and good temperament makes you fall in love, but good health keeps your love alive.

There's only one irrefutable truism about picking a new German Shepherd: No matter which one you pick, he will be the best one. In the years to come, you'll wonder how you came to be so lucky in picking the greatest dog on Earth.

A final note: Don't visit different breeders on the same day. Puppies can harbor communicable diseases that you could pass from one litter to another.

Making It Official: Papers

How can you be sure that your new dog is a bona fide German Shepherd Dog? Papers.

Papers are for more than housebreaking — they are proof of your German Shepherd's pure ancestry. They consist of a litter or individual registration certificate issued by a registry. In most cases, the registry is the American Kennel Club (AKC), but German imports are registered with the SV (short for *Verein fur Deutsche Schaferhunde* — the German Shepherd Club in Germany).

The AKC and the SV are not the only registering bodies. The United Kennel Club (UKC) is also a respected dog registry in the United States, and most developed countries have a national kennel club that registers dogs.

Many countries also have "imposter" registries — small registries that offer to register dogs even if the dogs lack proof of pure breeding. Be wary of dogs registered with one of these unknown organizations (no matter how highfalutin the registry's name sounds) because they often are no more registered or purebred than you are.

Don't confuse the registration certificate with a pedigree. A dog with a pedigree is not necessarily registered, although a dog registered with a legitimate registry must have a pedigree. *Registration papers* are the actual documents that record a dog's registration numbers. A *pedigree,* which lists your dog's family tree, is more often an unofficial document (although you can purchase certified pedigrees through the AKC, and the pedigree is part of the SV registration certificate). To an experienced breeder, it is a history of breeding decisions that can be traced through generations.

All registered German Shepherds have a pedigree as long as your arm; the length of the pedigree doesn't mean that one dog is somehow more pure than another.

Finally, remember that neither AKC nor SV registration is a seal of quality. AKC registration means only that the dog's ancestry is pure and registered (even that can be subject to faking, although DNA testing now makes that more difficult); many AKC-registered dogs are poor examples of their breed. SV registration at least implies that the parents have met certain minimal standards of quality; nonetheless, nothing can guarantee how an individual puppy will turn out.

AKC registration

AKC registration papers consist of a registration certificate or application form, which you complete and send to the AKC to register the dog in your name. If these papers are not available when you buy the puppy, AKC rules require the breeder to give you a signed statement or bill of sale that includes the breed, sex, and color of the dog, the dog's date of birth, the breeder's name, and the registered names of the dog's sire and dam (with their registration numbers if possible). In addition, the breeder should be able to show you a litter registration number by the time of the sale.

Some unscrupulous breeders promise to provide registration documents "soon" and never deliver them. By the time you figure out this scam, you are already too attached to the puppy to ask for a refund. If registration papers are not available when you buy the puppy, ask to see both parents' registrations and get a written statement that the proper documents will arrive within a mutually acceptable time frame.

Breeders often sell pet-quality dogs with Limited Registration, which means that if the dogs are bred, their offspring will not be registered by the AKC. Breeders do so because they don't think that the dogs should be bred, and the Limited Registration designation is extra insurance in case the new owners don't have the dogs neutered or spayed. Such dogs can still compete in AKC competitions (except for conformation — see Chapter 16). Limited Registration may be changed to regular registration at a later date, but only by the breeder. The breeder may want to make such a change after the dog has tested clear of hereditary disease, or if the dog turns out to have better conformation than initially expected.

SV registration

SV certification is far more extensive than its AKC counterpart. It includes a four-generation pedigree complete with breed survey information, color, hip certification, titles and show ratings, and information about litter mates. Unfor-tunately, because all the information is in German, it may be Greek to you.

How to read SV papers

SV papers may seem confusing at first glance, but once you know what the various German terms mean, you realize that SV registration provides an immense amount of information — far more than AKC registration papers do. Among the terms found on the SV papers are the following:

- **"a" Zuerkannt:** Hip certification
- **Anschrift:** Address
- **Besondere kennzeichen:** Special marks
- **Eltern:** Parents
- **Farbe und abzeichen:** Color and markings
- **Geschlecht:** Sex
- **Geschweister:** Litter mates
- **Grob-Eltern:** Grandparents
- **Haarart:** Coat
- **Inzucht auf:** Line breeding
- **KB:** Breed survey report
- **Lebenszeit:** Breed surveyed for life (no subsequent evaluations required)
- **Mutter:** Dam
- **Tatowier-Nr.:** Tattoo number
- **Urgrob-Eltern:** Great-grandparents
- **Vater:** Sire
- **Wurffjahr:** Year of birth
- **Wurftag:** Day and month of birth
- **Zuchter:** Breeder

The certification may be either white (with green borders) or pink; the pink papers are more desirable because they're issued only when both the sire and the dam are recommended for breeding. In either case, you find the following information:

- The first page contains information about the individual dog, such as his name, color, birth date, breeder, and registration number. The top right-hand corner may also contain the "a" stamp for hip certification and survey remarks, if any. It also contains information about ancestors who are found more than once on either the sire's or the dam's side of the pedigree, listing these dogs' names and the generation of the pedigree in which they can be found, with sire and dam sides separated by a dash.

- The second and third pages contain the dog's pedigree, complete with the color and survey reports of the parents and grandparents, as well the names of litter mates. Dogs in the pedigree who were recommended for breeding have asterisks preceding their names.

- The fourth page is used to record ownership transfers.

Papers are important if you plan to breed or compete with your dog. However, your German Shepherd doesn't need papers to be a fine animal, a staunch protector, a loyal companion, and your best friend.

Part III
Bringing Up Baby

The 5th Wave   By Rich Tennant

CHASING STICK

BOWL DRINKING

GOOD DOG   BAD DOG

"Okay, let's get into something a little more theoretical."

In this part . . .

Adding a new family member is intimidating, tiring, and, most of all, fun. It's intimidating because the choices you make now can influence your relationship with your Shepherd in the years to come. It's tiring because protecting, training, and nurturing a dog of any age, especially a puppy, takes a lot of work. And it's fun because you're embarking on the adventure of a lifetime.

The chapters in this part hold your hand while you make tough decisions regarding feeding, training, grooming, and safeguarding your new charge. Few puppies are born angels, and you'll probably need some extra guidance when your GSD's behavior takes a wrong turn. Setting a good foundation now is the best way to ensure a strong and prosperous relationship in the years to come.

Chapter 5

Shopping for Dog Stuff

. . . .

In This Chapter

▶ Getting what you really need to make life good for your Shepherd

▶ Knowing which products you *don't* want to buy

▶ Taking precautions with even the best products

▶ Stocking your doggy medicine cabinet

. . . .

*O*ne of the best things about getting a new dog is that it gives you an excuse to go on a major shopping spree. True, your new pup will just as likely ignore his fancy store-bought toys in favor of an old sock, or choose a pile of rags to sleep on instead of his new velvet pad, but you will have the satisfaction of knowing that you have the most spoiled-rotten dog in the neighborhood.

Even if you have more Spartan ideas for your German Shepherd, you need some fundamentals. This chapter tells you exactly what you need, and also tells you about some extras that are good to have.

Fencing Your Yard

The number-one German Shepherd accessory and lifesaver is a securely fenced yard. In today's world, a loose dog is at best an unwelcome visitor and at worst a dead dog. GSDs are gifted jumpers, climbers, diggers, and wrigglers who often find other dogs, playing children, racing bicycles, or the call of the wild irresistible. Having a fence in place ensures that your dog will stay within his own yard, which is best for his safety as well as the safety of others outside the fence.

If the dumbest thing you can do is to let your dog run loose, the next dumbest is to chain him up. Dog chains are the perfect recipe for strangled or aggressive dogs. They are not acceptable. Neither is a little dog pen stuck out in the back 40. Even if you live in the middle of the country, you need a fenced yard for your German Shepherd — a yard that he shares with the rest of the family.

Never tie your dog out in the yard, even on a trolley line. Doing so is cruel and foolish — and is the perfect way to create an aggressive, neurotic, unhappy dog. Plus, your GSD could hurt his neck, choke to death, or be attacked by strays running loose.

In warm weather, shade must be available. If your yard doesn't offer your dog a shady spot to rest in, consider getting a doghouse (see the "Doghouses" section later in this chapter). When the temperature rises and the sun is shining brightly, make sure that your GSD has extra cool water to drink, and bring him inside on occasion so that he can cool down.

A great summertime cooler is a kiddie wading pool. Introduce your dog to the pool as a pup, and he will learn to lounge in the water to keep cool on hot days.

Doghouses

If your dog will spend a lot of time outside, you may need to build or purchase a doghouse. The best doghouses have a removable top for cleaning and a doorway system that prevents wind and rain from whipping into the sleeping quarters — which means a design with two offset doors and an "entrance hall." One of the doors should have a hanging rubber or fabric doggy door-type flap. The floor should be slightly raised, and soft bedding should be in the sleeping quarters.

Invisible fences

Invisible fences have become popular alternatives to traditional fences, but they do have their shortcomings. Because they work only on a dog wearing a special shock collar that is activated by the buried boundary wire, they can't keep out loose dogs who aren't wearing such collars, nor can they keep out unscrupulous dognappers. In addition, an excited, determined, or fast-moving GSD can get over the boundary before he has a chance to stop and then find himself blocked out of the yard. Nonetheless, most owners report good results with these fences, and they're an option for a front yard in a neighborhood in which a regular fence would be out of place. The best approach is to teach your dog what the boundaries are.

Kennel runs

A secure kennel run can be a convenient asset that provides a safe outdoor area for your German Shepherd while you're away from home, although it's not a substitute for a fenced yard or a home. The run should be at least 8 feet high and preferably have a top. A dog can get more exercise in a long, narrow run than in a square run of equal area. If the run is separated from the house, set it up so that it is parallel to the house, which encourages the dog to run back and forth along its length. In a run that's set at a right angle to the house, the dog tends to stay at the end closest to the house.

The most convenient type of run has a doggy door leading to an inside enclosure, often another small run, an area in the garage, or a laundry area. This door affords your dog shelter in case of bad weather. If you can't provide a door leading to the inside, make sure that your kennel run offers both shade and shelter, such as a doghouse.

If you place a doghouse within the run, make sure that your dog can't jump on the top of the doghouse and then out of the kennel run.

Dirt flooring can become muddy and harbor germs, as well as encourage digging. Cement flooring is easy to clean but holds odors and is expensive. The best compromise flooring for a kennel run is pea gravel, which is fairly easy to keep clean by scooping and hosing.

Living It Up: Home Spaces

If you want your dog to consider your house a home sweet home, you want to set him up with a comfy space that he can call his own. This section discusses the various home spaces that you may want to consider providing.

Don't forget baby gates! They're better than closed doors for placing parts of your home off-limits. Do not use the accordion-style gates, however, because a dog can get his head stuck in them and asphyxiate.

Cages

Many new dog owners are initially appalled at the idea of putting their pets in cages (or "crates") as though they were wild beasts. At times, though, your GSD pup may seem like a wild beast, and a cage is one way to save your home from ruination and yourself from insanity.

A cage can provide a quiet haven for your pup. Just as you find peace and security as you sink into your own bed at night, your pup needs a place that he can seek out whenever he needs rest and solitude. If you use the cage properly, your GSD will come to think of it not as way to keep himself in, but as a way to keep others out!

A cage should be the canine equivalent of a toddler's crib. It is a place for naptime, a place where you can leave your pup without worrying that he will hurt himself or your home. It is not a place for punishment, nor is it a storage box for your dog when you're through playing with him.

Cages are convenient — sometimes so convenient that they're overused. Don't expect your dog to stay in a cage all day, every day, while you're at work. Confining a dog to a cage is not only unfair, and even cruel, but it can also lead to behavior problems. Locking an intelligent, active dog in a cage without stimulation can result in such frustration and anxiety that the dog begins to resent the cage and act uncontrollably when out of the cage.

Nonetheless, a cage has its place in training. Place the cage in a corner of a quiet room, but not too far from the rest of the family. Place the pup in the cage when he begins to fall asleep, and he will become accustomed to using it as his bed. Be sure to place a soft blanket in the bottom. By taking the pup directly from the cage to the outdoors when he wakes, the cage will be one of the handiest housebreaking aids at your disposal. (See Chapter 8 for information about housebreaking and other dog training.)

The ideal cage is large enough for a puppy to stand up in but not walk around in — cages in which a dog can walk around tend to be used as bathrooms. If your dog will spend long stretches of time in the cage, it should be large enough to stretch out in. If money were no object, you could keep buying ever-expanding cages as your GSD gets bigger, but a less-expensive option is to buy a large cage and then place a divider in it that you gradually move to accommodate the growing pup.

If you plan to travel with your cage, make sure that it fits in your car and that it is easy to transport.

Most cages are made of either wire or plastic. Fancy metal cages are also available — for a fancy price. They are the choice of the elite for shipping, but they're out of the average owner's price range.

> ✔ **Wire cages** provide better ventilation and view for your dog, and most (especially the "suitcase" models) are easily collapsible for storage or transport. They can be drafty and don't provide the coziness of plastic cages, though. Also, a bored dog may be tempted to pull things through the grates, effectively straining the new coat that you happened to place on top of the cage. Most wire cages are not approved for airline shipping.

✔ **Plastic "airline" cages** — the most common cages used for flying — are relatively inexpensive. They don't provide as good of ventilation but can be cozy, especially in winter. They take up more room in storage, however, because they break down only into halves.

Whatever type of cage you choose, pay special attention to the latching mechanism. Make sure that a determined dog can't spring the door. You want a latch that doesn't come loose if the cage is rattled, and that a dog can't get a muzzle or toe under and push up. Most latches that require two hand movements to open them are relatively dog-proof.

Beds

If you're like most people, you sleep in a bed. If you're like most new dog owners, you are adamant that your dog won't be sharing it. The chances of you sticking to that promise are much better if your dog has a bed of his own. Yet many dog owners go to bed at night and leave their dogs wandering aimlessly around the house without beds to call their own. When they discover the dogs sleeping on the sofa, they label the dogs as sneaky, but Shepherds need comfortable beds just as much as you do.

A bed can be a folded blanket, a baby crib mattress, a papasan cushion, a fancy dog bed, or anything moderately soft and preferably washable. You can place it in a corner, a box, a dog cage, or anywhere out of drafts and away from excitement. Whatever you use and wherever you put it, the most important thing is that it serves as a place your dog can call his own. The second most important thing is that you don't use the traditional wicker basket . . . unless you have an insatiable desire to play pick-up sticks.

Exercise pens

An exercise pen (or *X-pen*) fulfills many of the same functions as a cage. X-pens are transportable wire folding "playpens" for dogs, typically about 4 feet x 4 feet in size. An X-pen is a reasonable solution when you must be gone for several hours, because the pup can relieve himself on paper in one corner, sleep on a soft bed in the other, and frolic with his toys all over! It's like having a little yard inside.

An X-pen provides a safe time-out area when you need quiet time for yourself. But before leaving your pup in an X-pen, make sure that he can't jump or climb out — covers are available for incorrigible escapees.

If you use an X-pen, cover the floor beneath it with thick plastic (an old shower curtain works well) and then add towels or washable rugs for traction and absorbency. Again, don't expect to stick your GSD pup in an X-pen all day every day and still have a sane dog.

Collaring Your GSD

Few items of such importance are so incorrectly chosen for dogs than the simple leash and collar. Just like your clothing, one size does not fit all, and one style does not fit all occasions.

Collars

For collars, you can choose between buckle, choke, and martingale (see Figure 5-1):

- **Buckle collars with tags:** Every dog should have a buckle collar to wear around the house. On it should be your dog's license and identification tags (preferably the flat plate type). You will have to buy several buckle collars as your pup grows, but just get the nylon puppy collars, which don't cost much. When your dog reaches maturity, you can splurge on a handsome leather or web collar. (The rhinestone variety isn't very popular for German Shepherds.)

   The problem with buckle collars is that constant, long-term wear can wear away the dog's hair. You can avoid this problem by removing the collar at night while your dog sleeps. Another problem is that a buckle collar can slip over a dog's head if he tries to back out of it, and it gives the handler little control if the dog is strong and strong-minded.

- **Choke collars:** A choke (or slip) collar may be a better choice for walking a dog on a leash. Choke collars come in nylon or chain, with chain giving a bit more control.

   The main problem with choke collars of any type is their tendency to literally choke dogs to death. Countless dogs have gotten their choke collars caught on sticks, fences, car parts, or even a playmate's tooth and have died — sometimes in front of their desperate owners who could not dislodge them because of the dogs' frantic actions. *Never* leave a choke collar on a dog unattended. Doing so is like sending a child out to play with a hangman's noose around her neck.

   The best choice for GSD choke collars are called "fur-saving" chain chokes, which have very large oval links, each about 1 inch long.

✔ **Martingale collars:** A compromise between a buckle collar and a choke collar is a martingale collar, which tightens when pulled but can tighten only so much. Most martingale collars are made of nylon.

A *prong collar* is a special type of martingale collar. These collars have links with prongs that bite into the dog when the collar tightens. Needless to say, their use is controversial. If you're physically unable to control your dog, however, a prong collar may be your only safe choice. Get professional advice on the proper use of the collar in training the dog.

Just as you wear different outfits for different reasons, your dog can wear different collars in different situations. A buckle collar is best for around the house, but a choke or martingale is better for walking on lead.

A problem with any kind of collar is that controlling a dog by his neck is somewhat difficult. When the collar slips down low on the neck, the dog can throw his weight into it and pull with reckless abandon, oblivious to all your pulling. A *head collar* can control your dog better by controlling his head. This type of collar works on the same principle as a horse halter; where the nose goes, the body follows. Head collars are a humane and effective alternative for headstrong Shepherds.

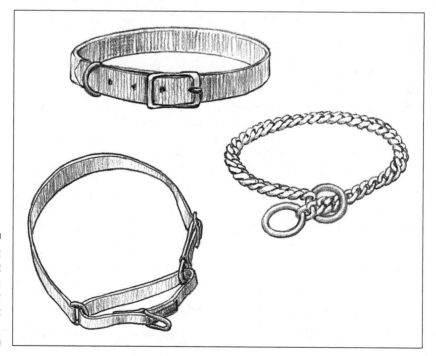

Figure 5-1:
Different
situations
call for
different
collars.

Giving your dog a chip on his shoulder or a tattoo on his thigh

Your dog needs at least two forms of identity: an identification tag on his collar (see the "Collars" section) and a second, nonremovable piece.

One option for this second form of identity is a tattoo. Although you can have a skull and crossbones or "Mom" tattooed on your dog, your social security number or your dog's registration number is easier to trace. These tattoos, usually placed on the inside of the dog's thigh, provide a relatively permanent means of identification (although they sometimes fade or are hard to read on a dog with dark skin or thick hair). You register the tattoo numbers with one of several lost pet recovery agencies, which will contact you if you report the dog lost or stolen. A determined dognapper could obscure the tattoo with subsequent tattooing, however.

The more permanent and informative means of identification is a microchip, which contains information about the dog and is placed under the dog's skin with a simple injection. Its shortcoming is that you need a special scanner to read it. (Most animal shelters, but few veterinarians, own them.) The number is registered with a microchip dog recovery agency, which will contact you if it finds your dog after he is lost or stolen.

Modern microchips are perfectly safe — they can't migrate through a dog's body. Some early microchips could migrate several inches from their original sites, but changes in their design have made microchips quite immobile.

The best solution to the "identity crisis" is all three forms of ID: tag, tattoo, *and* microchip. Of course, an even better solution is never to chance getting separated from your companion in the first place.

Harnesses that fit around the chest are seldom used on German Shepherds because they afford the least control of any restraining device. They were created to distribute weight so that a horse or sled dog can pull the most with the least effort. They're very safe for obedient dogs, but you'll be unable to control a Shepherd wearing a harness if he decides that he wants to go elsewhere.

Every dog should have an up-to-date ID tag on his collar. Flat tags are better than hanging ones because they're less likely to get caught on a playmate's tooth.

Leashes

As Chapter 15 explains in more detail, German Shepherds need exercise, and walking is a great form of physical activity for both you and your dog. Leashes also aid in training (discussed in Chapter 8).

For everyday use, get a sturdy web, nylon, or leather leash that is 4 or 6 feet long. Shorter leashes are better when walking in crowed places, and puppies can use lighter leashes. For early leash training, a light, adjustable show lead works well. These are one-piece collars and leads that have an adjustable head loop but no choking action.

The stupidest leash ever designed is the chain leash. You can't grab them because they cut your hand, and they're actually more likely to break than good web leashes are. Don't purchase chain leashes!

Retractable leashes are very popular and useful, but they're often carelessly used. They're not for use around other dogs or people, who too often get in the way and get tied up in the long line. Nor are they for use next to roadways; dogs are too apt to run in the road before you can put on the brakes. In addition, if you drop one of these leashes, it retracts toward the dog, which can cause the dog to think that the leash is coming after him, creating a horrifying chase in which the panicked dog runs faster and farther in a futile attempt to get away. Finally, be careful! People have lost finger parts when the line has whipped across their hands.

Getting the Scoop on Poop

The least glamorous thing on your shopping list is a poop scoop. It's also one of the handiest. If you have a yard, don't try to clean it with makeshift shovels and buckets; use something designed to make the job easy and less yucky. The two-part poop scoops are easier to use than the hinged ones. The ones with a rake are better for grass, and the flat ones are better for cement — think about where you'll be walking your dog and choose the appropriate type. If you walk your dog on city streets, a number of poop disposal baggy systems are available. Use them.

After you pick up the poop, where do you put it? It depends on your city's ordinances. You may just chuck it in the trash or in your own toilet. You can also get a dog-poop disposal system that digests dog wastes in a little bucket that you bury in your yard. These systems work great — as long as you don't have too many dogs!

Toying with Your Dog

German Shepherds may not be in the Toy Group, but they certainly are toy dogs — toy-loving, that is. Just as they do with children, toys play an important role in a dog's mental and physical stimulation. Dogs who have toys are

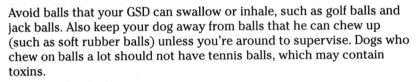

more confident in manipulating items with their mouths and are less likely to chew inappropriate items. Following are some popular toys that will amuse your GSD:

✔ **Balls:** The ball remains the standard dog toy. Hard rubber balls are ideal for tough-playing puppies. A large, partially deflated soccer ball also makes a great plaything.

Avoid balls that your GSD can swallow or inhale, such as golf balls and jack balls. Also keep your dog away from balls that he can chew up (such as soft rubber balls) unless you're around to supervise. Dogs who chew on balls a lot should not have tennis balls, which may contain toxins.

✔ **Fleece and other stuffed toys:** Fleece toys have become very popular, and most dogs love them. Again, they're not chew toys, and you should not allow your dog to play unsupervised with them if he might chew them up. Children's stuffed toys are good alternatives for dogs who are not great destroyers; long, stuffed snakes are a favorite. For safety's sake, first remove any eyes or nose ornaments that a dog could pull off and swallow.

✔ **Flying discs:** Many Shepherds love flying discs, but be sure to get the soft type made especially for dogs. The hard types can damage teeth if the dog tries to catch one.

✔ **Squeaky toys:** Most squeaky toys are not great choices for puppies or for any dog who chews toys apart. Many are made of plastic that a puppy can chew and swallow easily. In most squeaky toys, the squeaker is easy to dislodge and swallow. If you must get a squeaky toy for your dog, buy a squeaky stuffed animal or a toy made for children, in which the squeakers are usually better made. And never leave your GSD unsupervised with a squeaky toy. These are toys, not chewies, and should be used only when you're playing with the dog.

✔ **Sticks:** The traditional stick can be great fun. Make sure that the ends are blunt and that the stick isn't so long that your Shepherd can jab one end into the ground if he's holding the other end in his mouth — the dog can jab a hole in the roof of his mouth that way. And of course, make sure that your dog doesn't eat the stick!

You can also tie a rag on a rope and tie the rope on the end of a stick, run around the yard holding the stick and dragging the rag, and "troll" for your dog — as well as practice your sport fishing skills when you get a bite. It's best to play this game when your neighbors aren't looking.

✔ **Toys that hold food:** A good choice is a toy (such as Kong or Buster Cube toys) in which you can place food, such as peanut butter or dog kibble. The dog can spend a long time extracting the food from the toy. These toys are great for times when you must leave your dog alone — they'll keep him so busy that he won't remember to pine away in your absence.

> ✔ **Homemade toys:** Stuff a sock with a couple of other socks, knot it near the end, and leave a long "leg" for throwing and tug o' war, and you have one of the best toys money can't buy. Take an old plastic milk jug or soda bottle, and you have wacky, noisy throw toy that bounces erratically. Throw in a few dog biscuits or kibble, and you have a challenging puzzle.

Contrary to popular belief, old shoes do *not* make great dog toys. German Shepherds are smart, but they can't tell the difference between last year's old styles and this year's new ones — and when they come across your open closet, they may think that they've gone to toy heaven.

Choosing Chews

Shepherds love to chew. If you leave them to their own devices, they will chew shoes, furniture, walls, and anything else that will succumb to their vice-grip jaws.

You'll be far more successful in *redirecting* your dog's chewing than in trying to abolish it — do so by providing him with chews that tire his active jaws. The most popular chew items are those made of rawhide. These chews are usually safe, but some serious problems have been associated with rawhide chews. To start, rawhide from other countries is often processed with poisonous substances. Insist on rawhide made in the U.S.

Chewing rawhide has a minimal effect on cleaning teeth, but it can never take the place of brushing your dog's teeth (see Chapter 10).

Although it doesn't happen often, some dogs have had problems with impacted, undigested rawhide that have required surgery. Others have choked on large hunks of rawhide.

Safer alternatives are rawhide chews made of compressed rawhide bits, although they don't last as long as regular rawhide chews do. A variety of vegetable-based chews are also available. For gator-jawed dogs, hard rubber or nylon bones can last a long time and provide good dental cleaning.

For a special treat, a variety of disgusting animal parts are available: hooves, ears, knuckle bones, and others that are unmentionable in mixed company. Pig ears are a great treat but are high in fat and can cause diarrhea. Knuckle bones are a traditional good choice. Hooves tend to splinter and have been implicated in some problems. They're extremely hard, and if you keep them in the house, you may end up throwing them away in a fit of rage after stepping on one in the middle of the night for the tenth time.

Be careful when you handle these dog treats. Some people have caught salmonella from handling them and then placing their hands in their mouths. Dogs are apparently more resistant to salmonella.

While I'm on the subject of chews, I should remind you about anti-chews. Bitter-tasting sprays and liquids are available that dissuade dogs from chewing surfaces. After checking to make sure that it won't stain your items, apply these sprays to anything you don't want your dog to chew but that may be tempting — your shoes, your sofa, and so on.

Stocking Up on First-Aid Supplies

Dog medical emergencies are just as scary as human ones — and having the right supplies on hand can make a big difference in how a dog recovers. Keep the following items in your doggy medicine chest in case your dog becomes ill or is injured:

- Anti-diarrhea medication
- Antiseptic skin ointment
- Clean sponge
- First-aid instructions
- Hydrogen peroxide
- Instant cold compress
- Ophthalmic (eye) ointment
- Pen light
- Rectal thermometer
- Scissors
- Self-adhesive bandage (such as Vet-Wrap)
- Soap
- Sterile gauze dressings
- Syringe
- Towel
- Tweezers
- Veterinarian and emergency clinic numbers and poison control center number

For much more information about taking care of a sick Shepherd, see Chapter 13.

Chapter 6

Welcoming Your Dog Home

In This Chapter

▶ Safeguarding your German Shepherd indoors and out

▶ Making it through the first night

▶ Saving your rugs, furniture, walls, and sanity

▶ Introducing a new dog to your children and existing pets

▶ Socializing your pup

Your new German Shepherd faces the transition from canine litter member to human family member. Every day will be full of novel experiences and new rules. Your pup is naturally inquisitive and will need you to safeguard him from danger and guide him toward becoming a well-mannered member of the household. This chapter explains how.

Puppy-Proofing Your Home

When you're preparing to bring home a new dog, your best safety measure is your own diligence. You must impress upon your family or roommates the dire consequences that could occur if they carelessly leave a door open, slam a door without looking, allow the dog to dance around the lawn mower, or leave a puddle of antifreeze on the garage floor. Some people are just not safety- or pet-oriented, and making them exercise proper care can be difficult.

You can do your part by making it as difficult as possible for your pup to get into trouble. Any place your German Shepherd may wander must be German Shepherd–proofed. The first step is to do everything you would do to baby-proof your home. Get down at puppy level and see what dangers beckon.

Remember that a German Shepherd puppy is like a super-baby. Imagine a baby who can run faster than an adult, jump his own height, and chew through wires. That's a German Shepherd puppy. And that's why you have to be even more diligent in puppy-proofing than in baby-proofing.

Indoors

Watch for the following puppy hazards inside the house:

- ✔ **Doors:** Doors can be a hidden danger area. Make everyone in your family aware of the danger of slamming a door. Use doorstops to ensure that the wind does not blow doors shut suddenly or that the puppy does not go behind the door to play. Be especially cautious with swinging doors; a puppy may try to push one open, become caught, try to back out, and strangle himself. Clear glass doors are difficult for animals to see, and the puppy could be injured running into them. Place some stickers or decals on them at dog eye level. Never close a garage door with a puppy darting about. Finally, keep doors leading to unfenced outdoor areas securely shut. A screen door is a vital safety feature, but if you want one you can rely on, cover the screen with heavy hardware cloth; otherwise, your dog can rip right through.

- ✔ **Electrical cords, outlets, and appliances:** Puppies love to chew electrical cords and even lick outlets. Doing so can result in severe burns, loss of jaw and tongue tissue, or death from shock. Dogs can also pull electrical appliances down on themselves by pulling on cords. Keep cords tucked away, unused outlets covered, and appliances safely stowed out of reach.

- ✔ **Unstable furniture and other objects:** Jumping up on an unstable object (such as a bookcase) could cause it to come crashing down, perhaps crushing the puppy. Make sure that your furniture is anchored against walls or is well out of the way; if you have something fragile, consider using baby gates to keep the dog out of the room.

- ✔ **Staircases, balconies, and decks:** Don't allow a puppy near the edges of high decks, balconies, or staircases. Use baby gates, temporary plastic fencing, or chicken wire if needed in dangerous areas.

- ✔ **Other miscellaneous dangers:** Puppies have gotten their heads caught inside canisters and suffocated, have been crushed under rocking and reclining chairs, and have even lost tongues from being stuck to metal on freezing days. No matter how diligent you are, you have to think of avoiding even the craziest-sounding accidents. The most important thing is to supervise, just as you would a baby or toddler.

Also make sure that these potential household killers are well out of your dog's reach:

- ✔ Antifreeze
- ✔ Chicken bones, or any bone that could be swallowed
- ✔ Chocolate (especially baker's chocolate)
- ✔ Prescription and over-the-counter drugs
- ✔ Household cleaners
- ✔ Nuts and bolts or other small metal objects
- ✔ Paint thinner
- ✔ Pennies
- ✔ Pins, needles, and anything else in a sewing basket
- ✔ Rodent, snail, and insect bait
- ✔ Sponges
- ✔ Toilet cleaners and fresheners

Swallowed foreign objects can cause intestinal blockages that must be surgically corrected in order to save the dog's life. Swallowed pennies can dissolve in the stomach and cause zinc poisoning. Chapter 13 provides information about what to do in these and other emergency situations.

Outdoors

Dangers also abound within the yard. Check for bushes with sharp, broken branches at German Shepherd eye level, as well as trees with dead branches or heavy fruits in danger of falling. If you have a pool, be aware that although dogs are natural swimmers, you must show your dog how to get out of the pool in case he falls or jumps in. You do so by getting in the pool with your dog while both of you swim and letting the dog practice leaving the pool by the steps. Do not allow or encourage the dog to try to pull himself up the side walls, and do not let him near the pool unsupervised.

The number-one safety precaution is a secure fence. Make sure that your German Shepherd can't jump over it, dig under it, break through it, or let himself out of the gate because the latch is loose. (See Chapter 5 for more on fencing.)

Some outdoor plants are poisonous to dogs and other animals. If you have any of the following plants in your yard, either remove them or fence them off so that your dog can't get into them:

- Azalea
- Castor bean
- Corn cockle
- English holly berries
- Foxglove
- Jerusalem cherry
- Jessamine
- Jimson weed
- Milkweed
- Mistletoe
- Oleander
- Philodendron
- Rattle box
- Rhododendron
- Water hemlock

Surviving the First Day and Night

If possible, arrange to take a few days off work when you first bring your new dog home so that the two of you have some time to get to know each other. If not, try to bring the pup home on a weekend. Remember that the pup has probably been a member of a large family, and spending his first day at your house all alone may be extremely frightening. Let him roam around the house with you, reassuring and rewarding him with touch and praise. Doing so helps the pup form a bond with you.

When you get the pup home, take him to the spot that will be his outdoor bathroom. After he relieves himself, praise him, let him explore a little, and then offer him a small meal (see Chapter 7 for information about dog nutrition). Then take him back to his bathroom area so that he can relieve himself again.

Exploring

Don't push matters with your new puppy. Let the first day be a quiet one. The pup has already had enough excitement with the trip to his new home. Now just let him get to know you and his new surroundings.

Of course, you want to keep an eye on your Shepherd during this exploration process. Puppies, like toddlers, can get into trouble if unsupervised. Your puppy is a natural-born explorer and will follow his nose into every nook and cranny of your home. You can always extend the area of your home in which your dog is welcome, but it's a lot harder to tell your dog that he's no longer allowed in certain areas when he's used to wandering at will. To keep that roaming instinct in check, it's wise to establish which areas are allowed and which are off-limits on the pup's first day home.

The easiest way to keep your dog out of your pristine living room is simply to shut the door. You can also set up a baby gate or a cardboard panel. Eventually, you can teach your Shepherd to stay out by praising him for stopping at the doorway, but your young pup is not ready to assume such responsibility yet.

In general, you're better off restricting your puppy's access to one or two rooms in which you can easily supervise his activities. Many people find the kitchen to be a good place because it doesn't have carpeting. Expanding the area is always easier than decreasing it; if you intend for your puppy to live outside, you may wish to limit his indoor access to only one room. Most young puppies are not yet ready to be placed outdoors by themselves, however.

Turning in

When your German Shepherd begins to act sleepy, place him in his cage or designated sleeping area (see Chapter 5) so he knows that this is his special bed. Be forewarned, though, that this first night will not be easy for the pup. Chances are that he has always slept cuddled with his litter mates and mother; sleeping by himself will be disconcerting.

To combat the loneliness, you can try including a stuffed toy in the dog's cage, but even that won't take the place of a living body. Placing the pup's bed next to yours helps. The objective is for the puppy to learn to settle down and sleep without you fussing over him. This takes time (on his end) and patience (on yours). Tell him that he's a good dog when he's settled; if he learns that he'll get attention when he cries, he'll keep crying.

Accepting visitors

Chances are your friends and neighbors will be eager to see the new arrival. Your puppy has had enough excitement for one day, though, so discourage any but your pup's future family members from visiting at first. Besides, your Shepherd needs to know just which people are going to be his family. In addition, your pup is still susceptible to contagious diseases. Friends with dogs of their own, especially sick or unvaccinated dogs, should at the very least wash their hands thoroughly and remove their shoes before visiting. Actually, such friends shouldn't visit at all.

Should your German Shepherd sleep on your bed? Certainly not at first. Your pup needs to learn to sleep by himself, and he needs to have the security of a bed of his own. Consider this, too, before sharing a bed with a German Shepherd: No matter how large your bed, you will end up hanging off the edge while your dog stretches to his full length. In addition, a dog in bed can cause problems between couples when the dog decides to be jealous or overly protective. Finally, unless you change your sheets almost every day, you will be covered with hair and whatever else was on your dog's paws. Just as with other furniture (see the section "Setting Boundaries," later in this chapter), it's easier to invite your dog up later than it is to suddenly make the bed off-limits.

Don't count on getting much sleep this first night (or week). You need to be ready to take your puppy outside whenever he awakens. But start setting up good habits as soon as possible. Take your puppy to his spot when you go out, praise him for going quickly, and bring him back in if he doesn't go. Don't let him train you!

Setting Boundaries

Do you pride yourself on your beautiful home? Do you cherish your white velvet chairs and oriental rugs? Are you getting a little nervous envisioning a puppy in its midst? Come now, why on earth would you worry about unleashing a mobile set of barracuda teeth set on auto-chew, powered by four mud-tracking pistons and armed with a variety of orifices prone to randomly squirt out assorted yuck when you least expect it?

I know I said that you should treat your new German Shepherd like a real family member, but at least at first, think of your new dog as a very *sloppy* family member. German Shepherd pups don't wipe their feet, they chew like beavers, they're covered none too securely with fur, and they're not overly particular about where they deposit bodily waste. Your idea of a better home and garden is unlikely to mesh with your dog's. Unless you're trying to make your in-laws and neighbors quit coming over, you have to set up some house rules for your new family member, or your new family member will rule the house.

You can't prevent your dog from shedding, but you can cut down on how much shedding occurs by regular brushing, and you can control where it occurs by setting limits. You also can't prevent your dog from chewing, but you can redirect chewing to more appropriate items and prevent the dog from getting his teeth near your valuable items. In other words, you can't prevent your dog from being a dog — you wouldn't want to! But you can set limits.

Chewing

Part of a pup's exploratory tools are his teeth, and any chewed items left in his wake are your fault, not your pup's — *you* are the one who should have known better. Harsh corrections are no more effective than a firm "No" and removal of the item. If you come across a cherished item chewed to bits and feel compelled to lash out, go ahead — hit yourself in the head a few times for slipping up. It may teach you a lesson!

The best cure for chewing is the removal of all inappropriate items from the reach of the dog's jaws. Another good cure is age. Your puppy really will grow out of his need to gnaw everything in sight, but it may take a year or so for things to get better.

Shaking a puppy (or adult dog) as a means of discipline is no safer than shaking a baby. It's a good way to cause neck injuries or brain damage. In an adult, it's also a good way to get yourself bitten.

Getting on the furniture

Like all intelligent creatures, German Shepherds enjoy the creature comforts of chairs and sofas. Keep in mind that your nice furniture won't be nice for long after your dog sheds all over it, tries to dig a hole in it, dances on it with muddy paws, and chews on the arms while drifting off to sleep. If you don't want your dog on the furniture, keep him off from the beginning. Don't pick up the puppy and set him on your lap; instead, sit on the floor with him.

When your pup does get on forbidden furniture, simply say "No" and place him — don't fling him! — back on the floor. If you don't seem to be making progress, you can buy a device that emits a loud tone when the dog jumps on furniture (and in really hard cases, you can even get a mat that provides an electric buzz when the dog steps on it), but such devices shouldn't be necessary if you train your puppy gently and consistently from the beginning. Make sure that every family member knows the rules and understands that sneaking the puppy onto off-limits furniture does the puppy no favors.

But how can you treat your dear dog like a less privileged member of the family? You can make compromises. Your dog can learn that he is allowed only on certain pieces of furniture, or only if his special blanket is on the furniture. Your dog can have his own special bed, maybe next to your own. Restricting your dog doesn't mean making him second-class — it means making sure that he has a place to call his own.

General misbehavior

If your pup misbehaves, you can go berserk, or you can count to 3, and then 33, and end up with a far better trained dog in the long run. Dogs don't understand English, and they don't understand you losing your temper. They really do want to please you, but it's a strange world with strange rules that don't always make sense to fun-loving pups. The situation will get better, so make sure that you can look back at these precious months and remember the fun parts without being ashamed of your own lack of training in temper control. Your puppy will never be a puppy again. They really do grow up too fast.

The first few months are a time of incredible fun and hair-pulling frustration. Your pup will have flashes of intelligence and obedience matched by periods of apparent dumbness and disobedience. No matter how wonderful your dog is and how careful you are, you will lose a few cherished possessions and more than a few good nights' sleep — all of which is part of raising a puppy.

Introducing Your Dog to the World

Too many people, especially those who live in rural areas, forget that there's a whole big world out there, and if your dog spends his puppyhood down on the farm, it really will be a case of country come to town when you finally take him to the big city. You can't put this off because puppies are born basically fearless. As they open their eyes and begin to explore the world, they can't afford to be afraid of every new thing they see because everything they see is new. So when they're very young, up to the age of about 12 weeks, they take new experiences in stride. Therefore, the best time to introduce your dog to the world is from about 8 to 12 weeks of age. During this time, the puppy will not be frightened of new experiences and will come to accept them readily and happily. These happy memories will stay with the pup as he grows into adulthood. (See Figure 6-1.)

Figure 6-1:
By exposing your puppy to a variety of new experiences, such as children and the outdoors, you teach him not to be afraid of the world around him.

© Kent and Donna Dannen/AKC Stock Images

Of course, a dog without fear is a dead (or stupid) dog, and starting at around 12 weeks, puppies begin to get a little more suspicious of anything new. This suspicious nature continues to grow. If you wait until your pup is older, when he has become fearful of new experiences, you may never convince him that harmless things are indeed harmless. Therefore, you should expose your pup to as many novel experiences early in puppyhood as possible. Try to expose him to

- Children
- Strangers, both men and women
- Other dogs
- Cats and other pets
- Car rides
- Loud noises
- Traffic
- A variety of footing and surfaces
- Swimming

- ✔ Ball chasing and other appropriate games
- ✔ Bathing and grooming procedures
- ✔ Being alone
- ✔ Being in a cage
- ✔ Any specialized circumstances or equipment required of working or competition dogs

Remember, the idea is not to overwhelm but to expose — *and* to make it a good experience. Bring a pocket full of treats and hand them out liberally.

Many people arrange for their dogs to be exposed to everything — the dogs go with them to work, then to class, and then to a new experience every day. But the owners forget one thing: to expose the pup to being by himself. This omission is serious because separation anxiety is one of the largest sources of dog problems. Dogs are social animals who don't like to be alone, but most dogs have to be alone at some time or another. Start when your Shepherd is already tired, and leave him in a place where he is secure. Leave him for only a little while. Don't sneak out, but don't make a big deal of leaving, either. Just nonchalantly leave and return. Work up to longer times. If your dog does well with this exercise, great! If not, see Chapter 9.

What about disease? You're right, you can't trot your puppy all around town without worrying about him catching a disease. The thing about socialization, though, is that a little bit will do. Take your dog to a "clean" area (one in which unvaccinated dogs or puppies are unlikely to have been) a few times when he's young. If you expose him to other puppies, make sure that they have been vaccinated.

One more important thing about socializing puppies: A bad experience is worse than no experience at all. Puppies learn from outings, and they're just as likely to learn that strangers are mean as they are that strangers are kind. Be very careful that your pup doesn't get hurt or frightened. Don't think that if a little is good, a lot is better. For example, if you want your puppy to enjoy a stroll downtown and meeting new people, don't figure that by taking him to the Macy's Thanksgiving Day Parade, you will be socializing even more. You won't. You will overwhelm your pup and achieve the opposite result of what you expected.

Every dog is different. Some approach everything in life as though they owned the patent to it, and others are more naturally wary and lack confidence. The latter type needs a little more work, but don't think that by flooding a dog with crowds and new experiences you will miraculously make him brave. You need to build his confidence, and that only happens gradually. Just as with people, confidence comes from pride in a job well done, so the best thing for these dogs is to learn to do something. For a very young puppy, simple obedience may be the answer. For an older dog, agility is probably the best confidence builder. For some Shepherds, Schutzhund training (see Chapter 16) may prove the answer, but you have to be extremely careful in your training. Tracking or herding can also be great confidence boosters.

Taking Your Pup to School

In many towns, obedience groups offer puppy kindergarten classes. These classes are a great opportunity to expose your pup to nice people and other pups his own age. Especially if you have only one dog, he may not have many opportunities to interact with other dogs. But again, this doesn't mean that running amuck with his new buddies is necessarily a good thing, especially if your dog gets beat up or is the bully. You need to know when to step in and say, "Enough is enough!"

Ask your veterinarian's opinion about your pup's immunity status before taking him around other dogs. (See Chapter 11 for information about finding and working with a vet.)

In general, these classes are great, and you're lucky if you can find one in your area. Contact the American Kennel Club or your vet for the name of a nearby obedience training club or German Shepherd club. These clubs may offer their own classes or be able to suggest a good class for you to attend. While being exposed to new experiences, your pup can start practicing his first simple obedience exercises and learn to control himself in public. You can also get advice about common puppyhood problems. As with all classes, there are good ones and rotten ones, so check it out first and don't be shy about complaining or quitting if things don't seem right after you enroll.

Chapter 7

Feeding Your German Shepherd

Your Shepherd's athletic build — as well as his energy level, condition, health, and longevity — depends in part on which foods you set in front of him. Unlike humans, dogs are usually fed only one type of food, which makes choosing that food even more important and intimidating. All it takes is one dizzying trip through the dog food section of a supermarket or pet supply store to leave you utterly baffled.

Before you become paralyzed with indecision, keep in mind that dog nutritionists have done most of the work for you, and that as long as the food you choose meets some basic guidelines, it will be adequate to sustain your dog's life. It may not make him bloom with condition, however. For that, you do need to do a little investigating, as this chapter explains.

Going Bowling

To eat and drink, your dog needs separate food and water bowls. Although you can let him use your people bowls, most people prefer for the dog to have his own. Your choices are plastic, ceramic, and stainless steel.

✔ Look for stainless steel bowls. They last forever (except for the occasional dog who chews his bowl) and are easy to wash.

✔ Forget plastic. Dogs can chew it up, and many dogs are allergic to it. It's also hard to keep clean.

✔ Ceramic bowls are a nice aesthetic choice but can be awkward to clean and will harbor germs if they crack.

Get a good-sized food bowl, at least 10 inches in diameter. Most German Shepherds prefer a wide, rather than deep, bowl. Otherwise, their jaws bump against the sides when they try to eat.

Make sure that the bottom of the food bowl you purchase is flat or has nonskid material on it. Round bowls tend to tip when your dog is trying to get at those last morsels — or if your dog thinks it's more entertaining to dump the food on the floor than to eat it out of the bowl!

If the dog's bowl is outside and you develop an ant problem, you can buy a special ant-resistant bowl, or you can simply place the bowl in a shallow pan of water so that the ants would have to cross a moat to get to the food.

Choosing Your Dog's Chow

Once you have the dog's food bowl, you need to decide what type of food to put in it. When you first bring your puppy home, you can continue to feed him whatever he had been eating at his breeder's or former home, but you'll want to experiment to find a food that meets your growing dog's needs — and taste preferences. If you need to start with a new food, choose a high-quality food that's appropriate for your dog's age.

When changing foods, introduce a new food gradually. Dogs can get upset stomachs from sudden changes in diet.

Dry, semi-moist, or canned?

Although dogs are members of the order *Carnivora* ("meat-eaters"), they are actually omnivorous, meaning that a diet derived from both animals and plants best meets their nutritional needs. Most dogs do have a decided preference for meat over non-meat foods, but a balanced meal combines both meat- and plant-based nutrients. These nutrients are commercially available in several forms. Most Shepherd owners feed a combination of dry and canned food, supplemented with dog biscuits as treats. For example, a typical meal might be made up of dry to canned food in a 3:1 ratio, with dog biscuits given as occasional snacks. The exact amount depends on your dog's age, activity, metabolism, weight, and health.

- **Dry food** (containing about 10 percent moisture) is the most popular, economical, and healthy choice, but it's the least enticing form of dog food.

- **Semi-moist foods** (about 30 percent moisture) are tasty and convenient but are not an optimal nutritional choice for a dog's regular diet because they contain high levels of sugar as preservatives. Pay no attention to their meat-like shapes; they all start out as powder and are formed to look like meat chunks or ground beef.

✔ **Canned food** has a high moisture content (about 75 percent moisture), which helps make it tasty but also makes it comparatively expensive, because you're getting only fewer solid nutrients for your money. Keep in mind, too, that a steady diet of canned food does not provide the chewing necessary to maintain dental health.

✔ **Dog biscuits** can help provide the chewing action necessary to rid teeth of some (but far from all) dental plaque. (See Chapter 10 for more on dog dental care.) The better varieties of dog biscuits provide complete nutrition. Dog owners most commonly use them as snacks or treats.

When you add table scraps and other enticements to your dog's food, you disrupt the diet's balance. A few table scraps won't hurt, but a diet made up of a large percentage of scraps will almost certainly not be balanced, and that could be harmful to your dog's health (not to mention his waistline).

Protein and fat contents

The Association of American Feed Control Officials (AAFCO) recommends minimum nutrient levels for dogs based on controlled feeding studies. Unless you are a nutritionist, the chance of you cooking up a homemade diet that meets these exacting standards is remote. So the first rule is to select a high-quality, name-brand food whose label states that it not only meets the requirements set by the AAFCO but also has been tested in feeding trials.

Natural and homemade diets

More and more, people are cooking for their dogs just as they do for themselves and their families to ensure that they're eating a healthy, balanced diet. Homemade diets guarantee that you know what you're feeding your dog — and if your dog has certain allergies, you may *need* to cook for him.

Although knowing everything that's going into your dog's bowl is reassuring, it can also be troubling. Dogs are not people, so you can't just figure that what's good for your human family is good for your Shepherd. If you want to go the homemade or natural route, you need to bone up on canine nutritive needs. And because each dog is different, you need to experiment to be sure that your dog is getting what he needs.

Fortunately, a lot of information is available on homemade, natural diets for dogs. A particularly reliable source is the book *Holistic Guide to a Healthy Dog*, by Wendy Volhard and Kerry Brown, DVM (Howell Book House).

When you compare food labels, keep in mind that differences in moisture content make it difficult to directly compare the guaranteed analyses in different forms of food unless you first do some calculations to equate the percentage of dry matter. The components that vary most from one brand to another are protein and fat percentages.

- ✔ **Protein** provides the necessary building blocks for growth and maintenance of bones, muscle, and coat and the production of infection-fighting antibodies. The quality of protein is as important as the quantity of protein. Meat-derived protein is generally of higher quality; it is more easily digestible than plant-derived protein. Most Shepherds do fine on regular adult dry foods that have protein levels of about 20 percent. Canned foods appear to have a lower percentage because of their high water content.

  A good general rule is that three or four of the first six ingredients should be animal-derived. These ingredients tend to be tastier and more highly digestible than plant-based ingredients; more highly digestible foods generally mean less stool volume and fewer gas problems.

- ✔ **Fat** is the calorie-rich component of foods, and most dogs prefer the taste of foods with a higher fat content. Fat is necessary to good health, aiding in the transport of important vitamins and providing energy. Dogs that are deficient in fat often have sparse, dry coats. Yet foods that are too high in fat can also produce coat, weight, and other health problems. Only extremely active dogs should eat high-fat dog foods.

Choose a food that has a protein and fat content that suits your dog's life stage, adjusting for any weight or health problems. (Prescription diets formulated for specific health problems are available from your veterinarian.) Your vet or breeder can help you make this determination.

- ✔ **Puppies and adolescents** need particularly high levels of protein and somewhat higher fat levels in their diets, such as those found in puppy foods.

  German Shepherds are among the breeds predisposed to hip dysplasia (see Chapter 11). Studies have shown that extremely rapid growth can increase the probability of developing hip dysplasia. The current recommendation is to discontinue feeding puppy food and switch to a lower-protein food (about 21 percent to 24 percent) at about 3 months of age. The puppy will grow more slowly but will reach the same adult size.

- ✔ **Healthy adult dogs** should get average protein and fat levels found in adult-formulated premium dog foods.

- ✔ **Stressed, highly active, or underweight dogs** should get higher protein levels or even puppy food.

- ✔ **Obese dogs or dogs with heart or digestive problems** should get a lower-fat food.

- ✔ **Older dogs, especially those with kidney problems,** should get moderate levels of very high-quality protein. Studies have shown that high-protein diets do not cause kidney failure in older dogs, but a high-protein diet will do a lot of harm to a dog who already has kidney problems.

Testing Your Dog's Tastes

Mealtime is a highlight of a dog's day; although a dog will eventually eat even the most unsavory of dog foods if given no choice, depriving your family member of one of life's simple — and for a dog, most important — pleasures hardly seems fair. So shop around for a food that your Shepherd enjoys. If your dog doesn't like it by the end of the first bag, try another brand. Although many individual differences exist, the average dog prefers beef, pork, lamb, chicken, and horse meat, in that order. They also tend to prefer higher-calorie (and of course, higher-priced) dog foods.

Heed this word of warning as you experiment to find the right food: One of the great mysteries of life is how a dog who is renowned for his lead stomach and prefers to eat out of garbage cans can at the same time develop a violently upset stomach simply because you switched from one high-quality dog food to another. But it happens. When changing foods, do so gradually, mixing in progressively more and more of the new food each day for several days.

Also beware of this: Dogs often seem to prefer a new food when first offered but balk after the novelty has worn off. Only after you buy a cupboard full of this alleged ambrosia do you discover that it was just a passing fancy.

Knowing What Not to Feed a Dog

Avoid feeding any of the following to your dog:

- ✔ **Alcohol:** Many dogs like the taste of beer, but dogs can become intoxicated very easily. Some dogs have been killed while intoxicated, and others have died from drinking too much alcohol.

- ✔ **Bones that could be swallowed whole:** Swallowing these bones can cause choking or intestinal blockage.

- ✔ **Chicken, pork, lamb, or fish bones:** These bones can be swallowed, and their sharp ends can pierce the stomach or intestinal walls.

- ✔ **Cooked bones:** Cooked bones tend to break and splinter.

- ✔ **Chocolate:** This human treat contains theobromine, which is poisonous to dogs.

- ✔ **Mineral supplements** (unless advised to do so by your veterinarian): Adding minerals can upset the balance of other nutrients, causing health problems.

- ✔ **Onions:** Onions can cause red blood cells to break down, sometimes causing serious illness in dogs who eat them.

Also avoid food that has been sitting on the shelf for a long period. One sign that a food may be old is that grease is seeping through the bag. Dry food loses nutrients as it sits, and the fat content can become rancid. Also avoid bags that have holes in them or show any evidence of bugs. Steer clear of bags on which you can see tiny webs or moths, too (they love dog biscuits); these are signs of insect infestation. Always strive to buy and use only the freshest food available.

Thirsting for Water

Water is essential to your Shepherd's health and comfort. Your dog's body is made up of mostly water, and many of his organs require proper hydration in order to function properly. Dehydration is one of the first things your veterinarian looks for when you bring in an ill dog to be examined; if a dog is dehydrated and can't drink, the veterinarian will give fluids intravenously.

Fortunately, in most cases you can keep your dog properly hydrated simply by providing a bowl of fresh water at all times. Adding ice cubes will encourage your dog to drink.

Don't keep your dog's water bowl full simply by topping it off every day. This habit allows algae to form along the sides of the bowl and gives bacteria a chance to multiply. Instead, empty, scrub, and refill the water bowl daily. And keep it filled. If the water bowl runs dry, your dog may turn to the toilet bowl as an especially deluxe alternative source. It should go without saying that drinking from the toilet is not a healthy practice — and definitely not conducive to dog kisses! Make it a habit to keep the lid down.

Deciding How Often to Feed Your Dog

Dogs are creatures of habit who like to eat on very regular schedules. Of course, your dog will probably eat whenever you feed him and as often as you offer him food, but setting up a healthy feeding schedule and sticking to it is in the dog's best interests. The schedule depends on the dog's age:

- ✔ **Very young puppies** should be fed three or four times a day on a regular schedule. Feed them as much as they care to eat in about 15 minutes.

- ✔ **Puppies aged 3 to 6 months** should be fed three times daily.

- ✔ **Young dogs aged 6 months to 1 year** should be fed two or three times daily.

- ✔ **Adult dogs** should be fed twice daily.

Some people let their dogs decide when to eat by making food available at all times. This is not a good idea for several reasons. First, a lack of appetite is often the first sign of a health problem. A self-feeding dog may seem picky, but he may be sick. You need to know which is the case. Another reason not to let your dog self-feed is that if you have other pets or children in the house, they may get into the dog's food — not a good thing.

Your healthy dog should be eager for his meals. He should gobble them down within 15 minutes. Don't encourage fussy eating by giving him any more time than that.

Weighing In on Fat and Thin

Just as important as feeding the right *type* of food is feeding the right *amount* of food. If you overfeed or underfeed your dog, he will become overweight or underweight — neither of which is a healthy state.

A Shepherd of the proper weight should have a slightly hourglass figure whether viewed from above or the side. There should be no roll of fat over the withers or rump. The stomach should be slightly tucked up. The ribs should be easily felt through a layer of muscle. A GSD is an athlete and should have an athlete's body: lean and muscular. (Figure 7-1 shows a German Shepherd at the appropriate weight.)

Ribs easily felt through
layer of muscle

No roll of fat

Stomach slightly
tucked up

Figure 7-1:
A German
Shepherd
should
be lean and
muscular.

Gail Painter

The amount of exercise your dog gets also affects his weight. See Chapter 15 for information about exercise for German Shepherds.

Shedding the pounds

The dog's wild ancestor, the wolf, evolved to survive feast and famine, gorging following a kill but then waiting several days before another feast. In today's world, without the period of famine, dogs who feast daily can easily become obese. Obesity predisposes dogs to joint injuries and heart problems and makes many pre-existing problems worse. An obese GSD can't enjoy one of the greatest pleasures in life — the ability to run, jump, and frisk with boundless energy.

Overfeeding a German Shepherd puppy is one of the worst things you can do. Studies have shown that overfed GSD pups are more likely to develop hip dysplasia. It's not that overfeeding causes hip dysplasia; rather, if a dog has a genetic predisposition to be dysplastic, overfeeding makes him more likely to actually become dysplastic.

It's easy to tell that you're overfeeding an adult when the dog becomes fat; trying to decide whether you're overfeeding a puppy is much harder. A puppy with rolls of fat is probably being overfed. One with a pot belly may have internal parasites, however. Your pup should maintain a trim figure, neither fat nor thin. Special large-breed puppy foods are available that are formulated to provide proper nutrition without encouraging overly fast growth.

If you have an overweight German Shepherd, use the following guidelines to get him fit and trim again:

- ✔ Feed your portly pooch a high-fiber, low-fat, and medium-protein diet dog food. (The section "Choosing Your Dog's Chow," earlier in this chapter, explains how to determine a dog food's fat and protein contents.) Commercially available diet foods, which supply about 15 percent fewer calories per pound, are preferable to feeding less of a fattening food. New research has shown that higher-protein (about 24 percent), low-fat diets are best. Home-prepared diets that are both tasty and less fattening are also available. Your veterinarian can usually provide printed recipes.

- ✔ Watch the snacks that you feed your dog. Many people find that one of the many pleasures of dog ownership is sharing a special treat with their pets. Rather than giving up this bonding activity, substitute a low-calorie alternative such as rice cakes or carrots. Make sure that family members aren't sneaking the dog forbidden tidbits.

- ✔ Keep the dog out of the kitchen or dining area at food preparation or mealtimes so that you aren't tempted to let him nibble on the scraps that may fall to the floor.

- ✔ Schedule a walk immediately following your dinner to get your dog's mind off of your leftovers — doing so will be good for both of you.

If your dog remains overweight, seek your veterinarian's opinion. Several health problems (including heart disease, hypothyroidism, Cushing's disease, and the early stages of diabetes) can cause the appearance of obesity and should be ruled out or treated. A dog whose stomach is enlarged, but who has no fat around the shoulders or rump, is especially suspect and should be examined by a vet. However, most cases of obesity result simply from eating more calories than are expended.

Putting on weight

Just as some dogs have trouble with excess weight, others have trouble keeping their weight up. Often, a dog will suffer a temporary loss of appetite. How you overcome this problem depends on its apparent cause.

- ✔ Many picky eaters are created when their owners begin to spice up their ordinary food with especially tasty treats. The dog then refuses to eat unless the preferred treat is offered and finally learns that if he refuses even the proffered treat, another even tastier enticement will be offered. If you and your dog are playing this game, try a couple of dog food brands. If your Shepherd still won't eat, you may have to employ tough love. Give your dog a good, tasty meal, but don't succumb to blackmail or you may be a slave to your dog's gastronomical whims for years to come. Eventually, the dog will eat what you offer him — a hungry Shepherd won't hold out forever!

✔ A sick or recuperating dog may have to be coaxed into eating. Usually, cooked fresh meat prepared with broth and rice will do the job; consult with your veterinarian.

✔ If the dog suddenly loses his appetite or loses weight, take him to a veterinarian. Such problems can be warning signs of a physical disorder. Also see a vet if the dog's appetite fails to pick up or if he simply can't gain weight. Some GSDs have enzymatic deficiencies that you can treat by adding digestive enzymes to their food (see Chapter 12). You are the best judge of whether your dog's appetite has changed. For some chow hounds, a day without inhaling each meal is cause for concern; for other dogs who may be generally less enthusiastic eaters, it may take a week of pickiness before you realize that a problem is brewing.

Chapter 8

Training Your Dog

German Shepherds are among the most intelligent dogs. Intelligent dogs can be a challenge because they need mental stimulation. Remember, idle minds are the workshop of the devil — and idle German Shepherd minds work overtime! Training is a great way to keep your dog's mind occupied, and as an added bonus, a trained dog actually minds what you say.

There's no such thing as an untrainable dog, but many untrained dogs exist. A surprising number of these untrained dogs have been "trained," but trained ineffectively. Their owners usually give up and decide that their dogs are dumb or that dog training works only for dog whisperers or people who devote their entire lives to training dogs. You can train your dog without devoting your life to it, however. You just have to know the rules.

This chapter walks you through the various aspects of dog training, from the all-important housetraining to lead training to Sit, Stay, and more.

The Ten Commandments of Training

Why do some people seem to be natural-born dog trainers? Because they have a sense of how to communicate with their dogs, and they also follow some basic rules. Following these rules is absolutely essential to your success in producing a well-behaved dog. If you obey these ten commandments, I can virtually guarantee that you'll be pleased with the results of your training sessions.

1. **Think like a dog.** Dogs live in the present. If you punish or reward them, they can only assume that you're acknowledging their behavior at that moment. So if you discover a mess, drag your dog to it from his nap in the other room, and scold, the dog will get the impression that he is being scolded for napping (or that you are mentally unstable). Good lesson!

2. **You get what you ask for.** Dogs repeat actions that bring them rewards, whether or not you intend for them to. Letting your dog out of his cage to make him quit whining may work momentarily, but in the long run you'll end up with a dog who whines incessantly every time you put him in a cage. Make sure to reward only those behaviors that you want to see more often.

3. **Mean what you say.** Sometimes a puppy is awfully cute when he misbehaves, and sometimes your hands are full, and sometimes you just aren't sure what you want from your dog. But lapses in consistency are ultimately unfair to the dog. If you feed your dog from the table "just this one time" because he begs, you teach him that although begging may not always result in a handout, it just might pay off tonight. This intermittent payoff produces behavior that is resistant to change — just like a slot machine jackpot. You could hardly have done a better job of training your GSD to beg if you tried!

4. **Say what you mean.** Your GSD takes commands literally. If you teach that "Down" means to lie down, what must the dog think when you yell "Down" to tell him to get off the sofa where he was already lying down? Or "Sit down" when you mean "Sit"? If "Stay" means not to move until given a release word and you say, "Stay here," as you leave the house for work, you are telling your dog that you want him to sit by the door all day until you get home.

5. **Guide, don't force.** Your German Shepherd already wants to please you; your job is simply to lead the way. Forcing a dog to do something can distract or intimidate him, actually slowing down learning.

6. **Punish yourself, not your dog.** Striking, shaking, and choking are extremely dangerous, counterproductive, and cruel; they have no place in the training of a beloved family member. Plus, they don't work. Owners sometimes try to make it "a correction the dog will remember" by ignoring or chastising him for the rest of the day. The dog may indeed realize that his owner is upset, but he won't know why. Besides, chances are that *you're* doing things the wrong way, not your dog.

7. **Give your dog a hunger for learning.** Your GSD will work better and will be more responsive to food rewards if his stomach is not full. Never try to train a hot, sleepy, or tired dog.

8. **You can be a quitter.** You, and your dog, have good days and bad days. On bad days, quit. It makes no sense to continue when one or the other is not in the mood for training. Do one simple exercise and then do something else. Never train your dog when you're irritable or impatient.

9. **Happy endings make happy dogs.** Begin and end each training session with an exercise that the dog can do well. Keep sessions short and fun — no longer than 10 to 15 minutes. Dogs have short attention spans, and you'll notice that after about 15 minutes, your dog's performance begins to suffer unless a lot of play is involved. Continuing to train a tired or bored dog will result in the training of bad habits, as well as resentment for the dog and frustration for the trainer. Especially when training a young puppy, or when you have only one or two different exercises to practice, quit while you're ahead. Keep your dog wanting more and you'll have a happy, willing obedience partner.

10. **Once is enough.** Repeating a command over and over or shouting it louder and louder never helps anyone, dog or human, understand what is expected. Your GSD is not hard of hearing. Repeating or shouting a command only adds to your dog's confusion and anxiety. Instead, give your command once in a calm voice and then help your dog follow it.

11. **The best-laid plans don't include dogs.** Nothing ever goes as perfectly as it seems to in the training instructions. You may encounter setbacks, but you can train your dog as long as you remember to be consistent, firm, gentle, realistic, and patient — and have a good sense of humor.

Yeah, I know. You got an extra commandment, no charge.

A meeting of the minds

What if dogs ruled the earth? You wake one day to find yourself in a backward world with a collar around your neck and a German Shepherd holding the leash. The dog is barking and whining, and one of its whines sounds like "Tis!" Suddenly, you're jerked by the neck and pushed to the ground. Then the dog walks away and whines, "Yats," so you go to follow and whammy — a jerk backward with the leash. Better not do that again. So the dog walks away again and yanks the leash while barking, "Emoc!"

What have you learned from this experience? Number one, being trained (if that's what you call it) stinks. It's confusing, unfair, unpredictable, and unfun. As if that's not enough, your trainer apparently thinks that you're either stupid or stubborn.

What if you had a different trainer? This one first whines, "You, emchtaw!" so you look over and you're handed your favorite snack. Then your new trainer whines, "Tis," and slides a chair under your rump. You sit and are again handed your favorite snack. Then the dog says, "Yats," and steadies you in your seat as she backs away. Then the dog calls, "Emoc!" and beckons you. When you get there, more snacks! Learning what these words mean wouldn't take you long, and you might start thinking that you've finally found that easy job you've been looking for all your life.

Remember to look at things from your dog's point of view. Doing so might help you to quit being stupid.

Making Training Fun by Rewarding Good Behavior

The best obedience dogs, drug-detection dogs, and police dogs have one thing in common while they're at work — their tails are wagging. They enjoy every minute, not only because the work itself is pleasurable, but because the reward following it is also fun. Did that attitude come about because they were dragged, slapped, and choked? Of course not! It came about because their trainers knew how to make training a game. Just like people, dogs may go through the motions of a job they're forced to do, but they will never do it well unless it's fun.

Old-fashioned dog training methods based on force are difficult, ineffective, and no fun for either dog or trainer. Punishment may tell a dog what not to do, but it can't tell a dog what he should do, and it can't make a dog want to do it. Your role should be teacher, not drill master; your goal is to teach through guidance, not punishment.

Your first assignment is to find out what your dog loves. A special treat? A chance to chase a ball? A big hug? Whatever it is, make it your secret training ally. Save this special treat for training rewards, and don't give it out too freely.

Dog owners have been told for years that dogs should work only for praise, but praise alone is not a strong motivator for most dogs. Praise can become a stronger motivator if you always praise immediately before giving a food reward. In this way, praise becomes a secondary reinforcer. Eventually, you can wean the dog from the food and he will come to work in large part for praise, but you should still give food or games as rewards intermittently.

Many years ago, people believed that dogs should not be trained with food. Yet professional animal trainers and animal learning scientists knew that food training produces excellent results. Only recently has food-motivated training become accepted in training the family dog, and owners are finding dogs that learn faster, mind more reliably, work more eagerly, and have more trusting dog/owner relationships.

Just for clicks

Professional dog trainers go one step further than food rewards: They use a signal, such as that from a clicker, to tell the dog instantly when he has performed correctly. They then follow the signal with a food reward. Trainers use a clicker signal because it is fast, noticeable, and something the dog does not encounter in everyday life. To apply this technique to the instructions in this chapter, issue a clicker signal before you give a treat.

You initially use food to guide the dog into position and then reward him when he is in place. After he knows what is expected, you hold the food out of sight and give it to him only when he has performed correctly. Ultimately, you wean the dog from getting a food reward each time but still give one every once in a while. This randomized schedule — as in slot machine pay-offs — has proven to be very effective in both animals and humans.

Food is a great teaching aid, but eventually the best-trained dogs work for fun — the fun of the work and the fun of a special game or treat following the work.

Commanding a Good Performance

Issuing commands is essential to proper training. You can't expect your dog just to do what you want him to — you must tell him that you want him to do something, and you must specify what it is that you want him to do. Make your commands consistent, clear, and concise.

The crux of training is anticipation. Your dog comes to anticipate that upon hearing his name and then a command, he will be induced to perform some action, and he will eventually perform this action without further assistance from you. A properly issued command has four parts:

1. **Your dog's name.** You probably spend a good deal of your day talking, with very few words intended as commands for your dog. So you need to alert your dog that this talk is directed toward him by calling his name.

2. **The word that tells your dog what's coming next.** "Fritz, sit!" tells your dog that after he hears "sit," you will induce him to sit.

3. **An induction to perform the desired behavior.** Induce Fritz to sit either by luring him with a treat or by pushing him into position.

4. **A reward for performing the behavior you told him to perform.** Eventually, Fritz will make the connection that you always reward him for sitting when he hears the word *sit,* and he will find that it's easier to go ahead and sit without your help.

Many trainers make the mistake of simultaneously saying the command word *at the same time* they place the dog into position. The command should come *immediately before* the desired action or position. When the command and action come at the same time, the dog tends to pay more attention to your action of placing him in position and less attention to the command word, and the command word loses its predictive value for the dog.

Housetraining

You know you've lived with a puppy when the sound of running water awakens you from a deep slumber and you blindly stumble toward the source yelling, "Out!" Don't think that you can raise a puppy and never have to clean your carpets. All puppies go in the house until they're trained not to. For obvious reasons, housebreaking is the most critical type of training you can provide a dog who spends time indoors.

As dogs go, German Shepherds go in the house less often than most other breeds — maybe not at first, but they're fairly easy to housebreak. No matter how gifted your German Shepherd is, he probably will leave occasional "gifts" for you until he is around 6 months of age, and he may not be reliably housetrained until he's 1 year old.

If you want to eliminate household elimination, you need to heed the following housetraining rules.

Rule #1: Restrict your pup's unsupervised freedom in the house

If you plan to let your dog roam freely about the house, plan on stepping in a lot of soggy spots (or worse!) in remote areas. Your dog is not being sneaky; he's being a good little wolf. All canines have a natural desire to avoid soiling their denning area. As soon as wolf pups can teeter out of their dens, they walk away from the entrance to eliminate. The wolf den area is considerably smaller than your house, however, and your pup probably considers only his own bed to be the equivalent of the den. He may walk to another part of the room and eliminate there, not understanding that he has just soiled the carpet in *your* den!

The solution is to restrict your puppy to a wolf den–sized area when you aren't around to supervise. You can use your dog's cage as his den (see Chapter 5 for more on cages), but if the cage is too large, the puppy may simply step away from the area in which he sleeps and relieve himself at the other end of the cage. You can divide an overly large cage with a secure barrier until the puppy is larger or housebroken. Even so, your puppy may step just outside the door of the cage when you open the door and eliminate there. That's why you need to hustle your pup outside after he has awakened and you've let him out. If the cage is near a door to the outside, you have a better chance of getting the dog from the cage to the door accident-free.

If you can't place the pup's bed or cage near a door to the outside, you can fashion a runway out of portable construction fencing or even cardboard that you set in place when you let him out. You can also line the floor with plastic or scatter rugs.

Rule #2: "Just a second" is not in your pup's vocabulary

When a puppy has to go, he has to go *now* — not after you finish that last bite or this TV show. Puppies have very weak control over their bladders and bowels, so if you don't take them to their doggy outhouses often and immediately, they may not be able to avoid soiling. And when a pup soils in the house, he brands that area as his bathroom and is likely to go there again.

Learn to predict when your puppy will have to relieve himself. Immediately after awakening, and soon after heavy drinking or playing, your puppy will urinate. Right after eating, or if nervous, your puppy will have to defecate. Car rides also tend to elicit defecation. (*You'll* be the one riding with your head out the window!) Circling, whining, sniffing, and generally acting worried usually signal that the big event is imminent.

Even if the puppy starts to relieve himself, quickly but calmly scoop him up and carry him outside — the surprise of being picked up will usually cause him to stop in midstream.

If your pup does have an accident indoors, take care of it without letting him watch you. Clean and deodorize the spot thoroughly by sopping up as much urine as possible and then using a pet deodorizer/cleaner that neutralizes odors. Diluting the urine and then suctioning it out with a rug-cleaning machine, followed by deodorizer, is the best way to clean up. After you clean the spot, block the pup's access to that area for a week or more.

Steer clear of ammonia cleaners. Ammonia is a component of urine, so using an ammonia cleaner is like posting a sign that says, "Go here!"

If your adult dog starts to go in the house, check out the list of possible reasons in Chapter 12.

Rule #3: Know your puppy's limits

Learn how long you can expect your pup to hold it. A general rule is that a puppy can hold his bowels for at most as many hours as he is months old. For example, a 3-month-old can hold it for 3 hours. But remember that there are limits — your 12-month-old can't hold it for 12 hours. Even an adult should not be expected to hold it for more than eight hours.

You can't just stick a puppy in a cage all day while you're at work and think that you won't return home to a messy cage and a messy pup. If you can't be with your puppy for an extended period, you may want to recruit a family member, neighbor, or friend to take over for a shift.

If leaving your puppy with someone else is not possible, you may have to paper-train him. To do so, place newspapers on the far side of the room (or X-pen), away from the puppy's bed or water bowl; near a door to the outside is best. Place the puppy on the papers as soon as he starts to relieve himself. Be aware, however, that there are few more nauseating odors than that of urine-soaked newsprint.

Another option is to use sod squares instead of newspapers. Place the sod on a plastic sheet and, when soiled, take it outside and hose it off or replace it. By using sod, you train the pup to relieve himself on the same surface that he should use outside — and chances are you won't have any sod squares sitting on the floor next to your chair to confuse him. If you place the soiled squares outside in the area you want your dog to use as his bathroom, they will be prescented and will further encourage your dog to relieve himself in that outdoor area.

Some breeders train puppies to go on guinea pig food pellets in a shallow litter box. The scent seems to attract puppies, and if they happen to eat some of the pellets, they suffer no harm. The pellets are absorbent and disposable, too.

Rule #4: Know that punishment doesn't help

Dog owners have been rubbing their dogs' noses in their messes for years, but this form of punishment has never worked. Punishing a dog for a mess he made earlier is totally fruitless; it only succeeds in convincing him that every once in a while, for no apparent reason, you are apt to go insane and attack him. That "guilty" look you may think your dog is exhibiting is really a look of fear that you have once again lost your mind.

Even if you catch your dog in the act, overly enthusiastic correction only teaches him not to relieve himself in your presence, even when outside. This doesn't mean that you should ignore the peeing pup as he soils your carpet, though. You can clap your hands or make a loud noise to startle him so that he stops, or swoop him up and run for the door. You can add a firm "No," but yelling and swatting are actually detrimental to the dog's training.

Rule #5: Reward correct behavior

If punishment doesn't teach your pup, what will? Rewards. Punishment doesn't make clear what behavior you desire, but rewards make it clear very quickly. When the puppy relieves himself in his outside "toilet," remember to heap on the praise and let him know how pleased you are. Adding a food treat really gets the point across — keep some tidbits in a jar near the door.

Rule #6: Go outside with the dog

If you want your dog to go outside for his duties, you need to go outside and watch him. Most owners think that they're doing their part by opening the door and pushing the pup outside. After five minutes, they let the pup back in, and the pup promptly relieves himself on the rug. Bad dog? No, bad owner. Chances are the pup spent his time outside trying to get back inside to his owner. Puppies do not like to be alone, and knowing that you're on the other side of the door makes the outdoors unappealing. If the weather was bad, the pup probably huddled against the door so that he wouldn't miss the opportunity when you opened the door again.

The solution? Go outside with the pup every time. Don't take him for a walk, and don't play with him; simply go with him to his relief area, say, "Hurry up" (for some curious reason the most popular command words), and be ready to praise and perhaps give a treat after the pup does his deed. Then you can go to his outdoor play area or go back inside.

Teaching the Basic Commands

You want a well-behaved dog in addition to a housebroken one. It's never too early or too late to start your German Shepherd's education. With a very young GSD, train for short periods. By the time your dog reaches 6 months of age, he should know Sit, Down, Stay, Come, and Heel.

A common problem in the training of any dog is that the dog's attention wanders. You can teach your dog to pay attention to you by teaching him the "Watch me" command before going on to the other commands. Say, "Wolfman, watch me," and give him a treat or other reward when he looks in your direction. Gradually require him to look at you for longer and longer periods before rewarding him.

Come

If your dog knows only one command, that command should be to come to you when called. Coming on command is more than a cute trick; it could save your dog's life. Your puppy probably already knows how to come; after all, he comes when he sees you with the food bowl, or perhaps with his leash or a favorite toy. You may have even used the word *Come* to get his attention then; if so, you have a head start. You want your puppy to respond to "Wolfman, come" (use his name in place of "Wolfman," of course) with the same enthusiasm as he would if you were setting down his supper. In other words, "Come" should always be associated with good things.

Think about what excites your dog and makes him run to you. For most young German Shepherds, the opportunity to chase after you is one of the grandest games ever invented. And of course, most young GSDs will jump at the chance to gobble up a special treat. Combine these two urges and use them to entice your dog to come on the run.

The best time to start training is when your German Shepherd is a young puppy, but it's never too late. You need a helper and an enclosed area — a hallway is perfect for a very young pup. Have your helper gently restrain the puppy while you back away and entice him. Do whatever it takes at first: Ask the pup if he wants a cookie, wave a treat or a prized toy, or even crawl on your hands and knees. The point is to get the pup's attention and get him struggling to get away and get to you. Only at this point should you call out, "Wolfman, come!" with great enthusiasm, at the same time turning around and running away. Your helper releases the pup at the same time, and you let him catch up to you. Reward him by playing for a second, and then kneel down and give him a special treat.

Repeat this exercise several times a day, gradually increasing the distance, taking care never to practice past the point where your pup begins to tire of the game. Always keep up a jolly attitude and make the pup feel lucky to be part of such a wonderful game.

After your puppy has learned the meaning of "Come," move your training outdoors. With the pup on a leash, command, "Wolfman, come!" enthusiastically and quickly run away. When he reaches you, praise and reward him. If he ignores you for more than a second, tug on the leash to get his attention, but don't drag him. Your dog can't put off responding to the Come command until he feels like coming. In addition, the longer you separate the tug from the command, the harder it will be for him to relate the two, and in the long run, the harder the training will be. After the tug, be sure to run backward and make the pup think that it was all a grand game.

Next, attach a longer line to the pup, allow him to meander about, and, in the midst of his investigations, call, run backward, and reward. After a few repetitions, drop the long line, let your shepherd mosey around a bit, and then call. If he begins to come, run away and let him chase you as part of the game. If he doesn't come, pick up the line and give it a tug, and then run away as usual.

If at any time your GSD runs the other way, never give chase. Chase the line, not the dog. The only game a German Shepherd likes more than chasing you is being chased by you. The dog will always win. Chase the line, grab it, give it a tug, and then run the other way.

As your dog becomes more reliable, begin to practice (still on the long line) in the presence of distractions, such as other leashed dogs, unfamiliar people, cats, and cars. In most of these situations, you shouldn't let the dog drag the line, but hold on in case the distractions prove too enticing.

Some dogs develop a habit of dancing around just out of reach, considering your futile grabs to be another part of this wonderful game. You can prevent this habit by requiring your dog to allow you to hold him by the collar before you reward him. Eventually, you can add sitting in front of you to the game.

Never have your dog come to you and then scold him for something he's done. In the dog's mind, he's being scolded for coming, not for any earlier misdeed. Nor should you call your dog to you only at the end of an off-lead walk. You don't want him to associate coming to you with relinquishing his freedom. Call him to you several times during the walk, reward and praise him, and then send him back out to play. Of course, it bears repeating that your dog shouldn't be off lead anywhere he could run away or get into danger.

Sit

Sit is the prototypical dog command, and for good reason: It's a simple way of controlling your dog, and it's easy to teach.

The simplest way to teach a dog to sit is to stand in front of him and hold a treat just above his eye level. Say, "Wolfman, sit," and then move the treat toward him until it's slightly behind and above his eyes. You may have to keep a hand on his rump to prevent him from jumping up. If your dog backs up instead of sitting down, place his rear against a wall while training. When the puppy begins to look up and bend his hind legs, say, "Good!" and then offer the treat. Repeat this process, requiring him to bend his legs more and more until he must be seated before he receives the praise and reward.

Teach stationary exercises like Sit, Down, and Stay on a raised surface. Doing so enables you to have eye contact with your dog and gives you a better vantage point from which to help your dog learn. It also helps keep your little one from being distracted and taking off to play.

Stay

You may have noticed that you can get your dog to sit, but he may have a habit of bouncing back up after you reward him. Require him to remain sitting for increasingly longer times before giving the reward. You can also teach the Stay command, which is another handy thing for your dog to know.

A dangerous habit of many dogs is to bolt through open doors, whether from the house or the car. Teach your dog to sit and stay until you give him the release signal before walking through the front door or exiting your car.

Have your dog sit and then say, "Stay," in a soothing voice. (Don't precede the command with the dog's name, because the dog will tend to jump up and be halfway to you by the time he realizes that you followed the command with "Stay.") If your dog attempts to get up or lie down, gently but instantly place him back in position. Work up to a few seconds, give a release word (such as "Okay!"), and praise and give a tidbit. Next, step out (starting with your right foot) and turn to stand directly in front of your dog while he stays.

Work up to longer times, but don't ask a young puppy to stay for longer than 30 seconds. The object is not to push your dog to the limit but to let him succeed. You must be patient, and you must increase your times and distances in very small increments. Finally, practice with the dog on a lead by the front door or in the car. For a reward, take him for a walk.

Staring into your dog's eyes as if hypnotizing him to stay is tempting, but doing so has the opposite effect. He perceives staring as a threat and can be intimidated, causing him to squirm out of position and come to you, his leader. Instead, look to the side of your dog, behind your dog, at your feet — anywhere but directly into the dog's eyes.

Down

When you need your dog to stay in one place for a long time, you can't expect him to sit or stand. This is when the Down command really comes in handy.

Begin teaching the Down command with your dog in the sitting position. Say, "Wolfman, down," show him a tidbit, and then move it below his nose toward the ground. If he reaches down to get it, give it to him. Repeat, requiring him to reach farther down (without lifting his rear from the ground) until he has to lower his elbows to the ground. Never try to cram your dog into the Down position, which can scare a submissive dog and cause a dominant dog to resist. Practice the Down/Stay command just as you did the Sit/Stay command.

Remember to use a distinctive command for Down when it means that you want your dog to stop jumping on you or to get off the furniture. Many people use the same word, which can be confusing for the dog. Instead, try "Off" or use the German word for Down when you want your dog to quit jumping up. For more information about teaching your dog not to jump up, see Chapter 9.

Heel

One of the many nice things about having a dog is taking him out in public. You know you look good strolling down the sidewalk with your German Shepherd stepping along smartly at your side. It's no fun if your dog drags you along behind him as he visits every fire hydrant and Poodle in sight. Not only that, but your dog will be out of control and will be perceived as a menace, and you will be exhausted by the end of what should have been a pleasurable walk. Walking alongside you on a lead doesn't come naturally to your GSD, but it can come easily.

Walking on a leash may be a new experience for a youngster, and he may freeze in his tracks once he discovers that his freedom is being violated. In this case, do not drag the pup, but coax him along a few steps at a time with food. When the puppy follows you, praise and reward him. In this way, the pup comes to realize that following you while walking on lead pays off.

Once your pup is prancing alongside you, it's time to ask a little more. Even if you have no intention of teaching a perfect competition Heel, you need to teach Heel as a way of letting your dog know that it's your turn to be the leader.

Have your German Shepherd sit in the Heel position — that is, on your left side with his neck next to and parallel with your leg. If your dog's front feet line up with your feet, that's close enough. Say, "Wolfman, heel," and step with your left foot first. (Remember that you step off on your right foot when you left your dog on a Stay; if you're consistent, the leg that moves first provides an eye-level cue for your dog.) During your first few practice sessions, keep him on a short lead, holding him in Heel position and of course praising him.

The traditional method of letting the dog lunge to the end of the lead and then snapping him back is unfair if you haven't first shown the dog what you expect. Instead, after a few sessions of showing the dog the Heel position, give him a little more loose lead and use a tidbit to guide him into the correct position.

If your Shepherd still forges ahead after you have shown him what you expect, pull him back into position with a quick, gentle tug of the lead, and then a release. If, after a few days of practice, your dog still seems oblivious to your efforts, turn unexpectedly several times; teach your dog that he must keep an eye on you. Keep in mind, though, that every time you do so, you cause your dog to heel a little bit farther back in relation to you. It's easier for your dog to keep an eye on you from behind you than from any other position. In the long run, more dogs have a problem with lagging behind than with forging ahead. In other words, don't go overboard when trying to correct forging. It tends to self-correct with just a little guidance.

As you progress, add some rights, lefts, and about-faces and walk at all different speeds. Then practice in different areas (always on lead) and around different distractions. You can teach your GSD to sit every time you stop. Vary your routine to combat boredom, and keep training sessions short. Be sure to give the Okay command before allowing your dog to sniff, forge, and meander on lead.

Keep up a pace that requires your GSD to walk fairly briskly — too slow a pace gives your dog time to sniff, look around, and in general become distracted. A brisk pace focuses the dog's attention on you and generally aids training.

Using the mother tongue

Many Shepherd owners train their dogs by using German commands:

- **Sit:** *Setz*
- **Down:** *Platz*
- **Come:** *Komm*
- **Stay:** *Bleib*

- **Heel:** *Bei Fuss*
- **Fetch:** *Bring*
- **No:** *Nein*
- **Watch:** *Achtung*
- **Let go:** *Aus*

Going to Obedience School

Home schooling alone isn't the right choice for every dog, or every dog owner. Obedience school for dogs can be extremely useful if you approach it the right way. You have a few options here:

- You can send your dog to boarding school to be trained by a professional. Your dog will return to you educated and perfectly obedient — to the professional trainer. This is an expensive route to take, but it can work as long as you're willing to work with both your dog and the professional so that you can bridge your dog's obedience to you. Understanding the commands, and when your dog's apparent disobedience may be your fault, takes practice. Just as your dog must be trained, so must you.

- If you have neither access to a professional trainer nor the money to pay for one, you can train your own dog. Do it the right way, and both you and your dog will have a good time, looking forward to the challenge of the day's lesson and the rewards to follow.

- You can train the dog at home and join a dog obedience class.

Always do your dog's training at home. Your dog practices, perfects, and troubleshoots at class but learns new things at home, where there are fewer distractions. You learn how to teach your dog at class, then you go home and teach your dog, and then you come back next week and show what you've taught your dog. Then your dog shows off his genius in front of all his new friends.

Looking at the advantages of an obedience class

If you plan on competing in obedience, a class is a necessity. Obedience trials are held amid great distractions. It would be nearly impossible for your dog to pass without having some experience working around other dogs.

A big advantage to obedience school is the access you get to the instructors, who are highly knowledgeable about dog training and behavior. If you have problems, experienced instructors can help you deal with them. No two dogs are alike, and I guarantee that your dog will do something offbeat and weird that this book doesn't cover. That's when you need advice.

Finally, obedience classes are filled with people who share your interests. They're a great place to learn about dogs, share your dog's latest cute story with people who actually think it's cute, and meet a lot of really nice people. If you take the plunge into competition, it's a place to celebrate wins and laugh about flubs.

Finding a good class

Not all obedience classes are created equal, and some should never have been created at all. To find a good one, ask someone with a well-trained dog, preferably a German Shepherd, where he or she attends class. You can also get recommendations from a local GSD club. Even better, contact the AKC and ask for a local obedience club and about upcoming obedience trials in your area. Go to the trial and ask people with happy workers if they can suggest a good class. Then sit in on the class. If they're still using outdated yank and jerk methods, look elsewhere.

Typical classes that may be offered include the following:

- ✔ Puppy kindergarten (for socialization of young pups)
- ✔ Beginners (for older pups and adults just starting obedience training)
- ✔ Novice (for dogs who know the most basic of basics)
- ✔ Graduate novice (for dogs who know the AKC Novice obedience exercises)
- ✔ Open (for dogs working toward a CDX title — see Chapter 16)
- ✔ Utility (for dogs working toward a UD title — see Chapter 16)

Some clubs also offer home behavior classes, which emphasize good behavior around the house, and Canine Good Citizen classes, which teach basic good behavior in public. A few also offer agility or tracking classes. Schutzhund clubs offer obedience classes as well, usually emphasizing the exercises needed to pass Schutzhund trials (again, see Chapter 16).

Be a joiner! Your dog will appreciate his night out on the town with you. But be careful who you choose to spend your time with. Remember that if you are ever in a class and are asked to do something to your dog that you don't feel comfortable doing, just say no. Your friend's well-being is worth too much.

Chapter 9

Dealing with a "Bad Dog"

- -

In This Chapter

▶ Understanding why your dog destroys your stuff

▶ Barking, digging, peeing, pooping, jumping, and escaping — it's gotta stop!

▶ Understanding and overcoming aggression

- -

German Shepherds are the best dogs in the world. And you are no doubt among the best dog owners. So why are you having problems?

Even the best dogs with the best owners can do bad things. Well-meaning but misguided training advice from the next-door neighbor, or even dog trainers who don't have a scientific background in analyzing dog behavior, can make the situation even worse. The most common improper advice is to punish the dog, and if that doesn't work, to punish him some more. If punishment doesn't work the first time, why do owners think that it will work the second, third, or fourth time? As the misbehavior continues, the owners lay the blame on the dog. Finally, they label the dog as stupid or incorrigible and either ban him to the far reaches of the yard, offer him to "a good home," or take him to the pound.

As a first step in any serious behavior problem, have a thorough veterinary exam performed. Some behavioral problems have a physiological basis that needs to be addressed before the behavior can improve.

Veterinarians can sometimes offer advice, but few are extensively trained in behavior. Despite the popular perception of doggy shrinks asking neurotic dogs about their childhood, a real dog behaviorist is educated in canine behavior and therapy and considers both behavioral and medical therapies. The behaviorist holds either a Ph.D. in behavior or a veterinary degree and is certified as a companion animal behaviorist. Great strides have been made in canine behavioral therapy in recent years.

This chapter talks about some of the most common behavior problems in German Shepherds and gives you advice on how to deal with each situation.

Taming Doctor Destructo

One of the great joys of owning a German Shepherd is knowing that after a hard day at work, you can come home, be greeted by your loyal dog, and spend quality time relaxing and playing. Dream on! That might happen, but just as likely you will open your door and stop dead in your tracks, gasping, "Vandals! We've been ransacked!" The vandal is your loving dog telling you how much he loves you as only a dog can do.

Before I get to how your dog destroying your home is a token of his love for you, let me talk about the times when this is *not* the case:

- ✔ Puppies are natural demolition dogs, and they destroy for sheer ecstasy. The best cure (besides adulthood) is supervision and prevention. Remove everything your pup can get into — there's no need for a costly paper shredder or garbage disposal when you have a puppy loose in the house! And consider keeping your pup in a crate until age 2.

- ✔ Adult German Shepherds may destroy items because of frustration or boredom. The best way to deal with these dogs is to provide both physical interaction (such as chasing a ball) and mental interaction (such as practicing a few simple obedience commands) an hour or so before you leave. Several toys are available that can provide hours of entertainment; for example, you can fill toys with peanut butter or treats that your dog can spend a long time extracting.

Often, adult dogs continue their puppy search-and-destroy missions, but the cause is seldom boredom, and they won't simply outgrow it. German Shepherds are extremely devoted dogs, and their owners tend to be equally devoted. They chose GSDs in part because of the breed's desire to be close to its family. The problem for many Shepherds arises when their people leave them all alone — an extremely stressful situation for these highly social animals. They react by becoming agitated and trying to escape confinement. Perhaps they reason that if they can get out of the house, they will be reunited with their people.

The telltale sign of a dog suffering from this *separation anxiety* (the fear of being left alone or separated from particular people or even dogs) is that most of their destructive behavior is focused around doors and windows. In this situation, most owners believe that the dog is spiting them for leaving and punish the dog. Unfortunately, punishment is ineffective because it increases the dog's anxiety level, and he comes to both look forward to and dread his owner's return.

The proper therapy for separation anxiety is to treat of the dog's fear of being left alone. You do so by leaving the dog alone for very short periods and gradually working up to longer periods, taking care never to allow him to become anxious during a session. When you *must* leave your dog for long periods during the conditioning program, leave him in a different part of the house than the one in which the conditioning sessions take place. This way, you won't undo all your work if he becomes overstressed by your long absence.

When you return home, no matter what the condition of the house or how much you missed your dog, refrain from inciting a joyous reunion scene. Greet the dog calmly, or even ignore him for a few minutes, to emphasize that being separated was no big deal. Then have him perform a simple trick or obedience exercise so that you have an excuse to praise him. This process takes a lot of patience and self-control, but letting this situation continue is not fair to you or your dog. It will only get worse.

Helping a Dog Overcome His Fears

Known for their bravery, even the bravest German Shepherds can develop illogical fears or phobias. The most common are fear of strange people or dogs, fear of gunshots, and fear of thunder.

You may have heard that the best way to deal with a scared dog is to inundate him with the very thing he is afraid of until he gets used to it. This technique, called *flooding*, doesn't work because the dog is usually so terrified that he never gets over his fear enough to realize that the situation is safe. The cardinal rule of working with a fearful dog is never to push him into situations that might overwhelm him.

Never coddle your GSD when he acts afraid, either, because doing so reinforces the behavior. Teaching him a few simple commands (see Chapter 8) is always useful; his performing these exercises correctly gives you a reason to praise him and also increases his sense of security because he knows what you expect.

In the worst-case scenario, the dog is petrified at even the lowest level of exposure to whatever he is scared of. You may have to use anti-anxiety drugs in conjunction with training to calm your dog enough to make progress. This is when you need a behaviorist's advice.

Interacting with strangers

German Shepherds are characteristically cautious with strangers. Some dogs take this caution to an extreme and are downright shy. Shy dogs are like shy people in some ways: They're not so much afraid of people as they are of being the center of people's attention.

Unfortunately, the most common advice given to cure shyness in dogs is to have a lot of strange people pay attention to them. Doing so usually does little but petrify the dog and further convince him to fear strange people. The dog learns that for some reason, strangers are alarmingly interested in him. And if you force a dog who is afraid of people to be petted by someone he doesn't know, the stranger may well get bitten.

Instead, ask strangers to ignore a shy dog, even when approached by the dog. When the dog gets braver, have a stranger offer him a tidbit, at first not even looking at him. Later, let the stranger make more direct contact, eventually petting or speaking to the dog. If the dog has been taught to sit on command, this process is often easier because the dog knows what is expected of him.

Loud noises

Fear of thunder or gunshots is a common problem in older dogs. To see a normally courageous German Shepherd quivering in the closet at the slight rumblings of a distant thunderstorm is a sad sight, and it only gets worse with time.

The time to do something about this fear is at the first sign of trouble. Avoid fostering these fears by acting cheerful when a thunderstorm strikes and playing with your dog or giving him a tidbit.

Once a dog develops a noise phobia, try to find a recording of that noise. Play it at a very low level and reward your dog for calm behavior. Gradually increase the intensity and duration of the recording, and your dog should eventually lose his fear.

A program of gradual desensitization, in which you expose the dog to the frightening person or thing and then reward him for calm behavior, is time-consuming but is the best way to alleviate the fear.

Keeping a Dog from Digging Up Dirt

You may remember the days when your lawn was lush and green. You should have taken a picture, because those days are long gone. But just think of the extra physical exercise your thoughtful dog has arranged for you as you leap over holes and shovel the dirt back into them, not to mention the mental exercise you get as you ponder why you never have enough dirt to fill them back up.

If you remain unappreciative, however, the best you can do is to confine the digging to certain parts of the yard. The dog will do most of his digging when you're not around, so fence off those parts of the yard that you wish to remain presentable and let your dog in them only when you're there to supervise. You might also try giving your dog his own sandbox or area for digging; when he digs in the nice parts, redirect him to the digging area. And take heart — digging is a problem that time may cure. Digging is worst in young adults but gradually improves with age.

Don't try to teach a dog to stop digging by filling the hole with water and half-drowning the dog in it. This tactic doesn't work, and it's dangerous.

Quieting a Barking Beast

Having a doggy doorbell can be handy, but there's a difference between being warned of a suspicious stranger and being warned of the presence of oxygen in the air. The surest way to make your neighbors hate your dog is to let him bark day and night. Allow your dog to bark momentarily at strangers, and then call him to you and praise him for quiet behavior, distracting him with an obedience exercise if you need to. If your dog won't stop barking when you tell him to, distract him with a loud noise of your own. Begin to anticipate when your dog will start barking, distract him, and reward him for quiet behavior.

You may worry that you'll ruin your dog's watchdog ability by discouraging barking, but the opposite is true. A watchdog who cries wolf is useless. By discouraging your dog from barking at nonthreatening objects and encouraging him to bark at people sneaking around, you create the ideal watchdog.

Isolated dogs often bark because of frustration or as a means of getting attention and alleviating loneliness. Even if the attention gained includes punishment, the dog will continue to bark in order to obtain the owner's temporary presence. A dog stuck in a pen or tied to a chain in the backyard will bark as well. What else is there to do?

The simplest solution is to move the dog's quarters to a less-isolated location. Let the dog in the house or fence in your entire yard. Take him for long walks so that he can interact with you and other dogs. If your dog barks when you put him to bed, move his bed into your bedroom. If doing so is not possible, you must reward the dog's quiet behavior with your presence, working up to gradually longer and longer periods of quiet separation.

The distraction of a special chew toy, given only at bedtime, may help alleviate barking. Remember, too, that a sleeping dog can't bark, so exercise can be a big help.

A dog who must spend the day home alone is a greater challenge. Again, the simplest solution is to change the situation, perhaps by adding another animal — a good excuse to get two dogs!

For stubborn barkers, a citronella collar is sometimes effective. These collars spray a squirt of citronella (which dogs don't like) whenever the dog barks. They're safer and more effective than bark-activated shock collars.

Dealing with a Dog Who Forgets He's Housebroken

What happens when your housebroken dog appears to be "housefixed"? If your adult GSD soils the house, the problem could be physical or emotional.

A physical examination is warranted anytime a formerly housebroken dog begins to soil the house. You and your veterinarian need to consider the following possibilities:

- ✔ Older dogs may not have the bladder control that they had as youngsters; a doggy door is the best solution.

- ✔ Older spayed females may "dribble"; ask your veterinarian about drug therapies.

- ✔ Several small urine spots (especially if bloody or dark) may indicate a bladder infection, which can cause a dog to urinate frequently.

- ✔ Sometimes a housebroken dog is forced to soil the house because of a bout of diarrhea, and afterward he will continue to soil in the same area. In this case, restrict the area, deodorize it with an enzymatic cleaner, and revert to basic housebreaking lessons.

- ✔ A male dog may lift his leg inside the house as a means of marking his territory. Neutering often solves this problem, as long as it's performed before the habit becomes established; otherwise, diligent deodorizing and the use of dog-deterring odorants (available at pet stores) may help.

- ✔ Submissive dogs, especially young females, may urinate upon greeting you; punishment only makes this submissive urination worse. For these dogs, be careful not to bend over or otherwise dominate the dog, and keep your greetings calm. Dogs usually outgrow submissive urination as they gain confidence.

- ✔ Some dogs defecate or urinate due to the stress of separation anxiety; you must treat the anxiety to cure the symptom. Dogs who mess their cages when left in them are usually suffering from separation anxiety or claustrophobia. Other telltale signs of anxiety-produced elimination are drooling, scratching, and escape-oriented behavior.

  You need to treat separation anxiety (see the section "Taming Doctor Destructo," earlier in this chapter) and start cage training again, placing the dog in it for a short period and gradually working up to longer times. Dogs who suffer from cage anxiety but not separation anxiety do better when left loose in a dog-proofed room or yard.

Fencing In an Escape Artist

German Shepherds are smart dogs — sometimes too smart for their own good. Some Shepherds are especially good at applying their intelligence to finding escape routes from the yard. In most cases, their owners have helped them learn how to escape by making it easy at first and then seeing whether a minimal fix will work.

Take the example of the new Shepherd owner and the old fence. The new owner surveys the fence and decides that it may be tall and strong enough. When the dog demonstrates that the fence is *not* tall enough, the owner tries to fix the problem by adding an extension to make the fence a bit taller. The problem is that the dog just graduated from crime school and has learned a very bad lesson: Fences can be beaten. He will likely test the new fence. If the dog can jump over or dig under that one, too, the owner is in for a problem.

Adding to the fence bit by bit is exactly the way you teach a dog to jump Olympic heights; in fact, that's how Shepherds are trained for military obstacle courses. So why would you use the same technique to teach your dog not to jump? If you want your dog to stay in the yard, make your yard escape-proof from the beginning. Make the fence high — at least 4 or preferably 5 feet. Make it strong. Make it reach to the ground and below. You can bury wire under the dirt for about a foot inside the fence to discourage attempts to dig under it. In rural areas, you can even string electric wire across the top to discourage fence climbing. Whatever you do, do it right the first time.

Keeping a Good Dog Down

German Shepherds are big, heavy dogs, and big, heavy dogs can wreak havoc when they jump on people — especially small, frail people in nice clothes. Puppies naturally greet their mothers and other adult dogs by licking them around the corners of their mouths. This behavior translates to humans, but in order to reach your face, they need to jump up on you. Sometimes owners love this display of affection, but not when they're all dressed up or when company comes over.

Because you can't expect your dog to know the difference, teach him to sit and stay so that you can kneel down to his level for greetings. When your dog does jump up, simply say, "No," and step backward so that his paws meet only air. Teaching your dog a special command ("Jump up!") letting him know that jumping up is okay (when you're in your grungy clothes, for example) helps him understand the difference.

Shutting your dog in the other room when guests arrive will only make him more crazed to greet people and ultimately worsen the problem. The more people he gets to greet politely, the less excited he will be about meeting new people, and the less inclined he will be to jump up. Have your guests kneel and greet your sitting GSD just as you do.

Getting Over Aggressive Behavior

Despite how wonderful German Shepherds can be, many people are afraid of them. Some GSD owners derive immense (if perverse) enjoyment from this fear, but most protest that their dogs are just big pussycats. Nonetheless, some GSDs can be aggressive, and their large size and powerful jaws make this sort of behavior very dangerous. Understanding aggression could save you a lot of grief and your dog's life.

Telling whether a dog is just playing

Puppies and dogs play by growling and biting. Usually they play with their litter mates this way, but if yours is an only puppy, you will have to do. So many people have seen horror stories about dogs that when their pups growl and bite, they immediately label them as mean. You need to know the difference between true aggression and playful aggression. Look for these clues that tell you it's all in good fun:

- Wagging tail
- Down on elbows in front, with the rump in the air (the *play-bow*)
- Barks intermingled with growls
- Lying down or rolling over
- Bounding leaps or running in circles
- Mouthing or chewing on you or other objects

On the other hand, these clues tell you that you'd better watch out:

- Low growl combined with a direct stare
- Tail held stiffly
- Sudden, unpredictable bites
- Growling or biting in defense of food, toys, or bed
- Growling or biting in response to punishment

Simply because your dog is playing doesn't mean that you should let him use you as a chew stick. When your pup bites you, simply say, "Ouch! No!" and remove your bloodied stump from his mouth. Replace it with a toy not made of flesh and bone. Hitting your dog is uncalled for — he was just trying to play and meant no harm. Hitting also is a form of aggression that could give him the idea that he had better bite harder next time because you're playing the game a lot rougher. You don't want to encourage playful aggression, but you don't want to punish it, either. You want to *redirect* it.

Resolving dog-dog conflicts

If your dog is really acting aggressively rather than playfully, you need to decide whether the aggression is directed toward other dogs and animals or toward people. Aggression toward other animals does not mean that a dog will be aggressive toward people. Many dogs are aggressive toward strange dogs but friendly toward housemates, and many dogs chase small animals, such as cats.

Aggression toward strange dogs is a biologically normal trait of canines, but one that is not suitable for dogs in today's world. It's natural for your dog to defend his territory against strange dogs. The problem develops when you try to introduce a new dog into the home, or when your dog thinks that the world is his personal territory.

Conflicts at home

The steps for introducing dogs are outlined in the sidebar "Shepherding in a second pet." Despite the most proper of introductions, however, dogs within a household sometimes fight. A little sibling rivalry is one thing, but continued and escalating fights can be dangerous to your dogs and to your mental health. Simply separating the dogs is an option, but this is the last choice. Ensuring that you can keep the doors closed without a mistake for the rest of the dogs' lives is difficult — and having dogs like that is no fun.

Problems between housemates are mostly likely to occur between dogs of the same sex and same age. Seniority counts for a lot in the dog world, and a young pup usually grows up respecting his elders. Sometimes, however, a youngster gets aspirations to be top dog, or two dogs of about the same age never quite decide which one is the better leader. Then the trouble starts.

Remember to decide first whether this is natural rough-play behavior between the two. An occasional disagreement is normal, too. A disagreement that draws blood or leaves one dog screaming, or in which the two dogs can't be separated, is a potential problem. Repeated such disagreements spell trouble. Neutering one or both males in a two-male dominance battle can help, but neutering females will not.

Shepherding in a second pet

Having more than one dog has certain advantages and disadvantages. Two dogs are twice the fun of one, without being twice the work. Consider adding another dog or pet if you're gone most of the day and your German Shepherd would otherwise be at home alone. Most dogs enjoy having a canine companion, but don't worry — they'll still be loyal to you.

Problems arise with fighting between dogs, especially between dogs of the same sex. Two males are most likely to fight, but two females can be persistent and vicious in their fighting. A male/female combination works best, but only if at least one of the dogs is neutered. It also works best if one dog is older than the other so that the elder dog is the undisputed leader of the pack.

When introducing dogs, do so on neutral ground. Have both dogs on a leash and walk them alongside each other, letting them focus on a lot of diversions. When they seem trustworthy around each other, feed them together, again on neutral ground. Ignore the newcomer around the older dog, and always make a fuss over the old dog when the new dog comes around. You need to reinforce the older dog's feelings of leadership by always petting and feeding him first and letting him know that he's still the special one.

The same procedures apply to introducing your pup to cats and other pets, except that you can't take them to neutral areas. Feed both animals in the presence of one another, and consider using a muzzle or cage for the protection of both. Don't leave the animals together unsupervised until you're absolutely sure that they're getting along.

You're likely to be bitten if you try to separate fighting dogs. Instead, throw a bowl of water on the contestants, spray them with a hose, or drop cans on a hard floor to startle them. You may be able to distract them with tidbits or the offer of a run. Dragging the combatants to a doorway and trying to close the door between them sometimes works, too.

Soothing the underdog and punishing the bully is human nature, but you'd be doing the underdog the worst favor you could. If your dogs are fighting for dominance, they're doing so in part because in the dog world, the dominant dog gets the lion's share of the most precious resources. Your attention is the most precious resource your dog can have. If you give your attention to the loser, the winner will only try harder to beat the daylights out of him so that your attention will go where it should go — to the winner. You do your losing dog the best favor if you treat the winning dog like a king and the losing dog like a prince. This means that you always greet, pet, and feed the top dog first. It goes against human nature, but with dog nature.

Conflicts out and about

Aggression toward strange dogs can be more difficult to work with. This behavior is more often a problem with males, and neutering these dogs may help. The most basic "cure" is to avoid other dogs and always walk your dog on a leash. Don't allow your male to mark trees (or anything) along your route; in doing so, he is claiming that as his territory and will be more likely to defend it later. Train your dog to do some simple obedience, including the Come, Sit, and Stay commands — see Chapter 8. Bring tidbits, and when your dog sees another animal, have him perform these exercises and reward him. Do not wait until he acts aggressively to give the commands; doing so only reinforces his aggressive actions.

Many people pet and speak soothingly to their dogs when they begin to act aggressively, but doing so gives the dog the message that he is doing the right thing. Do not yell and scream, either; to the dog, you are entering into the fray and attacking the other dog as well. For the same reasons, do not run toward the other dog; your dog will interpret your behavior as attack behavior and be only too happy to help.

Sometimes your dog will chase other dogs not out of a desire to fight, but out of a desire to catch. In this case, your dog is treating another (usually small) animal as prey. Its behavior differs from typical aggressive behavior in that no growling or posturing is involved. Dogs chase down the perceived prey, grab it behind the neck, and shake or fling it. Introducing your dog to a variety of small dogs, with your dog on lead, may give him the idea that dogs come in many sizes. Practicing basic obedience may help, too, but many dogs forget all training when the stimulus to chase arises.

Because this problem is potentially deadly, you can't take chances. You may want to get a radio-controlled shock collar, but even that may not help reliably. The best precaution is not to run your dog off lead anywhere small animals are also off lead.

Keeping a dog from being aggressive toward humans

Aggression toward humans is one of the most severe behavioral problems a dog can have. The potential for human endangerment often leads to the dog's demise. Many times the dog is dearly loved, but the owners can no longer cope with the threat to human safety.

Dog aggression toward humans can be roughly divided into aggression toward family members and aggression toward strangers. Aggression toward family members or other people known to the dog tends to be the most troubling. Because of the gravity of this problem, it's best to seek the counsel of a certified companion animal behaviorist.

Dominance aggression

Much has been made of dominance problems in dogs; they probably occur less often than people think, but when they do occur, the result can be aggression toward family members. This aggression most often occurs as a result of competition over a resource (such as trying to remove food or a toy, encroaching on sleeping quarters, or trying to step past the dog in a narrow hall) or during a perceived display of dominance by the owner (such as petting, grooming, scolding, leading, or bending over the dog). Dogs may act more aggressively toward family members than strangers and treat the family members in a dominant way, such as by walking stiffly, staring, standing over them, and ignoring commands. Punishment usually elicits further aggression.

Dominance aggression is more common in males than in females; occasionally (but not always), castration can help. Your veterinarian can give your intact (unneutered) male dog a drug that temporarily causes his hormonal state to mock that of a neutered dog as a test to see whether castration might help. Spaying a female does not help cure (and may even hinder) dominance aggression.

Owners of such dogs inevitably feel guilty and wonder, "Where did I go wrong?" The fault is not entirely theirs. Although some of the owner's actions may have helped create the problem, these same actions would not have produced dominance aggression in dogs who were not predisposed to the problem. In a predisposed dog, an owner who acts in ways that foster the dog's opinion of himself as king can lead to problems.

Actions such as the following convince a dog that he ranks over a person:

- Petting the dog on demand
- Feeding the dog before eating your own meal
- Allowing the dog to go first through doorways
- Allowing the dog to win at games
- Allowing the dog to have his way when he acts aggressively
- Fearing the dog
- Not punishing the dog for initial instances of aggression

Treatment consists of putting the dog in his place, without direct confrontations. Your dog has the ability to win in a serious direct confrontation with you. If you try to beat him into submission, you will just as likely end up the loser. At least at first, it's best to avoid situations that might lead to a showdown. If, however, your dog only growls and *never* bites, you may be able to nip the behavior in the bud before you get nipped yourself by scolding or physically correcting the dog. If your dog is likely to bite but you still want to try to correct his behavior, talk to your veterinarian about temporary drug therapy to calm him sufficiently during initial training, and consider having your dog wear a muzzle.

You must cease and desist any behaviors that tell the dog he is the boss. As much pleasure as you may get from petting your dog absentmindedly as you watch TV, you can't. From now on, your dog must work for his petting, his praise, and even his food. The work will be simple — obeying basic commands from you. He must sit when you tell him to sit and wait for you to go through doorways first. When your dog thrusts his head into your lap to be petted, you must ignore him. When you want to pet your dog, you must first have him obey some simple commands, and then pet him sparingly as a reward. Yes, it's tough love — but it may be your dog's only chance.

Do not roll a dominant dog onto his back into a submissive position. Attempting this move with a dominant dog is a good way to get bitten!

Aggression due to fear

Another cause of aggression toward people is fear. If a dog has come to fear overzealous physical punishment, he may bite his owner, or he may bite a stranger who approaches and tries to touch him. In both cases, the dog is biting out of perceived self-defense.

Obviously, punishment for this type of aggression only makes matters worse. The cure is to refrain from placing the dog in fearful situations or to try to alleviate the fears. To do so, follow the directions for working with a shy dog.

Aggression toward strangers

Aggression toward strange humans is not only dangerous, but also a lawsuit waiting to happen. Some dogs are afraid of strangers and bite when approached by them. Others actively go after strangers, treating them as they would intruding dogs. Still others bite visitors to their homes. You must treat each case differently.

- A dog who bites strangers out of fear must have his fear treated, and never be put in a situation in which a stranger is forced upon him.

- A dog who goes after strangers is very likely being territorial and must be corrected and scolded. When a stranger appears, require the dog to perform a few obedience commands, rewarding with a tidbit for good behavior.

- A dog who attacks visitors should be corrected and required to do some simple obedience moves when visitors come. Shuttling the dog into another room only increases his aggressive tendencies. You want your dog to associate visitors with good times. Eventually, you might even have your visitors give your dog treats.

Regardless of the cause of the aggression, don't take chances. Keep your dog on lead at all times around strangers, and keep him muzzled.

When divorce is the best course

What if you get a German Shepherd and it just doesn't work out? The only thing worse than getting a dog and not keeping him for his entire life is getting a dog and keeping him *against your will* for his entire life.

If you've reached the conclusion that dog ownership is not for you, try to find a home for your dog while he's still a cute puppy. If you got the dog from a breeder, you can contact the breeder and ask if he or she wants the dog back. This is one of the major advantages of buying from reputable breeders; they should always take the dog back, no matter what the dog's age (although you should not necessarily expect your purchase price to be returned).

Following are other options for divorcing your dog:

✔ You can try to find a new owner through a newspaper ad. Never advertise your dog as being free, however; vile people exist who collect free animals for horrific purposes.

✔ You can contact the German Shepherd Club of America Rescue, who may provide a foster home and will do their best to find the best new owner. You can reach them at 408-247-1272.

✔ As a last resort, you can take your dog to an animal shelter, who will take over the responsibility of finding him a new home. If your have a cute puppy or if your dog is obviously a purebred German Shepherd, his chances of being adopted are fairly high.

Never take your dog to the country and let him go to fend for himself. Such dogs routinely are shot, are killed by cars, or starve.

You are allowed to make one such mistake in your life. Do not think that things will go better with another dog. In 99 percent of cases, the owner is the problem. Try a fish next time.

Chapter 10

Grooming Your Dog

*B*efore you protest that if you had wanted a sissy dog to brush and coif, you wouldn't have chosen a German Shepherd, take heed of this caution: Grooming is important not only for the sake of beauty, but also because it can prevent serious health problems. And it's a necessity because Shepherds shed — a lot. Expect to brush your GSD at least once a week, or even daily.

Just as with people, good dog grooming involves more than an occasional brushing of the hair. Keeping nails, teeth, eyes, and ears well groomed is just as (if not more) important. The good news is that you don't have to visit the Shampoodle Hut to keep your dog groomed to perfection. All you need is a little direction, and you can be your GSD's personal beautician. Consider this chapter a take-home beauty school course.

Making the Fur Fly: Brushing

You don't need a chest of fancy brushes to keep your Shepherd's hair just so — luckily, Shepherds never have bad hair days. They just have profusion of hair days! Shepherd hair doesn't tangle or mat, and dirt falls right out of it. You'll do just fine with a few tools, shown in Figure 10-1:

✔ You use a **pin brush** to brush the thicker undercoat and get down to the skin. You can brush the hair backward to loosen dead hairs, but be careful not to irritate the skin.

✔ A **bristle brush** is better for extended brushing periods and for puppy coats; it helps remove dead hair, distributes the natural oils, and is easy on the skin.

✔ A **slicker brush,** which has many fine bent wires, can help remove shedding hair, but it can cut the outer coat.

✔ An **undercoat shedding rake** (the best are Teflon-coated) is the best tool for peak shedding periods, when it can help you create a pile of shed undercoat roughly equivalent in size to your dog.

Dogs usually regard being brushed as an act of bonding, so the experience should be pleasurable for both of you. (Of course, all dogs have different limits, and no dog appreciates a marathon grooming session. If your dog gets impatient, take a break and come back later.) To groom your dog, start with the shedding rake or slicker brush and remove as much of the loose undercoat as possible. Then use the pin brush, and finish up with the bristle brush. For extra sheen, go over the coat with a fine-tooth comb and finish with a couple of swipes with a chamois cloth.

Figure 10-1:
These three tools are essential for grooming a German Shepherd.

Bathing Your Dog

You can lead a dog to water, but you can't make him get in — especially if he is a 100-pound German Shepherd who's never been taught the difference between a tub of water and a tub of battery acid. If you start early and handle the situation delicately, though, your dog can learn to tolerate, or even like, baths.

The frequency with which you bathe your Shepherd depends on how dirty he gets and how healthy his skin is. Most dogs who are not being shown do well being bathed two to three times a year — more often for dogs with skin problems, less often for indoor dogs with healthy skin.

Choosing a shampoo

The choice of shampoo is as personal as the choice of dog food (see Chapter 7). Dog skin has a pH of 7.5, while human skin has a pH of 5.5; bathing in a shampoo formulated for human skin can lead to scaling and irritation. You generally get better results with a shampoo made for dogs. If you're on a budget and your dog's skin and coat are healthy, a mild liquid dishwashing detergent actually gives good results *and* kills fleas.

No dog owner should be without a dog shampoo that requires neither water nor rinsing. These shampoos are wonderful for puppies, spot baths, emergencies, and quick clean-ups when time doesn't permit a regular bath.

If your dog has skin problems, several therapeutic shampoos are available:

- **Itchy skin:** Oatmeal-based anti-pruritics
- **Dry, scaly skin:** Moisturizing shampoos
- **Oily scaling:** Anti-seborrheic shampoos
- **Infected skin:** Anti-microbials

Flea shampoos

You may have heard that flea shampoos are the answer for killing fleas. Most shampoos (even people shampoos) kill fleas, but none — including flea shampoos — has any residual killing action on fleas. For that, see the section "Making Fleas and Ticks Flee," later in this chapter.

Taking the plunge

You need to start bath training when your German Shepherd is still a young puppy. Done right, bath time can be fun. Done wrong, it can leave you with a lifelong battle on your hands.

Start bath training with semi-baths. Fill the tub with warm water only to your dog's ankles. For the first bath, wash only his feet. The next bath, wash his feet and rear legs. Bring some treats into the bathroom with you as rewards for cooperation.

Remember to use water in which you would be comfortable showering. Keep one hand under the spray so that you can monitor the water temperature, and make sure that an unruly pup can't accidentally hit a knob and turn up the hot water.

If you bathe your dog in your own tub, place a nonskid mat in the bottom and help him in and out of the tub so that he doesn't slip. Also place a strainer over the drain so that you don't have to spend the rest of your day trying to unclog it. A hand-held sprayer is essential for indoor bathing as well.

Follow these steps for a successful indoor bath:

1. **Wet down the dog to the skin, leaving his head for last.**

   Avoid spraying water into the dog's ears. You can plug his ears with cotton, but even then you should avoid spraying water into them, as the cotton gets soggy easily.

   Your dog will want to make sure that you, too, enjoy the benefits of the bath by shaking water all over you. To keep your dog from shaking, keep one hand clenched around the base of one ear. When you let go, stand back!

2. **Once the dog is wet, apply shampoo, again leaving his head for last.**

   Mixing the shampoo with water makes it go a lot further and makes it easier to work with.

3. **After you work up a lather, start rinsing, working from the head back and down.**

   Rinsing is a crucial step, because shampoo remaining in the coat can cause dryness, itchiness, and even hair loss. Most GSDs don't require cream rinse, but you can add a small amount if you like. Cream rinse tends to make the hair lie flatter.

4. **Dry the dog.**

   After the bath, your dog will shake and splatter the entire area. Cover him with a towel as quickly as possible and rub vigorously.

Once a GSD's thick undercoat gets soaked, it takes a very long time to dry, so a blow dryer is a great help. Some dogs enjoy being dried with a blow dryer, but as with all things, the secret is to get your dog used to it a little at a time. Make sure to use a low heat setting.

5. **Use a wide-tooth comb or brush to get the dead hairs out.**

   Bathing dislodges loose hairs; a good time to get them out is when the coat is almost, but not entirely, dry.

6. **Step back and admire your Adonis of dogs.**

   Take a picture, because as soon as your dog gets a chance, he's going to dig a hole and give himself a mud bath to get rid of that horrible shampoo stench.

Don't let your dog outside on a chilly day when he's still wet from a bath. You have removed the oils from the coat and saturated your dog down to the skin, so he's far wetter than he would ever get by going swimming, and thus more likely to become chilled.

An alternative on hot summer days, but not on chilly days, is to use an outdoor hose to bathe the dog. In this case, find a nice spot on a clean surface that won't get muddy, and where your dog can't run away, and bathe as you would indoors.

Removing a Stink

Dogs smell like dogs, but when they smell like dead dogs, you have a problem. Doggy odor is not just offensive; it's unnatural. Don't exile the dog or hold your breath if he reeks of something awful. First try giving him a bath, and if that doesn't produce results, use your nose to sniff out the source of the problem.

- ✔ **Infection** is a common cause of bad odor; check the mouth, ears, feet, anus, and genitals.

- ✔ **Impacted anal sacs or perianal fistulas** (see Chapter 11) can contribute to bad odor.

- ✔ Generalized bad odor can indicate a **skin problem,** such as seborrhea.

In every case, your dog needs to see a veterinarian to cure the problem at its source. Don't ignore bad odor, and don't make your dog take the blame for something you need to fix.

In case of skunk, act fast! Use a commercial skunk odor remover, or mix 1 pint of 3 percent hydrogen peroxide, ⅔ cup of baking soda, and 1 teaspoon of liquid soap or citrus-based dog shampoo with 1 gallon of water. Wear gloves and sponge the mixture onto the dog. Leave it on for about five minutes, rinse, and repeat if needed. *Caution:* This solution may slightly bleach dark coats.

Vinegar douche also is reported to work well at removing skunk stink. Contrary to popular belief, tomato juice rinses don't work that well, and they'll leave your bathroom looking like the scene of a mass murder if your dog shakes (which he will).

Making Fleas and Ticks Flee

Your dog's skin is a major interface between him and the environment, and as such is vulnerable to a plethora of problems, many caused by fleas and ticks.

Preventing fleas

Fleas can make your dog's life miserable and also can cause secondary problems, such as tapeworms and skin maladies. Many German Shepherds develop flea allergies, so keeping these dogs absolutely flea-free is essential. Products that require a flea to bite the dog before killing or sterilizing the flea may not be optimal for these dogs, because even one flea bite can elicit an allergic reaction.

Recent advances in flea control have finally put dog owners on the winning side. In any but the mildest of infestations, the new products are well worth their higher purchase price. Putting an expensive product on your dog once every three months is a lot cheaper, not to mention more convenient, than reapplying a cheap one every day.

The following are common and effective flea-prevention treatments:

- **Imidacloprid (for example, Advantage)** is a liquid that you apply once a month to the dog's back. It gradually distributes itself over the entire skin surface and kills at least 98 percent of the fleas on the dog within 24 hours, continuing to kill fleas for a month. It can withstand water but not repeated swimming or bathing.

- **Fipronil (for example, Frontline)** comes either as a spray that you apply all over the dog's body or as a self-distributing liquid that you apply only to the dog's back. Once applied, fipronil collects in the hair follicles and then wicks out over time. Thus it resists being washed off and can kill fleas on a dog for up to three months. It is also effective on ticks for a shorter period.

✔ **Lufenuron (for example, Program)** is given as a pill once a month. Fleas that bite the dog and ingest the lufenuron in the dog's system are rendered sterile. This product is extremely safe. If you use it, however, you must treat all the animals in your household for the regime to be effective.

✔ **Pyriproxyfen (for example, Nylar and Sumilar)** is an insect growth regulator available as an animal or premise spray (for the house and yard). It's marketed in different strengths and formulations and can protect in the home or yard for 6 to 12 months and on the animal for 100 days.

Ultrasonic flea-repelling collars have been shown to be both ineffective on fleas and irritating to dogs. The rumor that feeding dogs brewer's yeast or garlic gets rid of fleas is untrue as well; studies have shown that both are ineffective against fleas. However, many owners swear that they work, and they don't seem to do any harm.

Removing ticks

Ticks can carry Rocky Mountain spotted fever, tick paralysis, Lyme disease, babesiosis, and, most commonly, "tick fever" (ehrlichiosis) — all very serious diseases. They can be found anywhere on a dog but most often burrow around the ears, neck, and chest and between the toes. The ticks that can do the worst damage are often the smaller ones that are harder to see, so check your dog carefully.

To remove a tick, use a tissue or tweezers, because some diseases can be transmitted to humans. Grasp the tick as close to the skin as possible and pull slowly and steadily, trying not to leave its head in the dog. Don't squeeze the tick; doing so can cause it to inject its contents into the dog. Then clean the site with alcohol. Often, a bump will remain after you remove the tick even if you get the head. It will go away with time.

Don't try to burn out a tick. Not only is this method ineffective, but it's also a good way to set your dog on fire.

Giving Your Dog a Pet-icure

As the old saying goes, a horse is no better than its feet. The same is true of a German Shepherd. And a GSD's feet are no better than his nails.

When you can hear the pitter-patter of clicking nails, the nails are hitting the floor with every step. When this happens, the bones of the dog's foot spread, causing discomfort and eventually splayed feet and lameness. And if you leave the dog's *dewclaws* (the rudimentary "thumbs" on the wrists) untrimmed, they can get caught on things more easily and be ripped out, or actually loop around and grow into the Shepherd's leg. You must prevent these problems by trimming your Shepherd's nails every week or two.

Dogs don't wear their nails down naturally by running around, as you might think. Canine nails evolved to withstand traveling 20 miles or so a day. Unless your dog is a marathon runner, you're going to need to help out.

Nail clippers are absolute essentials. Two types are available: guillotine and scissor. Both are good. Be sure to get heavy-duty clippers for an adult German Shepherd.

As you may have figured out already, most dogs don't relish the idea of getting their nails trimmed. To work your way up to the task, begin by handling your puppy's feet and nails daily. Once he's comfortable with that, start cutting the very tips of the nails every week, taking special care not to cut into the *quick* (the central core of blood vessels and nerve endings). After every cut, give your dog a tiny treat.

You may find it easiest to cut the nails by holding the foot backwards, much as a horse's hoof is held when being shod. This way, your GSD can't see what's going on, and you can see the bottom of the nail. There you can see a solid core culminating in a hollowed nail, as shown in Figure 10-2. Cut the tip up to the core, but not beyond.

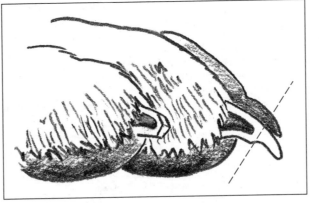

Figure 10-2:
You don't want to cut into the quick of a dog's nail.

On occasion, you will slip up and cause a nail to bleed. Most Shepherds are stoic and will only give you a grievous look that says, "I told you this would happen," but a few take the opportunity to tell the whole neighborhood that you're amputating their toes. Give a distressed dog another treat and apply styptic powder (available at pet supply stores) to the nail to stop the bleeding. If you don't have styptic powder handy, dip the nail in flour or hold it to a wet tea bag. And be more careful next time!

Cleaning Your Dog's Ears

A German Shepherd relies on his wonderful large ears to detect and localize sounds that you can't perceive and to look stunningly handsome and alert. A Shepherd has healthy ears, but even the healthiest ears may need occasional cleaning.

A dog's ear canal is made up of an initial long, vertical segment that abruptly angles to run horizontally toward the skull. This configuration provides a moist environment in which various ear infections can flourish, although the erect carriage of a GSD ear does aid in ventilation and health. Keeping your dog's ears healthy is fairly simple; check them regularly and do not allow moisture or debris to build up inside them.

So if you look in your dog's ear and you see a bunch of gunk, what do you do? It depends. If your dog shows no signs of discomfort or itching, you can try cleaning the ear yourself. Many veterinarians and dog catalogs sell products that dissolve wax and debris. You can also make a mixture of one part alcohol to two parts white vinegar. Armed with this potion, take your dog outside and follow these steps:

1. **Hold the ear near the base and quickly squeeze in the ear cleaner.**

   The more slowly you let it drip in, the more it will tickle.

2. **Gently massage the liquid downward and squish it all around.**

3. **When your dog can't stand it anymore (usually after about 15 seconds), jump back and let your dog shake it all out.**

   This is why you clean ears outside, because dissolved earwax is not a great thing to have on your walls. You may have to repeat this process a few times.

If the ear is so black with gunk that repeated rinses don't clean it right up, your dog has a problem that needs veterinary attention. If the ear is red, swollen, or painful, do not attempt to clean it yourself. Your dog may need to be sedated for cleaning and may have a serious problem. Again, see a vet.

Don't stick cotton swabs in the ear canal; they can irritate the skin and pack debris into the horizontal canal. And never use powders, which can cake in the ears, or hydrogen peroxide, which leaves the ear moist.

Dogs also can suffer from ear mites, which cleaning solutions do not kill. For information about this condition and how it's treated, see Chapter 13.

Keeping a Dog's Teeth Squeaky Clean

Just how intimidating do you think your German Shepherd would be if he had only gums to show when he snarled? With a lifetime of neglected tooth care, your dog may develop gum disease and need to have several of his teeth removed.

Tooth plaque and tartar are not only unsightly, but they contribute to bad breath and health problems as well. If it's not removed, plaque attracts bacteria and minerals, which hardens into tartar. Neglected plaque and tartar can cause infections to form along the gum line. The infection can gradually work its way down the sides of the tooth until the entire root is damaged. The tissues and bone around the tooth erode, and the tooth finally falls out. Meanwhile, the bacteria may enter the bloodstream and travel through the dog's body, causing infection in the kidneys and heart valves. What starts out as a simple tooth problem can eventually kill the dog.

Dry dog food, hard dog biscuits, and certain bones are helpful, but not totally effective, at removing plaque. Brushing your German Shepherd's teeth once or twice weekly — optimally daily — with a child's toothbrush and doggy toothpaste is the best plaque remover. If you can't brush, your veterinarian can supply cleansing solution that helps kill plaque-forming bacteria. Squirting this solution into your dog's mouth may help, but your dog may not tolerate it! If your dog won't stand for any of these treatments, you may have to have your veterinarian clean your dog's teeth under anesthesia as often as once a year — an expensive alternative.

Get your dog used to having his teeth examined and brushed while he's still a puppy. Even though people shouldn't eat after brushing, you may have to reward your pup with a tidbit at first for letting you brush one or two teeth. While brushing, get to know your dog's mouth so that you can spot any developing problems. (See Chapter 11.) Pay special attention to the teeth in the rear; the upper molars and premolars tend to be the worst. Don't worry about brushing the inside tooth surfaces; they tend to stay clean on their own.

Between 4 and 7 months of age, GSD puppies begin to shed their baby teeth and show off new permanent teeth. Often, *deciduous* (baby) teeth, especially the *canines* (fangs), are not shed, so the permanent tooth grows in beside the baby tooth. If this condition persists for over a week, consult your veterinarian; retained baby teeth can cause misalignment of adult teeth.

About occlusion

Correct *occlusion*—the way the teeth and jaws mesh when the mouth is closed — is important to good dental health. In a correct GSD bite, known as a *scissors bite,* the top *incisors* (the small front teeth) fit snugly in front of the bottom incisors. In an overshot bite, the top incisors are so far in front of the lower that a gap exists between them. In an undershot bite, the upper incisors are behind the lower incisors. Too large a gap between the upper and lower incisors can cause eating difficulties or result in the tongue lolling out of the mouth.

In most cases, little can be done to correct occlusion (and in fact, the AKC and most other dog showing organizations disqualify dogs who have had orthodontic procedures). In some cases, however, removal of puppy teeth may help the bite to correct itself.

The German Shepherd's expression is noble, alert, and intelligent, as befits the breed.

Gail Painter

German Shepherd puppies are masters of fun — and mischief! Keeping one out of trouble is a full-time job.

One day he may be your protector, but today he still needs you for protection.

Look to the parents for the dog your puppy will one day become.

"The first impression of a good German Shepherd Dog is that of a strong, agile, well muscled animal, alert and full of life" — AKC standard.

The German Shepherd is an explorer at heart. Make sure that your dog finds a safe place to satisfy his quest for adventure.

Black and tan German Shepherds have a sleek elegance.

White German Shepherds, although disqualified by the AKC standard, are nonetheless beautiful dogs and have their own devoted fanciers.

German Shepherds enjoy physical challenges; make an effort to share outdoor adventures with your dog.

An open field, a bouncing ball, and a strong arm can keep your GSD in top form.

A healthy German Shepherd can enjoy an active life well into older age, but any GSD should be checked for joint problems throughout his life.

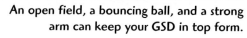

Agility competition is fun! Here a GSD emerges from the closed tunnel and sets his sights on the next obstacle.

© Tara Darling/AKC Stock Images

Retrieving a dumbbell is required in some obedience and Schutzhund exercises.

© AKC Stock Images/Mary Bloom

Gail Painter

The German Shepherd show stance, with one rear leg forward of the other, is unique in the world of AKC show dogs.

Some German Shepherds still perform their ancestors' herding duties.

Make his day! Police dogs enjoy their work, but they also like being regular pets at home with their handlers.

German Shepherds excel at many things, but none more so than being watchful and loving companions — true partners in life.

Until we meet again . . .

Part IV
Keeping Your Dog Healthy

The 5th Wave   By Rich Tennant

"Okay, this is getting ridiculous! Either teach your dog not to run away, or name him something other than 'Fire'."

In this part . . .

Nobody knows your dog like you do. Only you can pick up on the slight clues warning you that your Shepherd isn't quite up to snuff. But you have to know what to look for. You also need the help of a veterinarian in preventing, diagnosing, and treating problems. Your dog depends on you for a long and healthy life. True, sometimes a dog's genes dictate otherwise, and that's why you should be familiar with hereditary problems to which German Shepherds are susceptible. And true, there comes a time when even your best efforts are no longer of any help.

Being a good dog owner means spending time, money, and concern on your dog's health. The chapters in this part help you do so wisely.

Chapter 11

Working with Your Dog's Other Best Friend: His Veterinarian

In This Chapter

▶ Choosing a veterinarian

▶ Recognizing signs of illness

▶ Vaccinating a dog

▶ Saving your Shepherd from deadly heartworms

▶ Getting your dog to take his medicine

As good an owner and guardian as you try to be, there will come times when you need the help of a professional — a veterinarian trained in diagnosing and treating your dog's problems. By doing your part in protecting your dog from injury, vaccinating against diseases, and detecting the first signs of illness, you can cut down on your veterinary bills to some extent. Trying to play home vet can be flirting with disaster, however.

Your Shepherd's health care is a team effort that your veterinarian directs but that *you* undertake. Preventive medicine encompasses accident prevention, vaccinations, and parasite control, as well as good hygiene and grooming (see Chapter 10). An ounce of prevention really is worth a pound of cure.

Finding a Hospitable Hospital

No matter how diligent you are to give your dog the proper nutrition and exercise, he will eventually need professional medical attention. You also need a good veterinarian to monitor your dog's internal signs by way of blood tests and other procedures.

Just like human doctors, veterinarians vary in personality, skills, and so on. You want to find the one who best meets your dog's needs — and yours. When choosing a veterinarian, consider the following:

- ✔ **Availability:** The best vet in the world is no good to you if she is never in the office when you need her. If you work during the week, you may need to find a veterinarian with Saturday or evening hours, or one who allows you to drop off your dog for the day. Some vets even make house calls in mobile veterinary units.

- ✔ **Costs:** Some veterinarians include more sophisticated tests as part of their regular check-ups, which, though desirable, add to the cost of a visit. Unless money is no object, reach an understanding about procedures and fees before having them performed. A good vet should explain why a procedure is needed, whether it is optional for the health of your pet, and, if the procedure is expensive, about what the cost will be. It's difficult to compare prices from one veterinarian to another because you often get what you pay for. What seems like a really good deal may be so only because the vet cuts corners.

- ✔ **Facilities and staff:** The clinic should be clean and have safe, sanitary overnight accommodations. The staff should be proud to give you a tour if they aren't too busy. Trained veterinary technicians are a valuable asset to any clinic, but not all clinics have them. A clinic staffed by several veterinarians is usually better; the vets can confer about tough cases and are more likely to be available for emergencies.

- ✔ **Communication skills:** You and your veterinarian form a team who work together to protect your dog's health, so your rapport with your veterinarian is very important. The vet should listen to your observations and explain to you exactly what is happening with your dog. A vet who is familiar with German Shepherds and their special problems is a real asset.

- ✔ **Emergency arrangements:** Many veterinary clinics refer all clients to a central emergency clinic after-hours, but your veterinarian should still be reachable in cases of extreme emergency. Avoid a veterinarian with an unlisted phone number — but if your vet has a listed phone number, don't harass!

After you choose a veterinarian, bring your dog in for some routine checks, as shown in Figure 11-1. Doing so gives you a chance to evaluate your vet a bit more, gives your dog a chance to feel comfortable at the clinic, and, most of all, gives the vet a chance to get to know you and your Shepherd. If you establish yourself as a concerned and regular client, your veterinarian is much more likely to go the extra mile for you, whether it entails staying open late for your closing-time emergency or conferring with a specialist on your dog's case.

Figure 11-1:
By getting to know the dog in his "normal" state, the vet will be better able to diagnose and treat the dog if he becomes ill in the future.

© Kent & Donna Dannen/AKC Stock Images

Specialists

Most veterinarians are general practitioners, and most of their days are filled with routine cases, such as check-ups, vaccinations, spaying and neutering, skin allergies, and the more common illnesses. A good veterinarian will not hesitate to utter the phrases "I don't know" and "Perhaps you would like to be referred to a specialist." For any serious disease, always ask whether a specialist's opinion would be helpful.

Most specialists work at university veterinary teaching hospitals, although you can find some in private practice in larger cities. As with humans, expect to pay more for a veterinary specialist's opinion. Sometimes even a specialist can do nothing for a dog, but many owners find peace in knowing that they did everything they could and left no stone unturned.

Giving Your Dog a Checkup at Home

A veterinarian can treat a dog only after the dog's owner recognizes that the dog needs professional care. The only way to know whether your Shepherd may be sick is to be in tune with him when he's well. Take five minutes every week to perform a simple health check, examining the following:

- ✔ **Mouth:** Look for red, bleeding, swollen, or pale gums; loose teeth; sores on the tongue or gums; or bad breath. (Yes, dogs should have fresh-smelling breath!)

- ✔ **Eyes:** Check for discharge, cloudiness, or discolored whites.

- ✔ **Ears:** Watch for foul odor, redness, discharge, or crusted tips.

- ✔ **Nose:** Look for thickened or colored discharge.

- ✔ **Skin:** Check for parasites, hair loss, crusts, red spots, or lumps.

  If your dog has a sore that does not heal, or any pigmented lump that begins to grow or bleed, have a veterinarian check it immediately.

- ✔ **Feet:** Check for cuts, abrasions, split nails, bumps, or misaligned toes.

- ✔ **Anal region:** Watch for redness, swelling, discharge, or sores.

Also watch your dog for signs of lameness or incoordination, a sore neck, and loss of muscling, and for any behavioral changes. Run your hands over the dog's muscles and bones and check that they are symmetrical from one side to the other. Weigh your Shepherd and observe whether he is putting on fat or losing weight. Check for growths or swellings, which could indicate cancer or a number of less-serious problems. Look out for mammary masses, changes in testicle size, discharge from the vulva or penis, increased or decreased urination, foul-smelling or strangely colored urine, incontinence, a swollen abdomen, black or bloody stool, change in appetite or water consumption, difficulty breathing, lethargy, coughing, gagging, or loss of balance.

If your dog has any of these signs, call your veterinarian and ask about bringing your pet in to be checked.

Shepherds are sometimes so concerned with their tough-guy image that they are amazingly stoic, even when they're in pain. Because a dog may not be able to express that he's in pain, you must be alert to changes in demeanor. A stiff gait, low head carriage, reluctance to get up, irritability, dilated pupils, whining, and limping are all indications that your pet is in pain.

Gums

The simplest yet most overlooked checkpoint is a dog's gum color. Looking at the gums is simple, yet virtually no one does it — except your vet, who looks at the gums before anything else when your dog comes into the exam room. Get used to looking at your dog's gums — the one place you can see his blood without actually taking it out.

The neat thing about blood is that its color can say a lot:

- **Normal gum color** is a good deep pink.
- **Pale gum color** can indicate anemia or poor circulation.
- **White or tan gum color** can indicate shock, severe anemia, or very poor circulation.
- **Bluish gum or tongue color** indicates a life-threatening lack of oxygen.
- **Bright red gum color** can indicate carbon monoxide poisoning.
- **Yellowish gum color** can indicate jaundice.
- **Tiny red splotches on the gums** (called *petechia*) can indicate a blood-clotting problem.

All of these conditions (except, of course, normal, deep pink gum color) warrant a call to the emergency vet.

Don't confuse a red line around the gum line with healthy gums. A dog with dirty teeth can have gum disease, giving an unhealthy but rosy glow to the gums, especially at the margins around the teeth.

In addition to checking color, you can estimate *capillary refill time,* which is an index of blood circulation, simply by pressing on the dog's gum with your finger and then lifting your finger off the gum. The spot where you pressed will be momentarily white but should repink quickly as the blood moves back into the area. If repinking takes longer than a couple of seconds, circulation is poor, and you should have the vet examine your dog.

Temperature

Your dog's body temperature is another clue to what's going on inside him. You can't put your hand on your Shepherd's forehead and get an idea, and you can't have your dog hold a thermometer under his tongue. You can get a very rough idea by feeling your dog's ears, but for an accurate reading, you need to use a rectal thermometer.

The nose knows — or does it?

Contrary to popular belief, you can't tell whether a dog is well by whether it has a wet nose. Sick dogs can have wet noses, and well dogs can have dry noses.

Digital thermometers are much easier to use. Your dog will appreciate it if you lubricate it with a bit of Vaseline or K-Y jelly before inserting it.

Normal body temperature for a German Shepherd is about 100 to 102 degrees F. (As in humans, a dog's temperature is slightly lower in the morning and higher in the evening.) If your dog's temperature is 103 or above or 98 or below, call the vet and ask for advice. If it is 105 or above or 96 or below, go to the emergency vet immediately.

Pulse, heartbeat, and breathing rate

The easiest way to check your dog's pulse is to feel the pulse through the femoral artery. If your dog is standing, cup your hand around the top of his leg and feel around the inside of it, almost where it joins with the torso. If your dog is on his back, you can sometimes even see the pulse in this area. Normal pulse rate for a German Shepherd at rest is about 60 to 120 beats per minute. A dog with an excessively high or low pulse rate should be examined by a veterinarian.

You can feel your dog's heartbeat by placing your hand on his lower ribcage just behind his elbow. Don't be alarmed if it seems irregular; the heartbeat of many dogs is irregular compared to humans. Have your vet check it out, and then get used to how it feels when it's normal.

While you're at it, you can check your dog's breathing rate. Normal respiration rate for a German Shepherd at rest is about 10 to 30 breaths per minute. A higher rate in a resting dog is cause for a veterinary exam.

Hydration

Finally, check your dog's hydration. Pick up the skin on his back just above the shoulders so that it makes a slight tent above the body. After you release your hold, the skin should pop back into place almost immediately. If it remains tented and separated from the body, your dog is dehydrated. If dehydration is due to lack of water, give your dog lots of water and keep him quiet and still. If his condition does not improve, or if dehydration is due to vomiting or diarrhea, take your Shepherd to the veterinarian to be checked and to receive treatment, including intravenous fluids.

Vaccinating Your Dog

Many German Shepherds have succumbed to contagious diseases — diseases that could have been avoided with a simple vaccination. Don't let your precious pooch be one of them.

Vaccinations are available for several diseases. Some vaccinations are mandatory from a legal standpoint, some are mandatory from a good-sense standpoint, and some are optional. The following list explains the types of vaccinations that are available and when (and if) they should be administered.

✔ **Rabies:** Because rabies is inevitably fatal after symptoms appear, all dogs must be vaccinated against it. The initial rabies vaccination should be given at around 3 to 4 months of age, again one year from the first vaccination, and then once every three years (although to comply with local law, you may have to give a booster every year). Unvaccinated dogs remain the principal hosts for the disease in undeveloped countries.

✔ **Distemper:** The history of purebred dogs is riddled with stories of entire kennels being decimated by outbreaks of distemper. The production of a vaccine was one of the greatest developments in canine health. Today, distemper appears primarily in unvaccinated puppies. The initial symptoms are upper respiratory problems and fever, followed by vomiting, diarrhea, and neurologic signs such as difficulty walking or even seizures. Distemper is not always fatal, but curing it is a lot more expensive than getting a simple vaccination.

Very young puppies (about 6 weeks old) usually get a distemper/ measles vaccination because the measles fraction can give temporary immunity even in the presence of maternal antibodies. Subsequent distemper inoculations are given every three to four weeks until the pup is about 16 weeks old. Annual boosters are traditionally recommended.

✔ **Hepatitis:** Infectious canine hepatitis type 1 is caused by CAV-1, an adenovirus found mostly in foxes and dogs but also in coyotes, wolves, skunks, and bears. The disease is highly contagious, and there is no cure. Although this form of hepatitis can occur in adults, it most often occurs in young puppies. Some puppies survive, and others do not. Vets usually administer a vaccination with CAV-2 (which works just as well but doesn't result in the blue-eye reaction that CAV-1 caused when it was used years ago) along with the distemper vaccination.

- **Leptospirosis:** Leptospirosis is a bacterial disease that causes serious liver, kidney, and blood abnormalities. It's thought to be more prevalent in rural areas, where it is spread by the urine of infected wild animals. Vaccination for lepto protects for only about three to six months, and it works to prevent severe disease but does not protect against infection or all strains of leptospirosis. A small percentage of puppies have an adverse reaction (sometimes very serious) to the vaccination, thus some people prefer not to include lepto in their vaccination regimes. Talk to your vet about the pros and cons of including it in your dog's vaccination schedule.

- **Parvovirus:** In the late 1970s, an entirely new worldwide virus broke out that caused often fatal intestinal bleeding in dogs. The advent of a vaccination was a major triumph, although breeders still fear parvovirus because it's extremely contagious and can remain in the environment for years. Maternal antibodies often interfere with vaccination for parvo; for this reason, three vaccinations by the age of 16 weeks are recommended, with an optional fourth at around 18 to 20 weeks. Annual boosters are traditionally recommended.

- **Coronavirus:** Coronavirus causes extreme diarrhea, in rare cases resulting in death. Younger dogs are most adversely affected. A vaccination is available but is currently considered optional. Discuss it with your veterinarian.

- **Tracheobronchitis (kennel cough):** Kennel cough is highly contagious and tends to spread when dogs share closed spaces. It is characterized by a dry, honking cough that can last for weeks. Vaccinations are available, but many different infectious agents can cause kennel cough; the vaccines protect against the most common ones (CPIV, CAV-2, and bordetella), but not all of them. The effects of the vaccines also do not last very long.

  For these reasons, and because kennel cough is not fatal, some people prefer not to vaccinate for it. Nonetheless, kennel cough vaccination can be a good idea for dogs who are boarded or shown. The vaccines should be given a week before exposure or with annual boosters, usually by putting drops in the nose.

- **Lyme disease:** Lyme disease is known to cause severe problems in humans, but its effects in dogs are less clear-cut. A vaccination is available but is not universally accepted as necessary. Only dogs living in areas in which Lyme disease is prevalent should be considered candidates for Lyme disease vaccination. Consult with your veterinarian about the prevalence of Lyme disease in your area.

You often need proof of current vaccination to transport a dog by air, cross international lines, attend obedience classes, board at a kennel, or have the dog work as a therapy dog.

Puppy vaccinations

Puppy vaccinations are some of the most vital, but most confusing, vaccinations your dog will receive. A puppy receives his mother's immunity through nursing in the first days of life. This is why it's important that your pup's mother be properly immunized long before breeding, and that your pup be able to nurse from his dam. The immunity gained from the mother wears off after several weeks, and then the pup is susceptible to disease unless you provide immunity through vaccinations. The problem is that there's no way to know exactly when this passive immunity will wear off, and vaccinations given before that time are ineffective. So you must revaccinate over a period of weeks so that your pup is protected and receives effective immunity. That's why puppies get a series of shots instead of just one or two.

Your pup's breeder should have given your Shepherd his first vaccinations before he was old enough to go home with you. Bring the information about your pup's vaccination history to your veterinarian on your first visit so that the pup's vaccination schedule can be maintained.

Adult vaccinations

The German Shepherd is one of several breeds in which the immune system seems to act a little differently. For example, GSDs sometimes fail to gain immunity from certain vaccinations. One solution is to revaccinate them often, more so than with other breeds. The problem with this solution is that vaccinating can precipitate autoimmune diseases (in which the immune system turns on parts of the dog's own body in sort of a case of mistaken identity). GSDs also tend to be somewhat predisposed to autoimmune diseases.

The great vaccination debate

Traditional vaccination schedules vary, but they typically consist of annual booster shots. Several respected veterinary teaching hospitals have recently revised their vaccination protocols to include fewer booster shots. One such protocol suggests giving a three-shot series for puppies, each shot containing parvovirus, adenovirus 2 (CAV-2), parainfluenza (CPIV), and distemper, with one rabies vaccination at 16 weeks. Following this series, a booster is given one year later, and then subsequent boosters are given once every three years.

Other respected epidemiologists disagree and prefer the traditional vaccination schedule. The great vaccination debate is far from over, so confer with your veterinarian about current thinking on the matter.

One thing is for sure: No matter what their possible side effects, vaccinations are a good thing, and all dogs must be vaccinated for their own health as well as the health of others.

Recent studies have implicated "overvaccination" — repeated vaccinations of combined vaccines — with some autoimmune problems. Some veterinarians thus recommend staggering different types of vaccines and discourage overvaccination. They also discourage vaccination in any dog who is under stress or not feeling well. Many dogs seem to feel under the weather for a day or so after getting their vaccinations, so don't schedule your appointment the day before boarding, surgery, a trip, or a big doggy event.

Vaccinating is unlikely to affect your dog adversely, but if you're a worry-wart, you can ask your veterinarian about getting *titers* run every year instead of boosters. A titer can tell you whether your dog has sufficient immunity to a disease. The main problem with getting titers is that they're more expensive than vaccines. In addition, knowing how to interpret some of them is difficult.

Preventing Heartworms

One of a veterinarian's most important jobs is to prescribe medicine that keeps your dog from getting heartworms — deadly parasites carried by mosquitoes. If you live in a warm area, your dog may need to be on heartworm prevention year-round, but in a cooler climate, you may need to use prevention only during the warmer months. Your veterinarian can advise you whether year-round prevention is necessary in your area and will prescribe prevention medicine for you.

Several effective types of heartworm prevention are available, with some also preventing many other types of worms. Some require daily administration, and others require only monthly administration. The latter type is more popular and actually has a wider margin of safety and protection. The drugs don't stay in the dog's system for a month, but instead act on a particular stage in the heartworm's development. Giving the drug each month prevents heartworms from maturing.

If you forget to give the preventive as prescribed, your dog may get heartworms. Do not give a dog with suspected heartworms the daily preventive, because a fatal reaction could occur. The most common way to check for heartworms is to check the blood for circulating *microfilarae* (the immature form of heartworms), but this method may fail to detect the presence of adult heartworms in as many as 20 percent of tested dogs. An "occult" heartworm test, though slightly more expensive, tests for the presence of antigens to heartworms in the blood and is more accurate. With either test, the presence of heartworms will not be detectable until nearly seven months after infection.

Heartworms are treatable in their early stages, but the treatment is neither cheap nor without risks. If left untreated, heartworms can kill your pet. The best solution is to prevent them in the first place.

Scooting

Is it true that a dog who scoots his rear on the ground must have worms? No. Although scooting may be a sign of tapeworms, a dog who repeatedly scoots more likely has impacted anal sacs (see Chapter 13).

Some heartworm preventives also protect your dog from some other parasites (see Chapter 13). Discuss your options with your veterinarian.

Spaying and Neutering

One of the most important proactive things you can do for your dog's well-being is to neuter or spay your pet. Most veterinarians advocate neutering and spaying dogs who will not be used for breeding. These procedures negate the chance of accidental litters, do away with the headaches of dealing with a bitch in season or a male on the prowl for a date, and even afford some health benefits.

Spaying (surgical removal of the ovaries and uterus) before the first season drastically reduces the chances of breast or uterine cancer, as well as *pyometra* (infection of the uterus). Tumors of the mammary glands are among the most common of cancers in dogs, occurring mostly in females who were not spayed early in life. Spaying after the age of 2 years doesn't impart the protection from mammary cancer that earlier spaying does.

Castration (surgical removal of the testicles) eliminates the chance of testicular cancer with few, if any, adverse effects. And if you fear that a lack of testicles will somehow make your dog seem less macho, artificial implants (called Neuticles) are available so that no one can tell the difference.

Giving Your Dog Medicine

Chances are your dog will occasionally have to take medicine at home. For most dogs, taking medicine is no problem. The following list walks you through administering medicine in various forms:

- ✔ **Pills:** Open your dog's mouth and place the pill well to the back and in the middle of the tongue. Close the mouth and gently stroke the throat until your dog swallows. Pre-wetting capsules or covering them with cream cheese or other food helps prevent capsules from sticking to the tongue or the roof of the mouth.

If you have a dog who thinks you're trying to feed him thumbtacks, try hiding pills in cream cheese, hamburger, or peanut butter. Give a few decoy treats first so that he isn't suspicious and is more likely to gulp down the treat.

✔ **Liquid medicine:** Tilt the dog's head back, keep his mouth almost closed (but not tightly), and place the liquid in the pouch of the cheek. Liquid medicines are easier to give if you put the liquid in a syringe (without the needle!). Then hold the mouth almost closed until the dog swallows.

Liquid medications can be almost impossible to give if your Shepherd says, "No way!" You can try injecting the liquid into a blob of meat, cream cheese, or peanut butter, being very careful that it doesn't leak out. You can also try a sneak attack when your dog is sleeping, but only if you're absolutely sure that your dog won't become startled and bite. (This tactic seldom works more than once.) Or you can simply put the medicine on your dog's food if you're sure that he will lick the bowl clean. Of course, if you have to go to all this trouble, you really need to ask your vet whether the medicine is available in some other form!

✔ **Eye medications:** First, clean any goop out of your dog's eye, which can prevent the medication from contacting the eye. Then do your best to pry the eye partially open and place the drops or ointment in the inner corner of the eye. Because dogs have an extra eyelid and an extra muscle that pulls the eye back into its socket (neither of which people have), they can do a good job of appearing to be eyeless and making your job as difficult as possible.

✔ **Ear medications:** Clean any heavy debris from the ear, if possible. Then place the medicine as deep into the canal as you can. Remember that the ear canal first goes down vertically and then turns abruptly toward the center of the dog's head. Therefore, you should hold the head vertically at first so that the medicine can drop down to the curve and then turn the dog's head so that the ear you're medicating is turned upward.

Because most dogs are rarely this cooperative, your next choice is to massage the base of the ear in hopes that you squish the medicine inward. Remember that it's best to medicate ears outside, because as soon as you let go, the dog will shake his head and medicine will go everywhere.

Always give the full course of medication that your veterinarian prescribes. If a medicine is worth giving, it's worth giving a full course. Also, don't give your dog human medications unless your veterinarian has directed you to do so. Some medications for humans have no effect on dogs, but others can have a very detrimental effect.

Chapter 12

Dealing with GSD Hereditary Health Problems

. . . .

In This Chapter

▶ Knowing which health problems are more common in GSDs than other breeds

▶ Understanding the treatment options if your dog suffers from one of these conditions

▶ Recognizing hereditary eye and ear problems

▶ Screening for skeletal problems

▶ Dealing with digestive, neural, cardiovascular, and immunological problems

. . . .

*E*very pure breed of dog is predisposed to its own set of health problems, because every pure breed has its own subset of genes. In some breeds, selection for particular traits may inadvertently cause certain health problems. In other cases, a small number of dogs were used to found a breed, and if one of those dogs happened to carry a gene for a health problem, the problem could have become widespread throughout the breed due to the restricted gene pool. Finally, in breeds that have been extremely popular, careless breeding by owners who are unaware of health problems can cause genetic disorders to become more widespread.

Like all popular breeds, the German Shepherd has hereditary predispositions to several health problems. In this chapter are some of the more common problems that seem to have a hereditary basis in GSDs. Chances are you won't ever have to worry about most of them, but just in case you become worried about your dog's symptoms, I've organized this chapter by system of the body for easy reference.

Skeletal Problems

The skeletal system is the framework for your dog's body. Many large dogs, including German Shepherds, are predisposed to skeletal problems that can lead to lameness.

Hip dysplasia

Hip dysplasia is the most well known hereditary problem of dogs, and the German Shepherd has been the poster child for this disorder. The GSD is far from being the most affected breed, however.

Hip dysplasia occurs when the ball of the *femur* (thigh bone) does not fit properly in the socket of the pelvic bone, as shown in Figure 12-1. The fit is affected both by the depth and shape of the socket and by the laxity of the joint. With pressure on the joint, such as the pressure that occurs when a dog walks or runs, the combination of laxity and a shallow socket allows the ball of the femur to pop in and out of the socket. This movement further deterio-rates the rim of the socket, worsening the condition. This is why early diag-nosis and treatment are important.

Hip radiographs can diagnose dysplasia before outward signs of the disorder can be perceived. In the United States, radiographs are most often rated by either the Orthopedic Foundation for Animals (OFA) or the Pennsylvania Hip Improvement Program (PennHip).

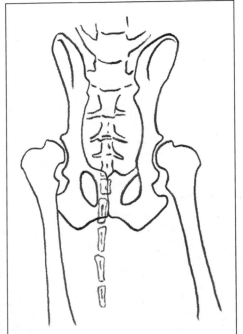

Figure 12-1:
Hip
dysplasia.

An OFA number deciphered

A dog with normal hips receives an OFA number, such as GSD23101G24MT. GS stands for German Shepherd Dog; 23101 means that this dog is the 23101th GSD to receive an OFA number; G stands for "good" (it could also be F for fair or E for excellent); 24 stands for the dog's age in months when X-rayed; M stands for male (F for female); and T stands for tattooed (M stands for microchipped).

The OFA is the most common hip certification. A panel of specialists subjectively rates radiographs based on a number of specific joint characteristics. A dog with "normal" hips (which includes ratings of excellent, good, and fair) receives an OFA number. Borderline ratings indicate that a dog should be rechecked in another six to eight months. Dysplastic hips include ratings of mild, moderate, and severe. Ratings are not given until dogs are 2 years old, but you can obtain a preliminary rating at an earlier age. Doing so can be important if you are buying or selling a young adult or if you want to initiate early therapy.

PennHip evaluation is available at a much younger age. It is based on objectively measured degrees of joint laxity, reported as a Distraction Index (DI), with lower numbers reflecting tighter (better) hips. PennHip–approved veterinarians must take the X-rays by using special procedures.

Breeders disagree about which method is better; thus many breeders elect to have two radiographs taken at the same time, submitting one to each registry. The only bad choice is no certification at all.

The "a" stamp given to German dogs includes those with normal, near-normal, and "still-permissible" hips, with the latter category including some mildly to moderately dysplastic dogs. Thus the "a" stamp is less informative and more inclusive than OFA or PennHip certification.

Hip dysplasia becomes progressively more crippling and painful. Mild cases may not need specific treatment, but dogs with more severe cases can live full lives if they're given timely surgery. If the condition is detected in a young dog before secondary changes (osteoarthrosis) have occurred, a procedure called a triple pelvic osteotomy (TPO) can be performed. In a TPO, the orientation of the dog's hip socket is surgically changed, allowing the femur head to fit better into the socket.

Older dogs or dogs with more advanced dysplasia are better candidates for total hip replacement, similar to the same procedure in humans. The ball of the femur is replaced with a metallic ball, and the socket is replaced with a Teflon cup.

A third procedure, which is less effective in large dogs, is simply to remove the head of the femur. Although it's less expensive than other surgical treatments, this surgery is not a good choice for young, active dogs. However, it may be a reasonable choice for an older dog who needs only to be comfortable walking around the house.

Elbow dysplasia

Elbow dysplasia occurs in many breeds, including the German Shepherd. Several different types of developmental problems can cause it; in GSDs, the cause is most often ununited anconeal process (UAP). The *anconeal process* is a small finger of bone that normally attaches to the head of the *ulna* (one of the long bones of the forearm) and works to stabilize the elbow by fitting snugly in a notch in the *humerus* (upper arm), where it hinges with the ulna.

In some dogs, the anconeal process never attaches properly to the ulna (see Figure 12-2), so the dog's elbow can shift from side to side when the dog puts weight on it. The anconeal process breaks loose, floats around, and causes irritation to the elbow.

A dog with elbow dysplasia has varying degrees of lameness of the front legs that originates in the elbow joint, which may be swollen and painful. Radiographs can diagnose the condition. To treat this condition, a vet surgically removes the loose piece.

Checking your dog's elbow clearance

The Orthopedic Foundation for Animals (OFA) maintains a registry for elbows, and all German Shepherd breeding stock should have an OFA elbow clearance. Dogs over 2 years of age with normal elbows are assigned a breed registry number. Abnormal elbows are assigned either Grade I, II, or III, with Grade III being the most severely affected. About 20 percent of the German Shepherds who have had their elbows X-rays submitted to OFA have been rated as dysplastic; most of them are Grade I.

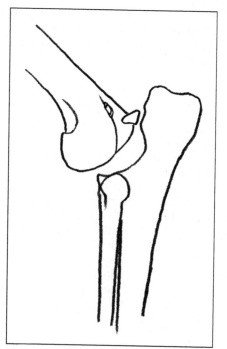

Figure 12-2:
Elbow dysplasia can cause lameness in GSDs.

Panosteitis

Panosteitis is an inflammation of the long bones resulting in lameness. The lameness often shifts from leg to leg. It is most common in growing dogs of large breeds, including German Shepherds. Symptoms may come on suddenly, usually at between 5 and 10 months of age, although some GSDs (unlike other breeds) may develop the condition at up to 2 years of age. The exact cause is not known, but the prognosis for a full recovery is excellent. Treatment consists of limiting exercise and giving the dog analgesics to help control pain — see your vet for details.

Osteochondrosis dissecans

Osteochondrosis dissecans (OCD) is lameness that occurs when a flap of cartilage becomes detached from the bone. Lameness starts gradually at around 7 to 10 months of age and gradually worsens. The most common site of the lameness is in one or both shoulders, but almost any joint can be affected. Sometimes absolute rest (meaning restriction to a cage) for several weeks helps, although lameness may actually worsen with rest. It gets better with mild exercise and is worst with heavy exercise. Surgical repair is usually preferable and is especially satisfying with OCD of the shoulder.

Pituitary dwarfism

Although technically an endocrine disorder rather than a skeletal disorder, *pituitary dwarfism* — failure to grow normally due to a lack of growth hormone — has profound effects on the skeleton. Caused by a simple recessive gene, it occurs more often in German Shepherds than in any other breed. You first notice affected dogs at about 2 months of age, when they're smaller than their litter mates. Their coats are wooly, lacking guard hairs, and often hair is missing from their bodies but remains on the heads and legs. Their bark may be shrill, and the dogs may be more difficult to housebreak as a result of retarded mental development.

Specialized testing can lead to a positive diagnosis. This condition is treated with growth hormone replacement, but treatment must be started early, will not totally cure the dog, may have side effects, and can be expensive.

Neural Problems

The neural system is the computer and wiring of the body. Neural problems can cause lack of coordination, paralysis, pain, and numbness.

Cauda equina syndrome

Cauda equina syndrome is more common in large breeds, particularly German Shepherds. No screening tests are available, and a hereditary component, if any, is not known.

Technically, cauda equina syndrome can result from several abnormalities, but narrowing of the lumbosacral vertebral canal is the most common. When this canal narrows, it presses on the spinal nerve roots within the canal, resulting in pain and perhaps incontinence and paralysis of the hind legs. The pain is focused in the pelvic area; the dog also feels pain when he lifts his tail or extends his hind legs rearward. Pain during defecation is a common symptom as well. The muscles of the hind limbs may waste away, and the dog may drag his toes. These signs may come on slowly, over a period of months, and are often confused with signs of hip dysplasia and degenerative myelopathy.

Specialized X-rays or other imaging techniques are required for diagnosis. Electromyography provides the most definitive diagnosis. Mild cases can be treated with rest and medicine, but most cases tend to progress. Veterinarians usually see better results with surgical correction, which requires a good deal of postoperative commitment from the owner.

Because of the pain involved in this condition, prompt attention is essential.

Degenerative myelopathy

Degenerative myelopathy is a progressive disease of middle-aged and older dogs in which the dog gradually loses control of his hind limbs. The condition is painless but progressive. The earliest signs may include dragging a foot slightly or occasionally placing the top of the foot on the ground. Dogs may have difficulty rising or lying down. More obvious signs follow, including increasing clumsiness, weakness, and partial paralysis. Eventually, the hind limbs become completely nonfunctioning. The feet must be monitored for sores that can form due to being dragged. Ultimately, the front legs also become affected and paralyzed. Finally, the brain stem is affected, resulting in death. (Most dogs are euthanized before they reach this point.)

Although the cause of DM is unknown, some experts speculate that it may be an autoimmune condition in which the immune system attacks part of the nerve fibers in the spinal cord of the mid-back region. Specifically, the part that is destroyed is the *myelin sheath,* the fatty insulating covering of the nerve fiber that is important in conduction of nerve impulses. This same part of the nerve fiber is destroyed in the human condition of multiple sclerosis. Spinal fluid proteins may help differentiate DM from other spinal problems.

Stress and inactivity seem to worsen this condition. No cure is available, but a special diet, supplements (including vitamins B and E and epsilon-aminocaproic acid), physical therapy, and exercise may help slow or perhaps even halt its progression. The earlier DM is detected and treated, the better the prognosis. Unfortunately, the early signs often go unnoticed or are confused with those of hip dysplasia, delaying the start of treatment.

Digestive Problems

German Shepherds are predisposed to several digestive problems, the most life threatening of which is gastric dilatation volvulus.

Gastric dilatation volvulus

Gastric dilatation volvulus (GDV), also known as *bloat* or *gastric torsion,* is a life-threatening emergency in which gas and fluid become trapped in the stomach, as shown in Figure 12-3. It is most common in large, deep-chested breeds, including German Shepherds.

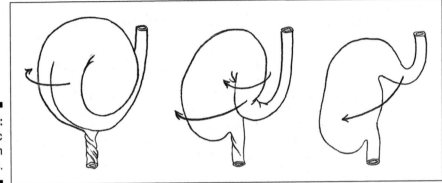

Figure 12-3:
Gastric
dilatation
volvulus.

Symptoms include distention of the abdomen, unproductive attempts to vomit, excessive salivation, and restlessness. A dog with these symptoms needs to go to the emergency clinic *immediately* — not tomorrow, and not even an hour from now.

The veterinarian will try to pass a tube into the stomach so that gases can escape. Often, the stomach has twisted and rotated on its axis, though, so the tube can't get into the stomach. These dogs require emergency surgery to save their lives. The rotation of the stomach cuts off the blood supply to the stomach wall (and sometimes other organs), which will die and subsequently kill the dog if surgery isn't performed quickly. During surgery, the veterinarian should tack the stomach in place to prevent future rotation. Dogs who bloat once often continue to do so.

In the largest study of bloat to date, several factors affecting bloat emerged. Dogs who are fearful, eat fast, and eat only one meal a day are more likely to bloat. Stress seems to precipitate a bloating episode. Dogs with stable temperaments, and dogs who eat some canned food and table scraps, are less likely to bloat. A dog with a close relative who has had the problem is more likely to have the problem, suggesting a hereditary component.

To be on the safe side, avoid other suspected risk factors. You should

- Feed your dog several small meals instead of one large meal a day.
- Include some canned food or table scraps.
- Not allow your dog to gulp food.
- Not allow your dog to be stressed around mealtime.
- Restrict your dog's water for an hour after eating.
- Avoid letting your dog run or jump for an hour after eating.
- Premoisten the dog's food, especially foods that expand when moistened.

Pancreatic exocrine insufficiency

Some German Shepherds eat voraciously yet fail to gain weight. In GSDs, this problem is often due to a lack of a pancreatic enzyme. Affected dogs produce a large volume of feces because they don't digest food efficiently. Your veterinarian can examine your dog's feces for excess fat and get a preliminary diagnosis, but a blood test is needed for definite diagnosis. You can treat these dogs by adding enzyme powder to an easily digested food, but you must treat them for the rest of their lives.

Inflammatory bowel disease

Dogs that have chronic diarrhea may be suffering from inflammatory bowel disease (IBD), a syndrome that may be due to a number of problems. In general, the condition involves hypersensitivity to substances in the bowel. Other symptoms may include vomiting, weight loss, unproductive attempts to defecate, and mucus in the stool. In extreme cases, anemia may result. The exact symptoms vary according to what part of the bowel is involved.

Vets usually run blood tests to rule out other possible causes, and fecal tests to rule out parasites. They diagnose IBD with a biopsy of the bowel mucosa. Feeding a controlled diet sometimes helps, and in some cases suppressing the immune system with drugs is helpful as well. Other drugs may also be useful.

A dog suffering from this condition should be fed a diet that's free of additives and preservatives and contains an adequate but not excessive amount of protein. The protein should come from a single source that the dog has no prior experience eating. Added dietary fiber may also be helpful. Because there's no such thing as an inherently hypoallergenic food, you may have to search for a novel source of protein. Lamb and rice foods used to be touted as hypoallergenic, but a dog is now likely to have eaten lamb previously. Your veterinarian can suggest sources of protein (such as venison, duck, or rabbit) that your dog may not have eaten.

Circulatory Problems

Disorders of the heart and blood are among the most common serious problems in dogs. In comparison to many other breeds, German Shepherds have healthy circulatory systems. They do have their predispositions, however.

Subvalvular aortic stenosis

Subvalvular aortic stenosis is a congenital heart defect in which the opening between the left ventricle and the aorta is abnormally narrow, obstructing the blood flow. The condition occurs most often in large breeds. Severe cases cause death by 3 years of age. In less-severe cases, the signs may not be noticeable, although some dogs may be weak and collapse when exercising. A veterinary cardiologist diagnoses the condition with an ultrasound. Open-heart surgery is the treatment of choice, but it's expensive and risky.

Patent ductus arteriosis

One of the most common congenital heart defects in dogs, patent ductus arteriosis is seen more frequently in GSDs than in other breeds. During fetal life, the lungs are not functional, so a vessel (the ductus arteriosis) allows blood to bypass the lungs. This vessel normally closes shortly after birth, but in some dogs it remains open, allowing blood to leak through it and placing a strain on the heart.

Affected dogs have a heart murmur and can be diagnosed conclusively with an ultrasound. Surgical correction is necessary to cure the condition. Left untreated, heart failure can result.

Hemophilia

Hemophilia is a hereditary blood clotting disorder occasionally found in German Shepherds. Affected dogs lack a factor needed to clot blood properly. Symptoms include pockets of blood beneath the skin, bleeding into the joints (causing lameness), and internal bleeding. Excessive bleeding during surgery or after a toenail is cut too short may be the first signs you notice. Blood tests can provide a definite diagnosis.

Immunological Problems

Your dog's immune system is his defense against microscopic intruders. Sometimes a dog's immune system isn't strong enough, and sometimes it is misdirected. In either case, problems can arise.

Immunoglobulin A deficiency

The immune system of a normal German Shepherd has a lower amount of immunoglobulin A (IgA) than is found in most other breeds. IgA is important for mucosal immunity, especially of the respiratory, gastrointestinal, and genital tracts. This lowered IgA may be related to some health problems, including bacterial overgrowth in the small intestine, although its significance is not known.

Autoimmune diseases

Autoimmune diseases occur when a body's own immune system turns against parts of itself. Specific types include autoimmune hemolytic anemia, autoimmune thrombocytopenia, systemic lupus erythematous, and discoid lupus erythematosus, among many others. No screening tests are available, and the hereditary component, if any, is not known.

Other German Shepherd problems, such as perianal fistulas, pannus, and degenerative myelopathy, may have an autoimmune component. Treatment is with drugs to suppress the immune system. A variety of autoimmune problems that strike all breeds include the following:

- **Autoimmune hemolytic anemia,** in which the body destroys its own red blood cells, leading to severe anemia. Affected dogs may be feverish, be lethargic, and have whitish gums.

- **Autoimmune thrombocytopenia,** in which the body destroys its own platelets, leading to spontaneous bleeding. Signs may include *petechia* (small red spots on the surface of the gums and skin and within the eye).

- ✔ **Systemic lupus erythematosus,** which affects many organ systems. Symptoms may include a recurring fever, arthritis in several joints, and small ulcers of the skin on the face or toes.

- ✔ **Discoid lupus erythematosus,** in which ulcers arise on the nose and face. They are aggravated by exposure to ultraviolet light.

All of these conditions require prompt veterinary attention. Treatment is usually with drugs that suppress the immune system.

Pannus

Pannus may be yet another autoimmune disease, in which a triggering factor (which seems to be ultraviolet light) causes the body to destroy its own corneal cells. Also known as *chronic superficial keratitis* or *German Shepherd Dog keratitis,* pannus is a chronic inflammation of the eye's cornea, the normally clear outer surface. It most often appears in young to middle-aged dogs, first appearing as a reddish area around the rim of the cornea, usually of both eyes. The pigmented area gradually expands toward the center of the cornea, leaving the affected areas covered with a brownish surface. Without treatment, the cornea will become opaque and the dog will become blind. Treatment consists of avoiding ultraviolet light (even fitting the dog with sunglasses) and instilling immunosuppressive drugs into the eyes.

Perianal fistulas

Perianal fistulas (also known as *anal furunculosis*) are chronic draining tracts in the tissue around the anus. They occur more often in German Shepherds than in any other breed. The exact cause is not known, but the condition may be related to an autoimmune problem, the configuration of the tail in which the broad tail is seated snugly over the anal area, or an overabundance of sweat glands around the anus. Symptoms may include open sores around the anus, foul odor, constipation, painful defecation, weight loss, and lethargy. Affected dogs may lick their anal region more than is normal.

Left untreated (and sometimes even with the best of treatment), dogs with perianal fistula can suffer so much pain that they must be euthanized. Antibiotics won't cure the problem, but they can help with secondary infections that often arise from fecal contamination. Drugs to suppress the immune system are also usually prescribed. Surgical excision of the affected tracts, and sometimes amputation of the tail, may help, but a chance of fecal incontinence exists. Several types of surgical procedures are available; owners of affected dogs should seek the best surgical center to perform the operation.

Cancer

Cancer occurs relatively frequently in all breeds of dogs. Some breeds seem to be predisposed to certain types of cancer; unfortunately, the German Shepherd is one of them.

For example, *hemangiosarcoma,* a malignant cancer of the circulatory system, is seen more often in GSDs than in any other breed. No screening tests are available, and the hereditary component, if any, is not known. Most often, hemangiosarcoma occurs as a tumor on the spleen or heart. As the tumor grows, internal bleeding may occur. Affected dogs may suddenly appear disoriented, collapse, and exhibit signs of hypovolemic shock. They may also be extremely thirsty. Perhaps most noticeable, their gums may be almost white.

If the tumor is on the spleen, the spleen can be removed. Not all tumors of the spleen are malignant, so it's a good idea to have a biopsy done and wait for the results before making a decision. If the tumor is malignant, or if it is on the heart, treatment is usually unrewarding. Unfortunately, most dogs with hemangiosarcoma succumb either to its primary effects (internal bleeding that cannot be stopped) or to cancer spread to other organs.

Osteosarcoma (bone cancer) occurs more frequently in large breeds, including the German Shepherd. It develops most often on a long bone of a leg and can sometimes be seen as a lump. More often, the owner first notices the dog limping; osteosarcoma is very painful. Owners face the terrible decision of amputation that must be made quickly, as time is of the essence to prevent the spread to other parts of the body. Dogs adjust to the loss of a limb fairly easily, but factors such as age, weight, arthritis, and other joint problems factor into how well the dog can cope with only three legs. Unfortunately, even with the best therapy, survival time for dogs with osteosarcoma is usually only a few months.

Mammary gland tumors are among the most common cancers in dogs, occurring mostly in females who were not spayed early in life. Spaying after the age of 2 years doesn't impart the protection from mammary cancer that earlier spaying does. Approximately 50 percent of all mammary tumors are malignant. Therapy may include surgical excision and chemotherapy.

Lymphosarcoma is another of the more common cancers in dogs. This cancer affects the blood and lymph systems; symptoms may include swelling of the lymph nodes, especially in the lower neck area and behind the "knees." Chemotherapy can extend the lives of many affected dogs.

Parasites and Infectious Diseases

Some dog breeds are more prone to certain infections or parasites, perhaps because of immune system differences. Many breeds are predisposed to developing demodicosis due to mites. German Shepherds are also more susceptible to fungal infection (aspergillus) and protozoal infection (ehrlichiosis). The following sections explain these conditions and their treatments.

Demodicosis

Demodicosis (also known as demodectic mange or red mange) is a type of mange that's caused by increased susceptibility to the demodex mite. Most dogs have some mites, but in some dogs the mites proliferate and cause the dogs' hair to fall out. Demodicosis often runs in families and seems to be passed from dams to offspring, although the exact hereditary nature is unknown. See Chapter 13 for more information about this condition.

Aspergillosis

When most people think of fungal diseases, they think of relatively minor problems. Many fungal diseases are deadly, however, and aspergillosis is one of them. The fungus aspergillus is found in soil and decaying vegetation throughout the world. Dogs inhale the spores, and usually nothing happens. In some dogs, however, the fungus colonizes the nasal passages, gradually causing the bone to deteriorate. These dogs have a nasal discharge, often tinged with blood. They may also sneeze and have a painful nose.

In some dogs, the fungus spreads into internal organs, causing disseminated aspergillosis. More cases of disseminated aspergillosis are seen in German Shepherds than in any other breed. Affected dogs may lose weight, appetite, and energy and may also experience fever, lameness, back pain, or paralysis.

Infected dogs must receive veterinary attention. Treatment of nasal aspergillosis is involved and expensive but can be successful. Treatment of disseminated aspergillosis, unfortunately, is far less satisfactory.

Ehrlichiosis

Ehrlichiosis (also called tick fever or tropical canine pancytopenia) is an underdiagnosed yet serious disease that's spread by ticks. Some reports contend that GSDs are more susceptible to being chronically affected by the disease. Symptoms may include lethargy, loss of appetite and weight, fever, and spontaneous bleeding. Often, no strong signs of disease are present. Owners may complain that the dog just doesn't seem as playful or is not quite right. Other symptoms may include coughing, arthritis, muscle wasting, seizures, and anemia. The point is that no one or two symptoms of themselves suggest erlichiosis as an initial diagnosis. A vet makes the definitive diagnosis by getting a blood titer, in which antibodies to the disease are found.

Ehrlichiosis wreaks its havoc by parasitizing the dog's white blood cells, crippling the immune system. If diagnosed early, it can be treated effectively. If not, it can be fatal. If your dog has a host of seemingly unrelated symptoms, make sure that your vet rules out ehrlichiosis.

Chapter 13

Taking Care of a Sick Shepherd

*P*eople get sick. Dogs get sick. The difference is that people can tell you where it hurts. They can also tell you how bad they feel and what may have caused the problem. Dogs can't. Add to this the German Shepherd's stoic personality, and you have the ingredients for a full-blown, undetected problem.

On the other hand, running to the vet every time your dog sneezes is expensive. You want to keep your dog safe, but you also want to be sensible about when to turn to a professional for help and when to try to fix the problem yourself. When your dog is sick, you need to look at what he's telling you, narrow it down to the most common problems it may indicate, and then decide whether it's time to get a veterinarian's opinion. This chapter gives you the tools you need to do so.

If you haven't yet chosen a vet for your dog, you really should do so immediately. See Chapter 11 for advice.

Remember, though, that veterinarians are not always right — they are human beings just like you and me. Don't hesitate to question a veterinarian's diagnosis or treatment, seek a second opinion, and, most of all, become informed about German Shepherd health issues.

Vomiting

When people vomit, they usually feel nauseated. When dogs vomit, it's hard to tell how they feel. That's partly because dogs vomit much more readily than people do. After all, wolves and many dogs feed their young by bringing back food in their stomachs and vomiting it up on demand.

A typical dog vomit episode begins with retching, followed by vomiting on your best rug, and then within a minute another bout of retching and vomiting (hopefully by now not on your best rug). After all this, the dog usually appears to be just fine. If the vomiting continues, however, it is not typical healthy vomiting and is cause for concern.

Regurgitating immediately after meals can indicate an obstruction of the esophagus. Repeated vomiting can indicate that the dog has eaten spoiled food or indigestible objects or may have stomach illness — seek veterinary advice. Meanwhile, withhold food (or feed as directed for diarrhea) and restrict water. Repeated vomiting can result in dehydration, so if your dog can't hold anything down for a prolonged period, he may need intravenous fluids.

Overeating is a common cause of occasional vomiting in puppies, especially if they follow eating with playing. Feed smaller meals more frequently if vomiting becomes a problem.

Consult your veterinarian immediately if your dog vomits a foul substance resembling fecal matter (indicating a blockage in the intestinal tract) or blood (partially digested blood resembles coffee grounds), if he exhibits projectile or continued vomiting, if he also has diarrhea, or if he is dehydrated. Sporadic vomiting with poor appetite and generally poor condition can indicate internal parasites or a more serious internal disease and should also be checked by your veterinarian.

Diarrhea

Dogs, especially puppies, get diarrhea. The problem can result from overexcitement, nervousness, a change in diet or water, sensitivity to certain foods, overeating, intestinal parasites, viral or bacterial infections, or ingestion of toxic substances.

Do not allow bloody diarrhea; diarrhea with vomiting, fever, or other signs of toxicity; or diarrhea that lasts for more than a day to continue without seeking veterinary advice. Some of these symptoms can indicate potentially fatal disorders.

The appearance of the diarrhea can provide your veterinarian with important information, so take a good look at your dog's diarrhea (even though you may dread the thought of it!). The following are clues to the severity and possible causes of your dog's problem:

- What is the consistency?
- Does it contain blood or mucus? If so, how much?
- Can you identify foreign objects or parasites?
- What color is it?

You can treat less severe diarrhea at home by withholding or severely restricting food and water for 24 hours. (Note that dogs with some other illnesses may not be candidates for food or water restriction — talk to your vet first.) Give ice cubes to satisfy your dog's thirst. If necessary, administer human diarrhea medication in the same weight dosage as recommended for people. Feed nothing but a bland diet consisting of rice, tapioca, or cooked macaroni, along with cottage cheese or tofu for protein, for several days; the intestinal tract needs time off to heal.

Coughing

A persistent cough may indicate a serious problem, so an affected dog should be checked by a veterinarian. Coughing also irritates the throat and can lead to secondary infections if allowed to continue unchecked — not to mention that it can be miserable for the dog. Although coughing can have many different causes, including allergies, foreign bodies, pneumonia, parasites, tracheal collapse, and tumors, the most common causes of coughing in German Shepherds are heart disease and kennel cough.

- ✔ **Heart disease** results in coughing most often following exercise or in the evening. Affected dogs often lie down with their front legs spread and point their noses in the air in order to breathe better. A low-sodium diet and drug therapy can help alleviate the symptoms for a while, although eventually a point will come when they are no longer effective.

- ✔ **Kennel cough** (or *canine infectious tracheobronchitis*) is a highly communicable airborne disease that's caused by several different infectious agents. It is characterized by a gagging cough that arises about a week after exposure. After a few days, the cough takes on a honking sound. Inoculations are available and are an especially good idea if you plan to board your dog or take him to a class, a competition, or any place dogs congregate.

  Treatment consists of resting the dog and avoiding situations that may lead to coughing. Cough suppressants may break the coughing/irritation cycle. Left untreated, the cough can irritate the dog's throat and eventually cause more serious problems. The dog may need antibiotics if secondary infections arise from prolonged irritation.

Urinary Problems

If your dog has difficulty or pain in urination, urinates suddenly and often but in small amounts, or passes cloudy or bloody urine, he may be suffering from a problem of the bladder, urethra, or prostate. Dribbling of urine during sleep can indicate a hormonal problem. Your veterinarian can diagnose the exact nature of the problem by administering a rectal exam and a *urinalysis* (a test of the urine).

The following are the most common urinary problems in dogs:

- **Bladder infections,** evidenced by frequent urination in small amounts and sometimes blood in the urine, must be treated promptly to prevent the infection from reaching the kidneys. Blockage of urine can result in death. Inability to urinate requires immediate emergency veterinary attention.

- In males, **infections of the prostate gland** can lead to repeated urinary tract infections and sometimes painful defecation or blood and pus in the urine. Castration and long-term antibiotic therapy are required for improvement.

- **Kidney disease,** ultimately leading to kidney failure, is one of the most common ailments in older dogs. The earliest symptom is usually increased urination. Although the excessive urination may make it difficult for you to keep your house clean or your night's sleep intact, never try to restrict water from a dog with kidney disease. A low-protein, low-sodium, low-phosphorus diet can slow the progression of kidney disease.

- Increased urination can also be a sign of **diabetes** or a **urinary tract infection.** Your veterinarian can uncover the cause with some simple tests, and both conditions can be treated.

Skin Problems

Most of the problem cases a veterinarian sees every day involve the skin. German Shepherds are prone to several skin problems, which can result from parasites, allergies, bacteria, fungus, endocrine disorders, and a long list of other possible causes. This section talks about some of the most common problems; see also Chapter 12 for information on the conditions to which GSDs seem to be predisposed.

Allergies

Flea allergy dermatitis (FAD) is the most common skin problem that ails dogs. A fleabite (actually, the flea's saliva) anywhere on a dog's body can result in itchy, crusted bumps with hair loss around the rump, especially at the base of the tail. The solution is simple (at least in principle): Get rid of every single flea on your dog. The newer flea-control products (see Chapter 10) now make this approach realistic.

Dogs can also have allergic reactions to pollens and other inhaled allergens. Many allergies can manifest themselves between a dog's toes. Suspect them when you see the dog constantly licking his feet, or when the feet are stained pink from saliva. Some dogs have food allergies as well, which may cause itching of the skin and ears. New blood tests for antibodies are much easier and less expensive (though not as comprehensive) than the traditional skin testing, which usually must be done by a specialist. This testing gives you a clue about what substances to keep away from your dog. In some cases, drug therapy can be prescribed and may help.

Pyoderma and impetigo

Pyoderma, which manifests itself in pus-filled bumps and crusting, is another common skin disease. Impetigo is characterized by such bumps and crusting, most often in the groin area of puppies. Both are treated with antibiotics and antibacterial shampoos; see your vet for help.

German Shepherd Dog Pyoderma is a type of pyoderma that is so common in GSDs that it bears the name. A dog with this condition has severe, deep-draining sores over his lower back and hind legs. This disease often isn't responsive to antibiotics, and lifelong corticosteroid therapy may be necessary to ensure the dog's comfort. Limited evidence suggests that it may have a hereditary basis and may be aggravated by hypothyroidism, fleas, and allergies.

Hot spots

A reddened, moist, itchy spot that suddenly appears is most likely a *hot spot* (pyotraumatic dermatitis), which arises from an itch-scratch-chew cycle most commonly resulting from fleas or flea allergy. German Shepherds tend to get hot spots especially in hot, humid weather.

To treat a hot spot, wash the area with an oatmeal-based shampoo and use a blow dryer to dry the area thoroughly. Prevent the dog from further chewing by using an Elizabethan collar (available from your veterinarian, or you can fashion one from a plastic pail) or an anti-chew preparation such as Bitter Apple (available from most pet stores). Your veterinarian can also prescribe anti-inflammatory medication. As a temporary measure, you can give an allergy pill (such as Benadryl — ask your veterinarian what dosage is appropriate), which alleviates some itching and causes drowsiness, both of which should decrease chewing.

Many people have obtained good results by using Gold Bond medicated powder or even Listerine on the spots.

Seborrhea

Seborrhea occurs in an oily form and a dry form. German Shepherds usually get the dry form, in which the skin feels waxy and greasy and may be also crusty and dry. Dandruff is often present. This condition is often associated with excessive earwax and rancid odor. Sometimes the hair falls out when the root area becomes coated with grease. Most hair loss occurs on the dog's trunk. Seborrhea can be treated with special (usually tar-based) shampoos. They can greatly improve the skin's condition, but at present no cure is available.

Eye and Ear Problems

The windows to your Shepherd's soul are no doubt the parts that you look at the most. Perhaps for this reason, eye problems are usually detected fairly early. These signs can tell you that your dog may be having eye problems that you and your veterinarian need to address:

✔ Squinting or tearing can be due to an irritated cornea or a foreign body in the eye. Examine under the lids and flood the eye with saline solution, or use a moist cotton swab to remove any debris. If you don't see improvement after one day, have the vet take a look.

✔ A watery discharge without squinting can be a symptom of allergies or a tear drainage problem. Your vet can diagnose a drainage problem with a simple test.

✔ As your Shepherd ages, the lenses of his eyes naturally become a little hazy, which you'll notice as a grayish appearance behind the pupils. If this occurs at a young age, however, or if a lens looks white or opaque, ask your vet to check your dog for cataracts. With cataracts, the lens becomes so opaque that light can no longer reach the retina; as in humans, the lens can be surgically replaced with an artificial one.

✔ If your dog's pupils do not react to light, or if one eye reacts differently than the other, take him to the vet immediately. Nonreactive pupils can indicate a serious problem.

The eyes are such complex and sensitive organs that you should always err on the side of caution. Consult your vet at the slightest sign of a problem.

Signs of ear problems include inflammation, discharge, debris, foul odor, pain, scratching, shaking, and tilting of the head. Extreme pain may indicate a ruptured eardrum. Bacterial and yeast infections, ticks or ear mites (see the "Mites" section, later in this chapter), foreign bodies, allergies, seborrhea, and hypothyroidism are possible underlying problems. Ear problems can be difficult to cure after they have established themselves, so early veterinary attention is crucial.

Plant awns, which are barbed seeds from some types of wild grasses, are one of the most common causes of ear problems in dogs who spend time outdoors. They penetrate the skin and migrate into deeper tissues, including the brain, causing irritation, infection, and even death. If your dog comes down with this problem, keep his ear lubricated with mineral oil and seek veterinary treatment as soon as possible.

Changes in Behavior

Sometimes physical problems manifest themselves in behavioral changes. If your dog suddenly acts strangely or uncharacteristically aggressively, don't assume that he's stopped minding you; the dog may be ill.

When is a change in behavior more than a mood swing? Sometimes it's difficult to know. Some changes are natural consequences of aging or hormonal states. Sexually intact dogs, for example, may become more excited and unmanageable if they or others around them are in heat. Aside from such changes, though, most normal and fairly long-lasting behavioral changes are not so abrupt.

✔ A dog who is uncharacteristically lethargic could be sick, and the possible causes are endless. You need to narrow it down a bit: Does the dog also have a fever? If yes, consider an infection. If no, your dog may have pain somewhere. Sudden loss of vision can also cause sudden lethargy. Cancer, poisoning, and metabolic diseases can cause lethargy without fever. In general, you want to have your veterinarian examine your dog if the dog is experiencing extreme lethargy, lethargy that lasts for more than one day, or lethargy that is accompanied by a fever.

✔ Aggressive behavior is usually not a sign of disease unless the behavior is totally unprecedented. It can be a sign of pain, an endocrine problem, or a brain problem. Usually, such cases are best examined by a neurologist or a veterinarian who specializes in behavior.

✔ Sudden loss of balance can be due to an inner ear problem or to unknown causes. Either way, your veterinarian can prescribe drugs to make your dog feel better.

✔ In general, unprecedented persistent circling or pacing, disorientation, *head-pressing* (pushing the head against a wall or other stationary object), hiding, tremors, seizures, lack of bowel or urine control, and dramatic change in appetite are usually signs of a physical problem. If your dog has any of these symptoms, have your veterinarian check him over.

✔ Sudden pacing and restlessness combined with unsuccessful attempts to vomit can indicate bloat — a "go the emergency vet right now" situation. Do not "wait and see." Bloat (or *gastric dilatation volvulus*) is a fast and merciless killer, and it targets German Shepherds. See Chapter 12 for more information.

Parasites

Parasites can rob your dog of vital nutrients, good health, a pleasurable existence, and even a long life. The most common *internal* parasites set up housekeeping in the intestines and heart. You can find the most common *external* parasites on the skin and in the ears. Every one is either treatable or preventable.

Hookworms, whipworms, roundworms, threadworms, and lungworms are all types of internal parasites that can infect dogs of all ages but have their most devastating effect on puppies. Left untreated, worms can cause vomiting, diarrhea, a dull coat, listlessness, anemia, and death. When you take your dog to be vaccinated, bring along a stool specimen so that your veterinarian can check for these parasites, and have your puppy tested for internal parasites regularly. If your dog walks in public areas that other dogs frequent, you need to have him checked more often than if he is restricted to your own yard. Some heartworm preventives (see Chapter 11) also prevent most types of intestinal worms, though not tapeworms.

Don't think that only puppies from bad homes have worms. Most puppies do have worms at some point, even pups from the most fastidious breeders. This is because some types of larval worms become encysted in the dam's body long before she becomes pregnant — perhaps when she herself was a pup. There they lie dormant and immune from worming until hormonal changes due to her pregnancy cause them to be activated; then they infect her fetuses or her newborns through her milk. The classic wormy puppy has a dull coat, a skinny body, and a potbelly, but many pups with worms have few of these symptoms.

Because you can buy worming medication over the counter, many people figure that they can save a little money that way. Others have been taught that to be good dog owners, they should "worm" their dogs once a month. Over-the-counter wormers are largely ineffective and often more dangerous than those available through a veterinarian. And no dog should be wormed unless he actually has worms. No worm medication is completely without risk, and using it carelessly is foolish.

Roundworms

Among the most common internal parasites of dogs, roundworms are found in virtually every puppy. Most puppies get the larva before birth, and you can find eggs in the pups' feces by the time they are 3 weeks old. Dogs can get roundworms by ingesting their eggs, and the parasites can be spread to people as well as dogs. (If you've been looking for a scientific reason to avoid eating dog doo-doo, this is it!)

Puppies should be wormed at least twice for roundworms. Many protocols advocate more frequent worming, with worming at 2, 4, 6, and 8 weeks of age. Pick up dog feces regularly, and do not allow dogs to defecate where children play.

Infected puppies can become quite ill, with heavy infestations leading to convulsions or death. Most mortality occurs around 2 to 3 weeks of age. Symptoms include a rough coat, a potbelly, and wasting muscles. Sometimes adult worms are visible in the dog's vomit or feces. Have your veterinarian examine the pup, along with a stool sample, to confirm the diagnosis and prescribe the correct deworming medication.

Hookworms

Hookworms are actually a family of species, the most prevalent in dogs being *Ancylostoma caninum*. They are especially prevalent in warm, humid climates. Dogs can acquire hookworms before birth, through penetration of the larvae through the skin, or by eating the larva. Puppies with heavy infestations can become anemic and have bloody, black, or tarry diarrhea. Without prompt treatment, these puppies usually die.

Treatment consists of deworming, blood transfusions, and follow-up prevention. Once the intestinal tract has been cleared of worms, larva in the muscle tissue migrate to the intestines and repopulate them, so another deworming treatment is needed two weeks after the first.

Adult dogs usually build up immunity to hookworms, although some dogs have chronic hookworm disease. This disease is more common in dogs with compromised immune systems and dogs who live in the midst of feces.

Removing feces at least twice a week is the most cost-effective means of hookworm control.

Whipworms

Dogs get whipworms by ingesting their eggs. Eggs can live in the environment for up to five years, especially in cold climates. Unlike some other types of internal parasites, dogs do not develop immunity to whipworms.

Whipworms inhabit the large intestine, where they puncture blood vessels and have a blood feast at the dog's expense. A heavy infestation can cause diarrhea, anemia, and weight loss. Treatment consists of repeated deworming, often every other month for a year. Picking up dog feces is an essential part of controlling whipworms.

Tapeworms

Tapeworms plague some dogs throughout their lives. Several species exist, the most common by far being *Dipylidium caninum*. Tapeworms look like white, flat, moving worms on fresh stools, or they may dry up and look like rice grains around a dog's anus. They are one of the least debilitating worms, but their segments can be irritating to a dog's anal region, and they're certainly unsightly.

Fleas transmit this kind of tapeworm to dogs. No preventive exists except to rid your German Shepherd of fleas diligently (see Chapter 10).

Protozoal Parasites

Puppies and dogs also suffer from protozoa parasites, such as coccidia and especially *Giardia*. Growing in frequency is *Babesia*. Because they are not worms, worm medications are usually ineffective in treating these parasites. Your veterinarian can prescribe an appropriate medication.

- ✔ **Coccidia:** Coccidia are often associated with diarrhea, but many infected dogs show no symptoms. A stool sample is needed for diagnosis. Affected dogs respond well to supportive treatment and drugs. The most important preventive measure is removal of feces from the yard or any area the dog frequents.

- ✔ ***Giardia:*** *Giardia* is fairly common in puppies and dogs. It can cause chronic or intermittent diarrhea but may have no symptoms. A vet can diagnose it with a stool sample; it's more likely to be found in loose or light-colored stool. *Giardia* can be treated with drug therapy.

- ✔ ***Babesia:*** Potentially fatal parasites, protozoa of the genus *Babesia* are transmitted by ticks and parasitize the red blood cells. This causes the infected dog to become anemic, and may also precipitate an autoimmune response in which the dog's body begins to destroy its own red blood cells and platelets. Symptoms include fever, lethargy, loss of appetite, and, in severe cases, darkened urine.

Affected dogs can die within a week of the first appearance of these symptoms, so act quickly. Diagnosis is with blood tests. Note that the symptoms of babesiosis are similar to those of autoimmune hemolytic anemia, so if your dog is diagnosed with either of these conditions, make sure that your veterinarian also tests for the other possibility.

Mites

Mites are tiny organisms in the tick and spider family. Of the many types of mites, only a few cause problems in dogs.

Sarcoptic mange

Sarcoptic mange, also called *canine scabies,* causes intense itching that's often characterized by scaling of the ear tips. It also causes lesions, most of which are found on the dog's ear tips, the underside of the body, the elbows, and the forelegs. This type of mite is highly contagious and is spread by direct contact — it can even spread to people. Treatment requires you to repeatedly shampoo or dip the affected dog, as well as other household pets who have been in contact with him. Newer, more effective treatments are available from your vet.

Demodectic mange

Demodectic mange, also called *red mange* or *demodicosis,* is not contagious and is not usually itchy. The condition tends to run in families and is more common in certain breeds, including GSDs. It is characterized by a moth-eaten appearance, most often around the dog's eyes and lips. Demodectic mange affecting the feet is also common and can be extremely resistant to treatment.

Most cases of demodectic mange appear in puppies, and most consist of only a few patches that often go away by themselves. But in those cases that continue to spread, or in adult-onset demodectic mange, aggressive treatment with an amitraz insecticidal dip is needed. Your veterinarian will need to perform a skin scraping to confirm the diagnosis before prescribing treatment.

Cheyletialla mites

Cheyletialla mites live on the skin surface and cause mild itchiness. Unlike other mites, they are large enough to be seen with the naked eye (but a magnifying glass is better) — they look like small white specks in the dog's hair near the skin. Sometimes people confuse them with dandruff because they also *cause* dandruff, especially along the back. Many flea insecticides also kill these mites, but they're better treated with the special shampoos or dips that are available from your vet.

Ear mites

Ear mites, which are often found in puppies, are highly contagious and intensely irritating. An affected dog will shake his head, scratch his ears, and perhaps carry his head sideways. The ear mite's signature is a dark, dry, waxy buildup resembling coffee grounds in the ear canal, usually in both ears. This material is actually dried blood mixed with ear wax.

Many people assume that any ear problem is due to ear mites, but unless you actually see mites, don't treat a dog for them. You could make another problem worse.

Separate a dog with ear mites from other pets, and wash your hands after handling his ears. Ideally, you should treat every pet in your household if one of them has ear mites.

Coping with Emergencies

Even experienced dog owners have a difficult time deciding what constitutes a true emergency. When in doubt, err on the side of caution and call the emergency clinic or your veterinarian for a professional opinion. Consider the following situations emergencies:

- Being hit by a car
- Profuse bleeding; bleeding from the nose, mouth, ears, eyes, or rectum; or blood in the urine or stools
- Sudden extreme lethargy or collapse
- Difficulty breathing
- Drowning
- Heatstroke
- Temperature over 104 degrees
- Hypothermia or frostbite
- Repeated vomiting; vomit containing blood, coffee ground–like material, or fecal-like material; or unproductive attempts to vomit
- Restlessness with a swollen stomach
- Frequent watery diarrhea
- Poisonous snake or spider bite or multiple insect stings
- Suspected poisoning, especially antifreeze
- Clusters of seizures or a prolonged seizure
- Paralysis
- Pupils of the eyes unresponsive or unequal in size
- Squinting, painful eye with redness, and aversion to light
- Electric shock
- Extreme dehydration

Because there are no paramedics for dogs, you must assume the role of paramedic and ambulance driver in case of an emergency. Now is the time to prepare for this life-saving role. Know the phone number and location of the emergency veterinarian in your area and keep the number next to the phone; don't rely on your memory during an emergency situation. Always keep enough fuel in your car to make it to the emergency clinic without stopping for gas. Finally, stay calm, which will help your dog stay calm as well. In general:

- Make sure that you and your dog are in a safe location, and move the dog as little and as gently as possible. Never use force or do anything that causes extreme discomfort.

✔ Make sure that your dog's breathing passages are open, and check his pulse and consciousness. Remove his collar and check his mouth and throat for obstructions.

✔ Control any bleeding (see below).

✔ Check for signs of shock (very pale gums, weakness, unresponsiveness, faint pulse, and shivering). Treat the dog by keeping him warm and calm.

✔ Never remove an impaled object (unless it's blocking the dog's airway).

Most other emergencies give you a little more time to act — but not much. For the following situations, administer first aid and seek veterinary attention. Situations not described in this list can usually be treated with the same first aid as for humans. In all cases, the best advice is to get a vet's opinion.

✔ **Abdominal wounds:** Place a warm, wet, sterile dressing over any protruding internal organs and cover with a bandage or towel. Do not attempt to push organs back into the dog.

✔ **Abdominal bloating, restlessness, and attempts to vomit:** Go to the emergency clinic right now without delay. The problem could be gastric dilatation volvulus.

✔ **Animal bites:** Allow some bleeding; then clean the area thoroughly and apply antibiotic ointment. A course of oral antibiotics will probably be necessary. Your vet can determine whether to suture a large bite (over ½ inch in diameter) or a bite on the face or other prominent position.

✔ **Bleeding:** Control massive bleeding first. Cover the wound with clean dressing and apply pressure. Don't remove blood-soaked bandages; apply more dressings over them until the bleeding stops. If possible, elevate the wound site and apply a cold pack to it.

✔ **Burns:** Deep burns, characterized by charred or pearly white skin, are serious. Cool burned areas with cold packs or towels soaked in water, or immerse them in cold water. If over 50 percent of the dog is burned, do not immerse the dog; doing so increases the likelihood of shock. Cover the area with a clean bandage or towel to avoid contamination. Do not apply pressure or ointments. Monitor for shock.

✔ **Electrical shock:** A dog who chews an electric cord may collapse and have burns inside his mouth. Before touching the dog, disconnect the plug or cut the power; if you can't do so immediately, use a wooden stick to knock the cord away. Keep the dog warm and treat him for shock. Monitor his breathing and heartbeat.

✔ **Heatstroke:** Early signs of heatstroke include rapid, loud breathing, abundant thick saliva, bright red mucous membranes, and a high rectal temperature. Later signs include unsteadiness, diarrhea, and coma. In this case, wet the dog and place him in front of a fan, or immerse him in *cool* (not icy) water. Offer small amounts of water for drinking. Stop cooling when the dog's rectal temperature reaches 103 degrees F.

- **Hypothermia:** Shivering and sluggishness are signs that a dog has become excessively chilled. Later signs include a very low body temperature (under 95 degrees F), slow pulse and breathing rates, and coma. To treat this condition, warm the dog gradually. Wrap him in a warm blanket. Place plastic bottles filled with hot water outside the blanket, not touching the dog. Monitor the dog's temperature and stop warming when it reaches 101 degrees F.

- **Insect stings:** Dogs are often stung by insects on their face or feet. Remove any visible stingers as quickly as possible. Administer baking soda and water paste to bee stings and vinegar to wasp stings. Call your vet immediately if your dog has an allergic reaction, including swelling that could interfere with breathing or any change in consciousness.

- **Limb fractures:** With most fractures, it's safest to simply transport the dog to the vet as gently as possible, taking great care to prevent the affected limb from hitting something. If you must try to splint the leg, use lots of padding and tape the splint outside the padding. If the bone is exposed, place a sterile covering over it but don't try to push it back in.

- **Poisoning:** Signs of poisoning vary according to the type of poison, but they commonly include vomiting, convulsions, staggering, and collapse. If you're not sure whether your dog ingested poison, call the vet or poison control hotline and give as much information as possible; they can advise whether you need to induce vomiting or bring your dog in to be examined. If possible, bring the poison and its container with you. If the dog vomits, put the vomit in a plastic bag and bring it with you as well. Antifreeze and Warfarin are the most common deadly dog poisons.

- **Seizures:** A dog undergoing a seizure may drool, become stiff, or have uncontrollable muscle spasms. If you think that your dog is having a seizure, wrap him securely in a blanket to prevent him from injuring himself on furniture or stairs. Remove other dogs from the area. If the seizure continues for more than ten minutes or repeats itself, get the dog to an emergency clinic. More often, the seizure will be over in a few minutes. Call your veterinarian for advice, because seizures can result from poisoning, high fever, or other conditions that must be treated immediately. Taking careful note of all characteristics and sequences of seizure activity can help your vet diagnose the cause.

Never put your hands (or anything) in a convulsing dog's mouth.

- **Snakebites:** Poisonous snakebites are characterized by swelling, discoloration, pain, fang marks, restlessness, nausea, and weakness. Most bites are to the head and are difficult to treat with first aid. If your dog is bitten by a snake, restrain him and keep him quiet. Note the snake's markings so that you're able to describe them to the veterinarian. Only if you can't get to the vet immediately, apply a firm pressure bandage (not a tourniquet) between the bite and the heart. If the bite is on a leg, keep the leg lower than the rest of the body.

Chapter 14

Caring for an Aging Shepherd

In This Chapter

▶ Feeding and exercising an older GSD

▶ Taking into account special health concerns that come with age

▶ Saying good-bye

▶ Coping with loss of a true friend

One day, you will look at your youngster and be shocked to discover that his face has silvered and his gait has stiffened. He sleeps longer and more soundly than he did as a younger dog, and he's slower to get going. He may be less eager to play and more content to lie in the sun. Congratulations! Getting your dog to a healthy old age is a worthy accomplishment.

You can't turn back the clock — and besides, you learn to appreciate the different stages of your dog's life as you share the years together. Puppies are full of curiosity and mischief; who could resist them? Adolescents begin to blossom into adults, sometimes doing the goofiest things but astounding you with feats of loyalty and intelligence just when you think, "This dog is hopeless!" Adult dogs mature into truly dependable companions whom you can trust with your life. Anyone who has had a German Shepherd for his entire life, however, would probably assert that a senior GSD is really the best. With the wisdom of years, a GSD becomes almost humanlike in his ability to tune in to your emotions. An older GSD, his gait stiff, his face gray, and his eyes often hazy due to cataracts, is, in the opinion of many GSD fanciers, the most beautiful of all.

Dogs age at different rates, but by 6 years of age most German Shepherds are considered to be middle-aged, and by 10 years of age they are considered geriatric. The average life span for a German Shepherd is 10 to 12 years.

As a caring owner, you must understand and respect your senior dog's special needs. This chapter explains how to nurture a German Shepherd in the last years of his life and how and when to say good-bye to your trusted friend.

Keeping Your Senior Fit and Trim

Both physical activity and metabolic rates decrease in older animals, meaning that they require fewer calories to maintain their weight. If you continue to feed an older dog the same amount of food that you fed when he was younger, you put him at risk of becoming obese; an obese dog has a greater risk of cardiovascular and joint problems.

Some German Shepherds lose weight with age, which can be equally bad. Your dog needs a little bit of fat so that he has something to fall back on if he gets sick. Other Shepherds lose weight and may need to eat puppy food in order to keep on the pounds. High-quality (not high-*quantity*) protein is especially important for older dogs, which means that feeding a high-quality food is especially important for older dogs. Chapter 7 tells you how to select a high-quality dog food.

Most older dogs do not require a special diet unless they have a particular medical need. (Your veterinarian can tell you whether your dog needs special food.) Just make sure to feed several small meals instead of one large meal, and serve those meals on time.

Moistening dry food or feeding canned food instead of dry can help a dog with dental problems enjoy his meal. He may also enjoy eating while lying down or eating off of a raised platform, both of which reduce the stress on his neck and joints.

Many people have the macho idea that their dogs will never slow down with age. Dogs do age at different rates, but being in a state of denial about your dog's increasing age or decreasing abilities does not do him any favors. Older German Shepherds who had joint problems when they were young can now really begin to suffer with them.

It's important to keep your older GSD relatively active, but without putting too much stress on his joints. If your dog is sore the next day, you probably asked too much. You may have to walk with your dog and do your marathon running by yourself. If you and your dog enjoy hiking together, pare down your trips and camp in just one spot. Swimming is an excellent low-impact exercise as long as the dog doesn't get chilled and is never put in a dangerous situation. (See Chapter 15 for safe swimming tips.)

Understanding the Changes a Dog Undergoes as He Ages

You may have depended on your dog for years when he was younger. Now it's your turn to let your dog lean on you. You can be a much better caretaker and friend to your dog if you understand the kinds of changes he will experience and know how to cope with those changes to help him remain comfortable.

Behavioral changes

Older dogs tend to like a simple life. Although they're still up for adventure, you may have to tone that adventure down a bit, or at least shorten it. Long trips can be grueling for an older dog, and boarding in a kennel may be extremely upsetting. Consider getting a house-sitter whom your dog knows if you want to go on vacation. (Chapter 18 provides much more information about traveling with your dog or safely leaving him at home while you go away.)

An older dog may welcome a new puppy that encourages him to play, but if your dog is not used to other dogs, he will more likely resent the newcomer. Some older dogs become cranky and impatient when dealing with puppies or boisterous children.

Don't just excuse behavioral changes as a part of the aging process, however, especially if they come on suddenly. The changes could be symptoms of pain or disease — talk to your dog's vet.

Physical changes

Older dogs may experience hearing or vision loss. The slight haziness that appears in an older dog's pupils is normal and has a minimal effect on vision. However, some dogs (especially those with diabetes) may develop cataracts, which look almost white through the pupils. A veterinary ophthalmologist can remove the lens of the eye if a cataract is severe.

Dogs with gradual vision loss cope well as long as you keep them in familiar surroundings and follow extra safety precautions. For example, don't move furniture, and place sound or scent beacons (such as perfumed items or radios) throughout the house or yard to help the dog locate specific landmarks. Also lay pathways in the yard, such as gravel or block walkways, and create paths in the house with carpet runners. Block open stairways or pools.

Dogs with hearing loss can learn to interpret hand gestures and also respond to vibrations. You can teach hand signals the same way you teach voice commands; if your dog still has some hearing, the easiest way to teach hand signals is to precede your voice command with a hand signal.

Be careful not to startle a dog with impaired senses, because a startled dog may snap in self-defense.

Like people, dogs lose skin moisture as they age, and although dogs don't have to worry about wrinkles, their skin can become dry and itchy. Regular brushing can help by stimulating oil production.

Even in the healthiest dogs, something has to give way first, and often it is the hindquarters. Your dog may need help getting up and may need some steadying when he walks. You can wrap a big towel under his belly and steady him by using the towel as a sling. Hindquarter harnesses are also available. Of course, any rear weakness, especially in a German Shepherd, needs to be checked thoroughly by a veterinarian.

Staying Well Up in Years

Just like older humans, older dogs tend to be more susceptible to disease and other health problems because their immune systems may be less effective. Therefore, an older dog should see his veterinarian at least twice a year — blood tests can detect early stages of diseases that can benefit from treatment. Shielding your dog from infectious disease, chilling, overheating, and stressful conditions also becomes increasingly important.

At the same time, an older dog who is never exposed to other dogs may not need to be vaccinated as often or for as many diseases as a younger dog. Discuss your options with your veterinarian.

Following are some points to keep in mind about older dogs and signs of illness:

✔ Vomiting and diarrhea in an old dog can signal many different problems. Keep in mind that an older dog can't tolerate the dehydration that results from continued vomiting or diarrhea; do not let the condition continue unchecked.

✔ Older dogs tend to have a stronger body odor, but don't ignore increased odors, which could indicate specific problems, such as periodontal disease, impacted anal sacs, seborrhea, ear infections, or even kidney disease. Have your veterinarian check any strong odor.

✔ Arthritis is a common cause of intermittent stiffness and lameness. You can help by providing a soft bed, moderate exercise, and possibly drug therapy, and by putting a heating pad (preferably one that uses moist heat) on the affected area. New arthritis medications have made a huge difference in quality of life for many older German Shepherds, but not every dog can use them. Ask your veterinarian to evaluate your dog.

✔ In general, any ailment that an older dog has is magnified in severity as compared to the same problems in a younger dog. Some of the more common symptoms and their possible causes in older GSDs include the following (see Chapters 12 and 13 for more on these diseases and conditions):

- **Diarrhea:** Kidney or liver disease, pancreatitis

- **Coughing:** Heart disease, tracheal collapse, lung cancer

- **Difficulty eating:** Periodontal disease, oral tumors

- **Decreased appetite:** Kidney, liver, or heart disease; pancreatitis; cancer

- **Increased appetite:** Diabetes, Cushing's syndrome

- **Weight loss:** Heart, liver, or kidney disease; diabetes; cancer

- **Abdominal distention:** Heart or kidney disease, Cushing's syndrome, tumors

- **Increased urination:** Diabetes, kidney or liver disease, cystitis, Cushing's syndrome

- **Limping:** Arthritis, hip or elbow dysplasia, degenerative myelopathy

- **Nasal discharge:** Tumor, periodontal disease

If you're lucky enough to have an old GSD, you still must accept that the end will come. Heart disease, kidney failure, and cancer eventually claim most of these senior citizens. Early detection can help delay their effects but, unfortunately, can seldom prevent them entirely.

Understanding arthritis

Many, if not most, older German Shepherds suffer from some degree of arthritis, a degenerative joint disease. Understanding how arthritis affects the joints can help you help your dog cope.

Joints occur at the moving junction of two bones. The ends of the bones are covered with cartilage, which helps cushion impact and allows for smoother movement between the bones. The joint is enclosed by the joint capsule, the inner layer of which is the synovial membrane. The synovial membrane produces *synovial fluid,* a thick liquid that fills the joint cavity and provides lubrication and nourishment. Cartilage can be injured from excessive joint stress or from a pre-existing joint instability that allows the bones to bump together abnormally. Injured cartilage releases enzymes that break down the normally thick synovial fluid into a thin fluid that neither lubricates nor nourishes adequately, in turn resulting in further cartilage deterioration. If the dog continues to stress the joint, the damage will increase until it extends to the joint capsule and bone. Only at this point are sensory nerves affected so that the dog feels pain. This means that considerable joint damage has already been

(continued)

(continued)

done by the time your dog exhibits lameness from a pre-existing condition.

In arthritis, the synovial membrane surrounding the joint becomes inflamed, and the bone develops small bony outgrowths called *osteophytes*. These changes cause the joint to stiffen, become painful, and have a decreased range of motion. In cases in which an existing condition is exacerbating the arthritis, surgery to remedy the condition is warranted.

When considering surgery for a joint problem, keep in mind that the more the joint is used in its damaged state, the more arthritis will occur. Even though the surgery may fix the initial problem, the dog will still be plagued with incurable arthritic changes if too much damage has occurred. *Preventing* arthritis is the key.

Conservative treatment entails keeping the dog's weight down, attending to injuries promptly, and maintaining a program of exercise. Low-impact exercise such as walking or swimming every other day is best for dogs with signs of arthritis. Newer drugs, such as carprofen, are available from your veterinarian and may help alleviate some of the symptoms of arthritis, but they should be used only under careful veterinary supervision.

Some newer drugs and supplements may actually improve the joint. Polysulfated glycosaminoglycan increases the compressive resilience of cartilage. Glucosamine stimulates the synthesis of collagen and may help rejuvenate cartilage to some extent. Chondroitin sulfate helps to shield cartilage from destructive enzymes.

Saying Good-bye to Your Trusted Friend

Despite the best of care, a time will come when neither you nor your veterinarian can prevent your dear friend from succumbing to old age or an incurable illness. It seems hard to believe that you will have to say good-bye to a dog who has been such a focal point of your life — a real member of your family. That dogs live such a short time compared to humans is a cruel fact, but one that you must ultimately face.

Realize that both of you have been fortunate to have shared so many good times, and make sure that your GSD's remaining time is as pleasurable as possible. Many terminal illnesses make a dog feel very ill, and there comes a point when your desire to keep your friend with you as long as possible may not be the kindest thing for either of you. If your dog no longer eats his dinner or treats, this is a sign that he doesn't feel well.

For every person, the ultimate point is different. Many people put off doing what's best for longer than is really kind because they don't want to act in haste and be haunted by thoughts that the setback may have been temporary. And of course, they put it off because they can't stand the thought of saying good-bye.

Euthanasia is a difficult and personal decision that no one can make for you. Ask yourself the following questions as you face this decision:

✔ Does your veterinarian believe that your dog has a reasonable chance of getting better? Is it likely that your dog is suffering?

✔ Is your dog still getting pleasure out of life? Is he still enjoying most of his days?

✔ Does treating an illness mean that you will have to go into debt in exchange for just a little more time with your dog?

✔ Is the constant worry and stress taking too hard a toll on you and your family?

Of course you wish that if your dog has to go, he will fall asleep and never wake up. Unfortunately, that almost never happens. Even when it does, you're left with the regret that you never got to say good-bye. The closest way you can simulate this experience is with *euthanasia,* which involves giving an overdose of an anesthetic, which is painless. Essentially, the dog falls asleep and dies almost instantly. This process may take slightly longer in a very sick dog because his circulation is compromised, but the dog is still unconscious.

If you do decide that euthanasia is the kindest farewell gesture for your beloved friend, discuss what will happen with your veterinarian beforehand. You might ask about giving your dog a tranquilizer before leaving the house if he fears the vet's office, or about having the doctor meet you at home or come out to your car to meet you. Although it won't be easy, try to remain with your dog so that his last moments are filled with your love; otherwise, have a friend whom your dog knows stay with him. Try to recall the wonderful times you have shared and realize that however painful it is to lose such a once-in-a-lifetime dog, having to cope with the loss is better than never having had such a partner at all.

After losing such a cherished friend, many people say that they will never get another dog. True, no dog will ever take the place of *your* dog. But you may find that another German Shepherd is a welcome diversion that helps keep you from dwelling on the loss of your first pet — as long as you don't keep comparing the new dog to the old one. By getting another dog, you sentence yourself to the same grief in another 12 years or so, but wouldn't you rather have that than miss out on a *second* once-in-a-lifetime dog?

The loss of a companion may mark the end of an era for you, a time when you and your shepherd grew up or grew old together. But one could scarcely ask for a better life partner than a special German Shepherd — perhaps the most magnificent being ever created.

Coping with your loss

Many people who regarded their German Shepherds as members of the family nonetheless feel embarrassed at the grief they feel at their loss. Yet this dog often functioned as a surrogate child, best friend, and confidant. Partnership with a pet can be one of the closest and most stable relationships in life. Unfortunately, the support from friends that comes with human loss is too often absent with pet loss. Such well-meaning but ill-informed statements as "He was just a dog" or "Just get another one" do little to ease the pain — many people simply don't know how to react.

Many people understand and share your feelings; however, if you'd rather speak to a professional, many veterinary schools (such as the University of California at Davis, 800-565-1526, and Iowa State University, 888-ISU-PLSH) have pet bereavement counselors. You can also find information — and solace — on the Web by searching under "pet loss."

Part V

Having Fun with Your German Shepherd

In this part . . .

*F*inally, the fun part! People wouldn't have dogs if all they involved were work and worry. Dogs, and especially German Shepherds, are fun. If you have a German Shepherd, you already know that. You know the fun you can have every day playing and interacting with your dog. But do you know how to have safe fun on an outdoor adventure? Do you know how to keep your German Shepherd the athlete he was meant to be? Have you ever dreamed about making your dog a star in one of the many dog competitions available to GSDs? Or how about a star in one thankful person's life?

The following chapters get you started in the wonderful world of German Shepherds in all their glory, whether it's working, competing, playing, or just sharing a good time at home.

Chapter 15

Exercising Your Dog

. . . .

In This Chapter

▶ Giving your dog the best exercise

▶ Recognizing the perils of outdoor life

▶ Knowing what to do when your dog's dogs are dogging him

▶ Swimming and hiking with your dog

▶ Finding the dog who gets away

. . . .

One of the greatest joys of being a German Shepherd is running and running and running until everyone else around has dropped from exhaustion — and then running some more. One of the greatest joys of owning a German Shepherd is watching this show of athleticism.

One of the saddest sights, however, is a German Shepherd held permanent prisoner in a small pen or on a chain. The only sadder sight is a German Shepherd hurt — or worse — because his owner wasn't careful enough to make sure that he exercised in a safe place.

In this chapter, you can find out how to give your German Shepherd the exercise and play he needs without feeling like you're running a marathon yourself. And because the number-one reason for exercising your dog is to keep him healthy, I explain how to exercise and play with your dog *safely* — and what to do if your dog does come up lame.

Giving Your Dog the Runaround (Or Walkaround)

You'll probably find yourself walking your Shepherd for exercise. Walking a dog is excellent low-impact exercise for both of you, and is especially good for elderly dogs or dogs recovering from injuries. If you pick a regular time of day for your walk, you'll have your own personal fitness coach goading you off the couch like clockwork!

Marathon dogs

If you're into both marathons and titles, your German Shepherd can strive for the AD (which stands for *Ausdauerpruefung*) title, signifying that he passed an endurance test. This test involves completing a 12½-mile marathon in which he trots next to a bicycle, with a ten-minute break halfway through. See Chapter 16 for other title-earning activities in which you and your dog can participate.

For a walk around the neighborhood, use a 6-foot non-chain leash or a retractable leash. (See Chapter 5 for information about buying leashes for your dog.) Retractable leashes, as shown in Figure 15-1, are great for walks because they give a dog the freedom to explore beyond the sidewalk, but be especially vigilant when using them because the dog can still dart out into the path of traffic.

The best way to hold a leash securely is to insert your entire hand through the loop and grasp the leash just above the loop handle. Never hold a leash with just your hand or fingers around the loop — at the first sight of a squirrel or other critter, your dog could pull the leash right out of your hand.

As you walk, keep up a brisk pace, and gradually work up to longer distances. An adult German Shepherd should walk at the very least half a mile daily — walking several miles a day is better. Don't ask older or obese dogs to walk farther than they can comfortably manage, however. If your dog begins to limp, pant heavily, salivate, or slow down or lag behind you, you've gone too far.

Jogging on leash can be fun for an adult dog, too, but keep the following cautions in mind:

- ✔ You must work up to longer distances gradually.
- ✔ Avoid jogging in hot weather. Dogs can't cool themselves as well as humans can, and heatstroke in jogging dogs has taken the lives of far too many.
- ✔ Avoid jogging your dog on hard surfaces, which are jarring to the joints.
- ✔ Check the dog's footpads regularly for abrasions, tearing, or blistering from hot pavement, and remove any gravel you find.
- ✔ In winter, check between the pads for balls of ice, and rinse the feet when returning from walking on rock salt.

You can prevent the formation of ice balls by coating the dog's pads with Vaseline or butter; just be sure to wipe them off before going back in your house!

- ✔ Never jog, jump, or overexert a puppy, whose bones can be overstressed and damaged. Let a pup run until he's tired, but absolutely not a step farther.

Figure 15-1:
For safety's sake, keep your dog close at hand when he's on a retractable leash.

If you want to train your dog to be a marathoner, use the same conditioning techniques that you would for any marathon athlete. Build up gradually, and take a day off between long jogs for the muscles to recover.

Playing It Safe

You probably think that your German Shepherd is smart, trustworthy, and reliable off lead. And you're probably right — until the unpredictable occurs: another dog attacks or a cat runs underfoot, for example. Whatever the reason, the trustworthy dog forgets himself for just a moment, and that's all it takes for him to run in front of a car. Trust is wonderful, but careless or blind trust is deadly.

Keep the following cautions in mind when you take your dog on an outdoor adventure:

- ✔ Never allow your Shepherd to run loose in sight of traffic, even if that traffic is a mere speck in the distance. A German Shepherd can travel a great distance in a short time.

- ✔ Never unhook your dog's leash until you know the area well. For example, are there so many squirrels and rabbits that your dog could be lured farther and farther away while chasing them?

✔ Deer are a grave danger because they're irresistible to most dogs and can lead them on a merry chase that may end in tragedy. If deer may be in the area, keep your dog on his leash.

✔ Watch for poisonous snakes, alligators, or other animals that could attack your dog, and for small animals and dogs that your dog could attack.

✔ Look out for cliffs, roadways, and drainage culverts. The danger of falling off a cliff or running into a highway is obvious, but drainage culverts also can be deadly when they fill with fast-moving water after a storm. They can sweep away a dog who just wants to cool off.

✔ Avoid wilderness areas during hunting season. Hunters are generally a careful lot, but an errant shot could mean tragedy for you and your dog.

✔ Although it's tempting to be lazy and jog your dog beside a bicycle or car, doing so is dangerous. Your dog could see a cat or squirrel and either pull you over or run into your path. If you do elect to try the lazy way out despite these warnings, train your dog to understand "Heel" before you start, and have your dog in Heel position (except farther from you) when on the move. Attachments that tether your dog to the rear of your bicycle enable you to keep your balance much better if the dog pulls and also keep him away from your wheels and chain.

✔ *Foxtails* are barbed seeds that can cause serious problems for dogs. Once embedded in or inhaled by a dog, the seed's barbs allow it to migrate through the dog's body, sometimes causing abscesses and sometimes even entering vital organs. Symptoms include localized infections or apparent pain; irritation to the nose, eyes, ears, or feet; and strange behaviors in which the dog rubs and licks parts of his own body. Foxtails usually have to be removed under anesthesia.

✔ Don't let your dog walk on thin ice. A dog — especially a fairly large dog like a German Shepherd — can fall through just as easily as a person can.

Don't let this list of caveats scare you away from the great times the great outdoors has in store for you and your dog. Just bring your common sense and a sharp eye with you — and of course, your happy partner in adventure!

Hiking with Your Dog

German Shepherds are great hiking partners. Hiking carries with it certain risks for dog and person, however; you need to know what they are to ensure that you both have a safe and fun adventure.

For example, dogs can fall off of cliffs or mountainsides. Not only do dogs scamper about with little regard for their safety, but dog paws lack the grasping ability of human hands, and once they begin to slip, dogs can do little to stop themselves. To make things worse, mountain and foothill areas may be home to abandoned mineshafts and their air vents. Know your hiking area!

Although your German Shepherd may think that he can best any wild animal, a few animals can get the better of him. Porcupine quills continue to work their way ever deeper into the flesh with every movement. Skunks can make you and your dog miserable. Poisonous snakes, and especially rattlesnakes, are high on most people's lists of dreaded animals encountered in the wild, and their venom has proven fatal to many dogs.

Don't deprive your German Shepherd of outdoor adventure, but don't take chances with his safety. Before you unhook the leash, be absolutely certain that you know where every road, every cliff, and every conceivable danger to your dog is. Never go into the field unprepared. Always have a first-aid kit available, along with a means of transportation to and communication with an emergency clinic. Of course, it's just as likely that your German Shepherd will rescue you from an accident! They've saved many a hiker, but try not to put your dog to the test.

WARNING!

Living off the land is not a good idea

Most dogs will avoid eating poisonous plants, but don't take any chances: Don't let your dog sample the green cuisine when hiking. And one more warning: Although dogs don't react to poison ivy or poison oak, they can carry the irritants on their fur and transmit them to you when you rub it. Keep your dog away from these plants for your own good!

A highlight of going to the shore for dogs is the chance to sample the dead fish. Unfortunately, every year hundreds of dogs in the Pacific Northwest get so-called salmon poisoning from eating raw salmon, steelhead, trout, and other species that are infected with small flukes that in turn contain *Neorickettsia helminthoeca*. A few days to weeks after eating the infected fish, the dog gets progressively sicker. Left untreated, most dogs die within two weeks. If you visit streams or rivers in areas of northern California, Oregon, Washington, Idaho, or Alaska, do not allow your dog to scavenge along the shore.

The smallest freshwater threat comes from those things in the water you can't even see. *Giardia* is a microscopic organism found in many water sources; it is nicknamed "beaver-fever" because of its propensity to be carried by beavers. When your dog drinks that seemingly pristine water straight from nature, it may ingest Giardia and can become ill sometime later with stomach cramps and loose, mucous stools. Giardia is a common condition in dogs who sample wilderness waters, but water doesn't have to be from the wilds to carry microscopic dangers. Pollution, especially in agricultural, industrial, or even residential areas, is a much-too-common threat. Avoid water that has a peculiar odor, color, or surface oiliness or that is obviously fed by runoff from polluted areas. Always bring water and a collapsible bowl for your dog when you hike.

Dangerous waters

Even the best swimmers can't overcome strong surf or undertows, nor can they predict the rogue waves that frequent certain beaches. In general, the waves of the Pacific Northwest are the least predictable and the least forgiving. If a sign says that swimming is unsafe for people, it is unsafe for dogs as well.

You don't have to be at the ocean to experience dangerous water. Fast running water in rivers, creeks, and ditches has killed more dogs than rough surf. Some calm mountain streams lead to deadly waterfalls. Normally placid creeks can swell into killer torrents from upstream rain, especially in desert regions. Many ditches have steep banks or bulkheads that dogs can't climb. The aquaducts of southern California have drowned many a dog.

Cold northern waters pose special hazards. Hypothermic dogs can lose the ability to swim with the strength necessary to make it back to shore. Dogs can break through thin ice. Ice that breaks under a dog's weight will almost certainly not support yours, making rescue dangerous or impossible.

Don't forget that your dog may not be the only animal in the water. The cottonmouth, or water moccasin, lives in swamps, lakes, rivers, and ditches. It often basks on the shore during the day but is more active at night. You can identify this snake by the light coloration inside its mouth and its way of swimming with its head held out of the water. Its bite can be fatal.

Even more widespread is the snapping turtle. Snappers are aggressive and have bitten body parts off of curious dogs with their sharp beaks. Snappers are found around muddy-bottomed fresh water with abundant plant life, although nesting females can wander far from water.

The largest freshwater threat is the alligator. Alligators consider dogs an irresistible delicacy. Never allow your dog off lead or in the water in alligator territory!

Don't be scared off of enjoying water sports with your dog, however. By far the vast majority of dogs frolic in the water without a care and emerge perfectly safe. Just make sure that your dog is one of them. Enjoy water sports — but do so safely!

Going for a Swim

Many German Shepherds seem intent on proving that they can outdo retrievers when it comes to water sports. A body of water is great for keeping your dog exercised yet cool in hot weather. It's also great for dogs with joint disorders or dogs who are recovering from injuries.

Don't send an exhausted dog out into deep water or into water with an undertow. Dogs do drown. Take the same precautions with your swimming dog that you would with a swimming child.

If your Shepherd is hesitant about swimming, you can use the following method to coax him into it:

1. **Get into the water yourself.**

2. **Entice your dog into the water a little at a time.**

   The best way is to walk along in shallow water and only occasionally ask your dog to take a step or two over his head.

   If your dog likes to retrieve on land, bring a favorite toy to use as an enticement into slightly deeper water.

3. **Elevate the dog's rear end so that his front feet stay under the water's surface.**

   Most beginner swimmers try to swim by walking on water, reaching above the water's surface with their front feet while their rear ends sink.

4. **Be calm and comforting, and let your dog get out of the water several times.**

   Go slowly and avoid scaring your dog. Soon, your GSD will be cruising along.

Out of the Running: Treating Injuries

Like all athletes, your Shepherd may hurt himself and come up lame, despite your best efforts to prevent injuries. This section tells you what to do if your adventuring GSD does come up injured.

Limping

Limping may or may not indicate a serious problem. Complete rest and total inactivity are the best initial home care for any lameness. Rest your dog well past the time he quits limping. If the condition persists after three days, take your dog to the veterinarian for an examination.

Ice packs may help minimize swelling if applied immediately after an injury. The reduced tissue temperature lowers the metabolic rate and inhibits edema and the sensation of pain. Cold therapy can be helpful for up to a week following an injury.

Heat therapy can be beneficial to older injuries. Heat increases the metabolic rate of the tissue, relaxes muscle spasms, and can provide some relief from pain. Moist heat applied for 20-minute periods is preferable — take care to avoid burning. Other types of heat therapy are available that penetrate more deeply through the tissues, but because they also carry a greater risk of burn injury, only an experienced person should perform them.

In many injuries in which the limb must be rested, passive motion can be important in preventing muscle contraction and maintaining the health of the joint. All movements should be slow and well within the joint's normal range of motion. Massage therapy can be useful for loosening tendons and increasing circulation. Exercise therapy is also important, but exercise must be controlled. Leash walking and swimming are excellent low-impact exercises for recovering dogs.

Many injuries are quite painful and may require drug therapy for pain relief. Orthopedic surgeries can be particularly painful and almost always warrant analgesics. Pain has a self-perpetuating aspect — it's easier to prevent than to stop. Discuss with your veterinarian the pros and cons of various analgesics.

If a dog is lame and also exhibits swelling or deformation of the affected leg, extreme pain, or grinding or popping sounds, he could have a break or another serious problem. Do not further traumatize the fractured area by attempting to immobilize it; when in doubt, leave it alone and seek immediate veterinary attention.

Foot injuries

Split or broken nails, cuts, peeled pads, and misaligned toes are all common sources of pain. Examine the feet of a limping dog for these ailments, and do the following to treat them:

- **Split or broken nails:** Cut the nail as short as possible and soak it in warm salt water. Apply an antibacterial ointment and then a human fingernail mender, followed by a bandage. If the toe becomes swollen or hot, take your dog to the vet.

  If the webbing between the toes is split, it will continue to split further. This condition warrants a trip to the vet.

- **Cuts and peeled pads:** Carefully flush the pad with warm water and then apply an antibacterial ointment. Cover the area with gauze and wrap the foot with Vet-Wrap (a stretchable bandage that clings to itself). You can also add padding to cushion the foot. Change the dressing twice daily (or anytime it gets wet) and restrict exercise until the wound heals.

  If your dog has deep cuts or extensive peeling, have your veterinarian check for foreign objects or tendon damage. A deep cut directly above and behind the foot may sever the ligaments to the toes, causing them to lose their arch and the dog to limp. Seek immediate veterinary attention for this condition.

  If you need a quick fix for a minor injury, you can fashion a makeshift pad by adhering a thin piece of rubber or leather to the bottom of the pad with tissue glue, or you can apply a coat of Nu-Skin (available at drugstores) if the injury isn't too extensive. Remember, too, that peeled pads are very painful. A local anesthetic such as hemorrhoid cream or a topical toothache salve can ease some of the discomfort.

✔ **Misaligned toes:** Toes that are broken or displaced, or that have torn ligaments, can stick up or out at odd angles. They require immediate veterinary attention.

Persistent limping in puppies may result from one of several developmental bone problems and should be checked by a veterinarian. In an older dog, or a dog with a previous injury, limping is often the result of osteoarthritis. You can treat arthritis with buffered aspirin, but do so only under veterinary supervision. Your veterinarian can also prescribe better drugs that may help greatly. Anytime a young or middle-aged dog shows signs of arthritis, especially in a joint that has not been injured previously, have him examined by his vet.

If a toe is swollen, does not match its fellow toe on the opposite foot in shape and position, or makes a grinding sound when moved, or if the dog is in considerable pain, immobilize the toe and have a veterinarian check it. Meanwhile, minimize the swelling by applying cold packs or placing the foot in a bucket of cold water.

I discuss other possible causes of lameness in Chapter 12.

Leg injuries

The most common non-foot injuries are muscle injuries, which usually cause little lameness but pronounced swelling, or can be felt as indentations in muscles. Torn muscles may require surgery to ensure a complete recovery. If your dog has a muscle injury, treat it with an ice pack followed by at least a week's rest.

Knee injuries, especially of the cruciate ligaments, are common in dogs — especially overweight dogs. They can also occur when a dog is pushed sideways while running. Most cruciate tears do not get well on their own. Still, cruciate surgery requires a commitment to careful nursing and should not be undertaken casually.

Puppies are especially susceptible to bone and joint injuries and should never be allowed to jump from high places or run until exhausted. Both puppies and adult dogs should be discouraged from romping on slippery floors that could cause them to lose their footing.

Finding a Lost Dog

While you and your Shepherd are exploring the great outdoors, the unforeseeable may happen: You may get separated. In this event, you need to act quickly. Don't rely on the dog's fabled ability to find his way home — this phenomenon occurs a lot more often in movies than in real life.

Here are some pointers for rounding up your dog as soon as possible:

- Start your search at the very worst place you could imagine: usually the nearest road. If you're in your car, drive carefully; you don't want to drive so recklessly that you endanger your own dog's life should he run across the road.

- If you must leave the area in which your dog was lost, try to leave his cage, his blanket, some of your personal belongings, or even your open car outside in case he returns while you're gone.

- Gather pictures of your dog and take them door to door. Be sure to ask neighborhood children, who are often the first to notice a new dog.

- Talk to the delivery personnel who service the area.

- Post large posters with a picture of your dog or a similar-looking German Shepherd.

- Distribute fliers at the local animal control, police department, parking lots, and veterinary clinics.

- Take out an ad in the local paper. Mention a reward, but do not specify an amount. Some scam artists answer lost dog ads and ask for money to ship the dog back to you from a distance or to pay vet bills when they don't really have the dog. If your dog is tattooed, you can have the person read the tattoo to you in order to positively identify it. Never give anyone reward money before seeing your dog.

Never give out your dog's tattoo number or divulge secret identifying marks. Some dognappers steal dogs so that they can collect large rewards. More often, scam artists read lost-and-found ads and claim to have found dogs they have not. Ask for identifying marks and for an address or phone number; if the person can't provide either, he or she almost certainly does not really have your dog.

- If your dog is likely to run away if approached, mention that fact in your ad or flyer. Some well-meaning or reward-hungry people have run dogs away while trying to catch them.

Losing a dog is a heartbreaking experience, a loss without closure or explanation. Remember, the best time to find a dog is right after he gets lost. Too many people take too long to realize that their dogs are really not coming back on their own — time in which the dogs probably could have been found. This is one instance in which being an alarmist pays off. I'd rather cry wolf than cry tears over a friend I never got to say good-bye to.

Chapter 16

Showing Off Your Dog

Something about dogs, and maybe German Shepherds in particular, brings out the human need to proclaim, "My dog's better than your dog!" The crazier owners actually set out to prove it.

But dog competitions are more than frivolous contests. At their best, they're a way to strengthen the human-dog bond, develop a partnership to its fullest, and allow your dog to be all that he can be (without joining the army). Competitions also provide a relatively impartial opinion of which dogs have the right stuff to be the parents of tomorrow's German Shepherds. If you plan on breeding your dog, you owe it to his future puppies and their owners to prove your dog's mettle in some area of competition. Luckily, you have lots of choices. This chapter explains the various types of competitions and how they work.

Conforming to the Standard of Perfection

A German Shepherd's build reflects his athletic heritage. This build has always been an important consideration in the breed's development. At conformation shows, judges evaluate how well each dog conforms to the physical standard of perfection while standing and moving. In the United States, shows are held every weekend, and a variety of judges make the choices (usually the wrong choices, according to most of the exhibitors except for the winners).

As long as your GSD doesn't have any disqualifying traits (see Chapter 2), he is eligible to compete in conformation shows. *Winning* may be a little tougher. You need to train and groom your dog — and yourself — before you start lugging home trophies.

How the shows work

German Shepherds are shown unlike any other dog breed. Other breeds are expected to pose four-square, but the German Shepherd has a distinctive show stance that makes him look like an action figure ready to spring. The front legs are placed straight down and parallel, like most other breeds, and the left rear leg is placed so that the hock is perpendicular to the ground, like most other breeds. But the right rear leg has crept up farther and farther as the years have passed, so that now GSDs look like runners in their blocks, ready to take off. Figure 16-1 illustrates this stance.

Other breeds are expected to trot nicely at their handler's sides without pulling; German Shepherds are expected to run well in front of their handlers and lead the way around the ring. Most dogs do one turn around the ring and are through; Shepherds may make many laps at all-breed shows. Some specialty shows start to resemble the Daytona 500.

Figure 16-1:
The German
Shepherd
show
stance.

© AKC Stock Images/Mary Bloom

Other breeds are expected to look at their handlers, perhaps focusing on a morsel of food that the handler is holding. A German Shepherd is expected to look past his handler out of the ring. Here's where it gets a little tricky: The AKC frowns on a practice known as *double-handling,* in which people outside the ring attract the attention of a dog being shown. In fact, a judge can excuse a dog from the ring and refuse to judge him if he's being double-handled. Yet the German Shepherd ring is known as the mecca of double-handlers, all trying (mostly unsuccessfully) to be subtle as they race from one side of the ring to the other using all their ventriloquist training to make noises without showing any visible sign of their source. Just don't get in their way!

How to get your dog involved

Most local kennel clubs offer handling classes where you can learn the fundamentals of conformation showing. Many also hold occasional *match shows,* in which everybody is there for practice, including the judges. Don't take a match win or loss too seriously, and at any show, no matter how obviously feebleminded you think the judge is, keep your opinion to yourself.

If the idea of running around a ring leaves you cold, or if the idea of losing a lot is unappealing to you, you can hire a professional handler to show your dog for you. Handlers are very good at what they do, and they know how to get the most out of a dog; Shepherds have a habit of being too mellow when shown by their owners but look much more alert when seeking their owners ringside. As a result, your odds of winning are greater with a professional at first (as long as the professional is a GSD specialist). Contact an organization such as the Dog Handler's Guild (612-682-3366, or www.infodog.com/misc/dhg/dhgmain.htm) for a referral. Nonetheless, he's your dog, and there's nothing like the thrill of winning when you're at the other end of the lead!

You may enter any class for which your dog is eligible:

- **Puppy:** For puppies between 6 and 12 months of age. This class is often split into two classes: Puppy 6-9 months and Puppy 9-12 months.
- **12-18 Months:** For youngsters between 12 and 18 months of age.
- **Novice:** For dogs who have won fewer than a certain minimal number of first placements (depending on the class in which they were won).
- **American-Bred:** For dogs who were bred in the United States. This class is often used for dogs who are no longer youngsters or novices but are still inexperienced.
- **Bred-by-Exhibitor:** For dogs bred, owned, and handled by the same person (or an immediate family member).
- **Open:** For any dog over 6 months of age.
- **Best of Breed:** For dogs who have already earned their AKC Championships.

Participating in SV shows

Some GSD exhibitors prove their dogs at SV shows, which are held in the United States through the United Schutzhund Clubs of America (USA) and the Working Dog Alliance (WDA) section of the German Shepherd Dog Club of America. Classes are divided by age and sex, with no interage or intersex competition. Puppies are rated as very promising (VP), promising (P), or less promising (LP); older dogs are rated as very good (SG), good (G), or rarely sufficient, insufficient, or excused.

Working class entrants must have a working title (either Schutzhund or the SV herding title — see the "Schutzhund" section at the end of this chapter) and certified hips. Only these dogs are eligible to receive a rating of Excellent (V). The Excellent Select (VA) title is awarded only at prestigious national shows, and dogs must have slightly higher levels of working certification to be eligible.

The SV show ring is much larger, and a lot of running is involved. An outer ring is included for the double-handlers to run around and get the dogs' attention. Unlike AKC shows, double-handling is expected and has reached the level of an art form. Also, unlike AKC shows, the judge critiques every entrant. In all but the puppy classes, a couple of gunshots are fired to evaluate the dogs' temperament.

At a typical show, you enter the ring, pose your dog, trot around the ring, allow the judge to physically examine your dog while he's posed, trot in a straight line to and from the judge, pose again, trot again, and then (hopefully) run to the first-place marker. The judge chooses first through fourth place in each class. After all the classes within a sex are judged, the first-place winner from each class is called back into the ring to compete against the other first-place winners for Winners, with the dog selected Winners winning points toward his Championship title. The number of points can vary from 0 to 5, depending on how many dogs are in competition — the more dogs who are competing, the higher the number of points awarded to the winner. To become an AKC Champion (Ch), your GSD must win 15 points including two *majors* (wins of 3, 4, or 5 points at one time).

The Winners in each sex (that is, the Winners Dog and the Winners Bitch) then return to the ring to compete for Best of Breed against all the German Shepherds who are already Champions. (A dog who has already earned the Ch title is not required to compete in the classes.) The dog selected as the best GSD goes on to represent the breed in the Herding Group competition. German Shepherds have proven themselves to be formidable competitors in the group, and those who do win the Herding Group go on to compete for Best in Show. The winner of the most Best in Shows of all breeds in AKC history is (of course!) a German Shepherd bitch, Ch Altana's Mystique.

Because a German Shepherd is so much a true family member, having your noble dog placed last in his class can hurt. To survive as a GSD competitor, you must be able to separate your own ego and self-esteem from your dog's. Do not allow your dog's ability to win in competition cloud your perception of his true worth in his primary role: that of friend and companion. A dog who is last in his class but first in his owner's heart is far better off than an unloved dog who places first in any competition.

Scoring an A in Obedience

H.I.T. is obedience lingo for High in Trial: the supreme award given to the top dog at an obedience trial, and an award that is no stranger to German Shepherds. Generations of attention to temperament and intelligence have placed the GSD among the top competitors in trials.

Several organizations, including the AKC, the Canadian Kennel Club (CKC), and the United Kennel Club (UKC), sponsor obedience trials for all breeds with progressively more difficult levels. The lowest level of AKC Companion Dog (CD) requires your dog to do the following:

✔ Heel on lead, sitting automatically each time you stop; negotiating right, left, and about turns without guidance from you; and changing to a faster and slower pace.

✔ Heel in a figure 8 around two people, still on lead.

✔ Stand still off lead 6 feet away from you and allow a judge to touch him.

✔ Do the exercises in the first item in this list, except off lead.

✔ Come to you when called from 20 feet away, and then return to the Heel position on command.

✔ Stay in a Sit position with a group of other dogs, with you 20 feet away, for one minute.

✔ Stay in a Down position with the same group, with you 20 feet away, for three minutes.

As the degrees get higher, the exercises get more difficult — but also a lot more fun. To earn the Companion Dog Excellent (CDX) degree, a dog must

✔ Heel off lead, including executing a figure 8.

✔ Come when called from 20 feet away, but drop to a Down position when told to do so partway to you, and then complete the recall when called again.

✔ Retrieve a thrown dumbbell when told to do so (see Figure 16-2).

✔ Retrieve a thrown dumbbell, leaving and returning over a high jump.

✔ Jump over a broad jump when told to do so.

✔ Stay in a Sit position with a group of dogs, with you out of sight, for three minutes.

✔ Stay in a Down position with a group of dogs, with you out of sight, for five minutes.

Figure 16-2:
To earn the CDX title, a dog must retrieve a thrown dumbbell.

The Utility Dog (UD) degree is a chance for your canine Einstein to really show off! This title requires a dog to

- Heel, Stay, Sit, Down, and Come in response to hand signals.
- Retrieve a leather article scented by the handler from among five other unscented articles.
- Retrieve a metal article scented by the handler from among five other unscented articles.
- Retrieve a glove designated by the handler from among three gloves placed in different locations.
- Stop and stand on command while heeling and allow a judge to physically examine him with the handler standing 10 feet away.
- Trot away from the handler for about 40 feet until told to stop, at which point he turns and sits until directed to jump one of two jumps (a solid or bar jump) and return to the handler.
- Repeat the preceding exercise, but jump the other jump.

A judge scores every exercise. To receive a passing score, a dog must pass each exercise and receive 170 out of a possible 200 points. Each passing score is called a *leg,* and earning a title takes three legs.

Sound easy? Then why stop there? How about a Utility Dog Excellent, which requires your dog (who must already have his UD) to earn legs in both Open (CDX) and Utility classes at the same trials, not once but ten times?

Or how about an Obedience Trial Champion (OTCH, pronounced "otch")? All that's required is for your dog (already a UD, of course) to place first or second in either Open or Utility classes, including three first places, until he earns 100 points. For each placement, the dog is awarded a certain number of points, depending on how many dogs were in competition (but don't confuse this point scale with the conformation point scale; they are entirely separate). Few dogs of any breed have earned the OTCH degree, but German Shepherds are among them.

The United Kennel Club offers comparable obedience titles: U-CD, U-CDX, and U-UD. The UKC titles are a little bit tougher, but the UKC trials have a more relaxed atmosphere that many exhibitors find refreshing. Many people enjoy competing in both UKC and AKC obedience trials.

Obedience clubs often sponsor dog obedience classes, which are a must if you plan to compete in trials. They are a valuable source of training advice and encouragement from experienced obedience competitors, and also provide an environment filled with distractions similar to the one you will encounter at an actual trial. Perhaps most of all, they provide a ready source of shoulders to cry on for all those trials you should have passed.

If you enter competition with your GSD, remember this golden rule: Companion Dog means just that. Being upset at your dog because he made a mistake defeats the purpose of obedience as a way of promoting a harmonious partnership between trainer and dog. In the scope of life, failing a trial is an insignificant event. Never let a ribbon or a few points become more important than a trusting relationship with your companion.

Tracking Down Titles

Of all the dog sports available to all the breeds, tracking is the least popular. Why? Could it be that people don't enjoy sharing a quiet, misty morning in the field with their dogs? That they don't enjoy watching a dog do what humans can scarcely comprehend? That they don't want to teach their dogs one of the most useful skills a dog can know? These reasons seem unlikely.

Of all the breeds that participate in tracking trials, German Shepherds are among the most common. Could it be because German Shepherd people are a little different from other dog owners? Probably. Could it be because German Shepherds are good at tracking? Definitely.

The following list describes the AKC titles available in this sport:

- A dog earns the **Tracking Dog (TD)** title by following a 440- to 500-yard track with three to five turns laid from 30 minutes to 2 hours before.

- A dog earns the **Tracking Dog Excellent (TDX)** title by following an older (three to five hours) and longer (800 to 1,000 yards) track with five to seven turns, in some more challenging circumstances. One of these circumstances is the existence of cross tracks laid by another track layer about 1½ hours after the first track was laid. In addition, the actual track may cross various types of terrain and obstacles, including plowed land, woods, streams, bridges, and lightly traveled roads.

- A dog earns the **Variable Surface Tracking (VST)** title by following a three- to five-hour track, 600 to 800 yards long, over a variety of surfaces such as you might normally encounter when tracking in the real world. At least three different surface areas are included, of which at least one must include vegetation and at least two must be devoid of vegetation (for example, sand or concrete). Tracks may even go through buildings and may be crossed by animal, pedestrian, or vehicular traffic.

- A dog earns the **Champion Tracker (TC)** title by earning the TD, TDX, and VST titles.

The SV offers the FH and FH2 titles for tracking.

The way you should start training your dog depends on what motivates your dog. For chow hounds, you can begin by walking a simple path and dropping little treats along it. The dog will soon learn that he can find treats simply by following your trail. As training progresses, you drop the treats farther and farther apart, until eventually you leave only the mother lode of treats at the end of the trail.

If your dog is motivated more by the desire to be with you, you can have a helper hold your dog while you hide a very short distance away. Then have the helper allow the dog to find you. Gradually increase the distance and make sure that the dog is using his nose to locate you.

Of course, the actual tracking tests require considerably more training, but you're on the right track in teaching your dog to follow his nose!

Jumping into Agility

German Shepherds set the standard for military and police dogs and early on excelled in jumping, sprinting, climbing, balancing, and crawling, overcoming just about any obstacle in their path. For years, pet owners wondered why only these dogs got to have all the fun. Today, the sport of agility — the fastest-growing dog sport in the United States — enables dogs of all breeds to hone their skills on an obstacle course made up of open and closed tunnels, an elevated walk-over, an A-frame climb-over, a seesaw, weave poles, a pause table, and several types of jumps. Not surprisingly, German Shepherds take it all in stride.

The obstacles are arranged in various configurations that vary from trial to trial. Handlers can give unlimited commands but can't touch the obstacles or the dogs or use food, toys, whistles, or training or guiding devices in the ring. Dogs lose points for refusing an obstacle, knocking down a jump, missing a contact zone, taking obstacles out of sequence, and exceeding the time limit. To get a qualifying score, a dog must earn 85 out of a possible 100 points with no nonqualifying deductions.

Classes are divided by height, with most GSDs competing in the two highest height divisions (18 to 22 inches and 22 inches and over, at the withers). These dogs jump heights of 20 and 24 inches, respectively.

The obstacles and their requirements are as follows:

- **The A-Frame** requires the dog to climb over two 8- or 9-foot boards, each 3 to 4 feet wide, positioned so that they form an A-frame with a peak about 5 to 5½ feet off the ground.

- **The Dog Walk** requires the dog to climb a sloping panel and walk across a suspended section and down another sloping panel. Each panel is 1 foot wide and either 8 or 12 feet long; the horizontal bridge section is 3 or 4 feet high.

- **The Seesaw** requires the dog to traverse the length of a 1 foot x 12 foot sloping panel supported near its center by a fulcrum base, so that when the dog passes the center, the plank teeters to rest on its other end.

- **The Pause Table** requires the dog to stop and either sit or lie down for five seconds on top of a table approximately 3 feet square and 16 or 24 inches high (depending on the height category).

- **The Open Tunnel** requires the dog to run through a flexible tube that's about 2 feet in diameter, 10 to 20 feet long, and curved so that the dog can't see the exit from the entrance.

- **The Closed Tunnel** requires the dog to run through a lightweight fabric chute that's about 12 to 15 feet long, with a rigid entrance of about 2 feet in diameter.

- **The Weave Poles** require the dog to weave from left to right through a series of 6 to 12 poles spaced 20 to 24 inches apart.

- **The Single Bar Jumps** require the dog to jump over a narrow bar without knocking it off.

- **The Panel Jump** requires the dog to jump over a solid-appearing wall without displacing the top panel.

- ✔ **The Double Bar Jump (or Double Oxer)** requires the dog to jump two parallel bars positioned at the jump heights specified for the Single Bar Jump, and situated a distance of one-half the jump height from each other.

- ✔ **The Triple Bar Jump** requires the dog to jump a series of three ascending bars, in which the horizontal distance between adjacent bars is one-half the jump height and the vertical distance is one-quarter the jump height.

- ✔ **The Tire Jump (or Circle Jump)** requires the dog to jump through a circular object resembling a tire suspended from a rectangular frame, approximately 2 feet in diameter, with the bottom of the opening at the same height as the Single Bar Jump.

- ✔ **The Window Jump** requires the dog to jump through a 2-foot-square (or diameter) window opening with the bottom of the opening at the same height as the Single Bar Jump.

- ✔ **The Broad Jump** requires the dog to perform a single jump over a spaced series of either four 8-inch-wide or five 6-inch-wide sections.

Because safety is of utmost importance, all official jumps have easily displaceable bars in case a dog fails to clear them. All climbing obstacles have contact zones painted near the bottom that the dog must touch rather than jumping off the top. Contact equipment surfaces are roughened for good traction in both dry and wet weather.

The AKC titles, in increasing level of difficulty, are Novice Agility Dog (NAD), Open Agility Dog (OAD), Agility Dog Excellent (ADE), and Master Agility Excellent (MAX). The United States Dog Agility Association (USDAA) and United Kennel Club (UKC) also sponsor trials and award titles.

Many obedience clubs are now sponsoring agility training, but you can start some of the fundamentals at home, making your own equipment:

- ✔ Entice your dog to walk through a tunnel made of sheets draped over chairs.

- ✔ Guide him with treats to weave in and out of a series of poles made from several plumber's helpers placed in line.

- ✔ Make him comfortable walking on a wide, raised board.

- ✔ Teach him to jump through a tire and over a hurdle.

Contact the AKC, USDAA, or UKC for more information.

Herding

They're called German *Shepherds*. Get it? Then why do so many people seem surprised to see them acting like shepherds in herding trials? Remember that they were shepherds first; all the other great stuff developed later. They're in the Herding Group because sheep are in their genes.

Several organizations hold herding trials, with those sponsored by the AKC the most popular for GSDs in the United States. The AKC awards a series of titles:

- ✔ **Herding Test (HT)** and **Pre-Trial (PT)** are noncompetitive titles based on the display of basic herding instinct and ability.

- ✔ **Herding Started (HS), Herding Intermediate (HI),** and **Herding Excellent (HX)** represent progressively more demanding titles. A dog must earn three qualifying scores for each title.

- ✔ A dog earns a **Herding Championship (HCh)** by winning placements in the most advanced level after completing the HX title.

The basic moves required in herding are an *outrun* (in which the dog runs past the stock so that the stock is between the dog and handler), a *lift* (in which the dog begins to move the stock), a *fetch* (in which the dog brings the stock back toward the handler), a *pen* (in which the dog moves the stock into a small pen), and, for an HX title, a *shed* (in which the dog separates one or more head from the herd). Three types of courses are available: The A course requires working stock through obstacles and penning within an arena. The B course requires an outrun, lift, fetch, pen, and, for an HX, a shed. A dog performs the C course with larger flocks in more open areas.

The American Herding Breed Association (AHBA) also offers a variety of herding titles:

- ✔ **Herding Capability test (HCT)** consists of a test of basic instinct and basic stock-moving abilities.

- ✔ **Junior Herding Dog test (JHD)** consists of a simple course ending in a fence-line pen.

- ✔ **Herding Trial Dog trials (HTD)** include three successively more difficult levels (I, II, and III), all of which include an outrun, lift, fetch, drive, and pen.

- ✔ **Herding Ranch Dog trials (HRD)** include a greater variety of elements and tasks more like those a working stock dog might encounter.

  To earn these titles requires two qualifying scores using sheep, goats, ducks (except for HRD), geese, or sometimes cattle. A small initial following the title signifies which species that title represents.

- ✔ The **Herding Trial Championship (HTCh)** title is awarded after a dog earns ten additional qualifying scores after completing the HTD III or HRD III title.

German Shepherds are known more for their expertise in handling very large flocks in open areas, where they act almost as moving fences, constantly patrolling a boundary to prevent sheep from crossing. In Germany, and more recently in the United States, German Shepherds can demonstrate their ability to control large flocks in HGH trials. HGH, a herding title recognized by the SV and the USA, stands for *Herdengebrauchshund* (Herding Utility Dog).

Whereas AKC herding trials usually make use of flocks of five to ten sheep, SV trials use flocks of at least 200 sheep. The tasks a Shepherd faces in these trials include

- Jumping into a pen of sheep and encouraging them to leave the pen calmly.

- Keeping the sheep away from obstacles or passing cars when walking on a pathway.

- Keeping the sheep contained within a large grazing area by patrolling its boundaries.

- Circling the sheep and approaching them from the far side until the sheep move toward the handler.

- Keeping the sheep contained within a long, narrow grazing area by patrolling its boundaries.

- Keeping the sheep confined to the boundaries of a narrow road as they're moved along it.

- Preventing sheep from avoiding a bridge they are to cross.

- On command, gripping a sheep by grabbing it on the thigh, nape, or ribs without tearing the skin.

- Repenning the sheep.

- In general, demonstrating obedience, diligence, and self-reliance.

The best way to start herding is to find someone who's experienced in herding. Attend a herding trial and find out whether someone in your area can show you the ropes. Besides profiting from their experience, you can use their stock that is already used to dogs and, best of all, you don't have to buy the farm in order to keep the stock.

Scoping Out Schutzhund

Schutzhund is the epitome — the very title that says German Shepherd Dog. Schutzhund was developed specifically for German Shepherds (although other breeds may also compete) to test a wide range of attributes necessary for a working dog. A Schutzhund trial requires a dog to demonstrate his tracking, obedience, and protection abilities all in the same day.

What the heck does *Schutzhund* mean, anyway? It's German for "protection dog."

Schutzhund trials have never been as popular in the United States as they are now, nor have they ever been as controversial. This controversy is partly due to a public misconception that Schutzhund dogs are simply attack dogs. Unfortunately, this perception stems in part from some bad trainers who seem to share this idea. Attack or protection training without obedience training is not Schutzhund! You're better off not to train your dog at all than to train him only partially in this area. I can't overemphasize the importance of finding a proper instructor.

Even before competing in a Schutzhund trial, a dog must pass the *Begleithunde* (BH, or companion dog) test, which consists of a basic obedience evaluation and a traffic safety exam. No, your GSD doesn't have to parallel park, but he does have to demonstrate that he's under control around joggers, bicyclists, cars, strange dogs, and loud noises. The Schutzhund trial itself begins with a brief temperament evaluation in which overly aggressive or uncontrollable dogs are weeded out of the competition even before it starts. Then let the games begin! A dog must pass all three phases of competition on the same day to earn a Schutzhund title.

Dogs can progress from the easiest Schutzhund title (SchH1) through SchH2 to the most difficult level, SchH3. Each level requires a dog to demonstrate abilities in tracking, obedience, and protection.

Tracking

The first phase is tracking. Tracking for the SchH1 is actually a bit easier than the tracking required for a TD. The track is somewhat shorter, about 20 minutes old, and laid by the handler. The track for the SchH2 is more difficult, being slightly longer, older, and laid by a stranger. That for the SchH3 is even longer and older yet and requires the dog to locate three dropped articles. It is comparable in difficulty to the track for the TD degree (see the "Tracking Down Titles" section, earlier in this chapter).

Obedience

The second phase of a Schutzhund trial is obedience. The basic exercises for SchH1 include

- Heeling on and off lead (including heeling into a group of people and executing a figure 8, and ignoring two gunshots).
- While walking at heel, sitting on command and staying while the handler continues to walk.
- Downing while the dog and handler are walking, with the dog remaining down while the handler continues to walk, and then coming to the handler when called.
- Retrieving a thrown article on command, both on a flat surface and over a 1-meter jump.

✔ Going ahead of the handler for 25 paces and downing on command.

✔ Remaining in the Down position with the handler in view while another contestant performs the preceding exercises.

SchH2 adds a retrieve over a 5-foot wall and substitutes the flat retrieve article with a 1-kilogram dumbbell and the high jump retrieve article with a 650-gram dumbbell.

SchH3 exercises add a stand while the dog and handler are walking and a stand while the dog and handler are running (in both of these exercises, the dog heels at the handler's side until the handler commands the dog to stand, at which point the dog stops and stands while the handler continues to walk or run). They also substitute the flat retrieve article with a 4-pound dumbbell, and substitute the 5-foot wall with a 6-foot wall.

Protection

The third Schutzhund phase is protection.

For the SchH1 degree, the dog must search two *blinds* (structures that look like half-tents, in which a person can hide), and when he finds the "helper" (a threatening or attacking person dressed in heavy padding) must hold him in position by barking. When the helper attacks the handler, the dog must attack and hold the helper by biting him, even when the helper hits the dog twice with a fiberglass stick. The dog must pursue and stop a fleeing helper. In all cases, the dog must release the helper immediately when commanded by the handler. (Parts of a couple of these exercises are done on lead.)

For the SchH2 degree, the dog must search six blinds. Upon finding the helper, the dog must bark but return to the handler when commanded. When the helper tries to escape, the dog must stop him by biting hard and must release when the helper freezes. The dog must again bite the helper when the helper threatens the dog with a fiberglass stick. The dog must watch the helper as the handler searches him. The dog must walk next to the handler as they escort the helper ahead of them; when the helper turns and tries to attack the handler, the dog must stop the helper by biting.

For the SchH3 degree, the dog performs similar exercises as for the SchH2 but does the whole thing off lead.

A well-trained Schutzhund dog is a dependable protector and a trustworthy companion. A poorly trained one is a danger to society. Do it right or don't do it at all.

Chapter 17

Putting Your Shepherd to Work

In This Chapter

▶ Participating in search-and-rescue missions

▶ Acting as the eyes, ears, and hands for the disabled

▶ Keeping the peace

The German Shepherd is one of the most versatile breeds when it comes to competing successfully in a variety of fields (see Chapter 16). Despite this fact, most GSDs never enter a competition and never win a ribbon. They don't have to. They've already won the biggest prize of all: their owner's hearts. Some GSDs do even more, however, and win the hearts of others whose lives they touch or even save.

Early in their history, German Shepherds distinguished themselves as military and police dogs — roles in which they continue today. They have expanded their abilities to serve as bomb- and narcotics-detection dogs and search-and-rescue dogs. Many GSDs have devoted their lives to helping disabled people, proving themselves as capable guide dogs for the blind, hearing dogs for the deaf, and all-purpose assistants for the physically challenged. They also have served as comforters and friends to the sick or lonely. No breed of dog has served so faithfully in so many roles.

This chapter tells you about these roles that German Shepherds can play, and about how you and your dog can be heroes in your spare time if you so desire.

Finding Lost Souls

Dogs have long been known for their ability to follow scent trails and to locate hidden animals and people by scent. Although dogs have been used to hunt for lost people for decades, only recently has a concerted effort been made to produce educated search-and-rescue dog teams. National and local canine search-and-rescue teams are available for local emergencies and may also be prepared to fly across the country in cases of disaster. They may search miles of wilderness for a lost child or tons of rubble for a buried victim.

Whereas so many dog training activities seem to have little relevance in society, search-and-rescue is the exception. Your long hours of training just may save a life. Search-and-rescue dogs are the cream of the crop. If your GSD is capable of competing in obedience, agility, and tracking (see Chapter 16), he has the basics of a search-and-rescue (SAR) dog. But an SAR GSD is much more. These dogs must respond reliably to commands, negotiate precarious footing, follow a trail and locate articles, and use air scenting to pinpoint the location of a hidden person. Well-trained dogs can locate a person from a quarter mile away, buried under snow or rubble, or even underwater.

German Shepherds remain the favored SAR dog breed to handle this tall order. Their combination of hardiness, agility, endurance, ruggedness, intelligence, scenting ability, and tractability make them ideal for the job. An SAR dog is only half the team, however; handlers must also be trained in search techniques, wilderness survival, first aid, and a variety of other skills — not to mention being pretty hardy and rugged themselves. Developing an SAR team requires many hours of committed work — hours made worthwhile by grateful tears and saved lives.

For more information about getting yourself and your Shepherd involved in search and rescue, look up the American Rescue Dog Association at P.O. Box 151, Chester, NY 10918; or on the Internet at www.ardainc.org. This site can link you up with the ARDA unit nearest you. (Note that the dog on the group's logo is a German Shepherd!) You can find additional information about search and rescue at www.nasar.org, the Web site of the National Association of Search and Rescue.

Warming Hearts with Cold Noses

Is the idea of trudging through the wilderness in search of buried bodies a little too wild for you? You and your dog can still be lifesavers. Therapy dogs visit hospitals, nursing homes, mental health centers, prisons, and other facilities where they provide people with unconditional love, motivation to communicate, entertainment, and something warm and cuddly to hug.

Therapy dogs must be meticulously well-mannered and well-groomed, but most of all, they must be friendly. If a person grabs them, yells at them, or hugs them until they can't breathe, they must be gentle and unflappable. The person half of the team is just as important. The handler needs to understand how to deal with people with a variety of disabilities.

If you're interested in volunteering yourself and your dog, local and national therapy dog groups can provide training and certification. Therapy Dogs International (www.tdi-dog.org; 973-252-9800) is the oldest and largest organization certifying therapy dogs.

The Certified Therapy Dog letters are among the proudest your dog can attain. German Shepherds, with their uncanny knack for understanding human emotions, have warmed many hearts, dried many tears, and opened many arms — proving themselves to be true therapists in fur coats.

Serving People Hand and Foot

The German Shepherd was one of the first breeds to provide assistance to physically disabled people. This assistance can take the form of pulling a person in a wheelchair, picking up dropped objects, getting objects off of shelves that a person can't reach, opening doors, and pushing a 911 button in case of emergency. Although shepherds are used for this purpose, retrievers are somewhat more popular because of the extensive retrieving that is often necessary. Shepherds are fine retrievers, but retrievers are *great* retrievers!

Other service dogs specialize in sensing when a person is about to have a seizure. *Seizure alert dogs* alert the person who is about to have a seizure so that the person can prepare and get to a safe area before the seizure occurs. *Seizure response dogs* provide safety after a seizure has ensued, lying next to the person until it has subsided. Exactly how these dogs become aware of an impending seizure even before the person knows that one is coming on is unknown, but experts think that the dog smells a change in body chemistry associated with changes in brain activity. These dogs provide a measure of safety and confidence for their people.

Seizure dogs must know the difference between friend and foe, allowing helpers to approach the victim while discouraging those with bad intentions. For more information, contact Canine Partners for Life (www.k94life.org; 610-869-4902).

Being a Guiding Light

Most guide dog facilities breed their own dogs, although a few accept donated puppies that pass certain stringent criteria. Most facilities rely on puppy raisers to provide a home environment, well-rounded socialization, and basic obedience to youngsters. The puppies then go to school for formal training when they're 12 to 18 months of age. Relinquishing a puppy you've grown to love is tough, but perhaps the most rewarding thing you will ever do. At the school, the dogs receive intensive specialized training. Not all dogs graduate, but those who do have full lives ahead of them.

A working guide dog is expected to take direction from his handler; locate specified objects, such as curbs, doors, and steps; stop at obstacles, changes in elevation, or dangerous traffic situations; and reasonably ignore distractions during his work and even ignore commands from his handler if they would result in danger to the handler. The dog gives his visually impaired handler mobility, confidence, independence, and love — a true friend in the dark. Figure 17-1 shows a GSD guide dog at work.

Figure 17-1:
German Shepherd guide dogs provide their handlers with a greater degree of independence.

© Kent and Donna Dannen/AKC Stock Images

A real Buddy

After the First World War, many German soldiers were left blinded. Although dogs had been used for centuries to guide blind or visually disabled people, the German government's efforts following WWI were the first concerted efforts to train guide dogs for the blind. The breed of choice, of course, was the German Shepherd.

When a GSD breeder learned of the program and reported on it in an American newspaper, a blind American contacted her and asked if he could go to Europe for training. Morris Frank and his German Shepherd, Buddy, became the first American guide dog team.

The pair returned to the United States to promote the guide dog concept. Dorothy Eustis, the breeder who had trained Frank, came to the United States and founded The Seeing Eye in 1929. Since then, thousands of German Shepherds have provided eyes and a link to the world for their people. You can find information about The Seeing Eye on the Web at www.seeingeye.org or by calling 973-539-0922.

Hearing for Those Who Can't

Dogs can provide confidence for deaf or hearing-impaired people. Although most dogs for the deaf are small dogs rescued from humane organizations, German Shepherds can be trained to do the job. At the novice level, dogs are trained to alert the person to a smoke alarm, the person's name being called, and an alarm clock. A slightly more highly trained dog (home level) alerts the person to the doorbell, telephone, and oven timer. A certified hearing dog responds to these sounds but is also extensively socialized and obedience trained so that he is dependable in public as well as at home.

For more information, contact Dogs for the Deaf at 541-826-9220 or on the Web at www.dogsforthedeaf.org.

Taking a Bite Out of Crime

German Shepherds have become identified so closely with police work that many people know them only as police dogs. They remain among the most popular all-around police dogs in the world, challenged only by the Belgian Malinois.

The police dog, or K-9, has proved to be one of the most valuable officers on the force. Who else can pursue (and catch) a fleeing suspect, locate crime scene evidence, sniff out contraband, and control a crowd? And a K-9 does this without ever drawing a weapon — except for those glistening choppers.

In addition to their official duties, police dogs act as ambassadors for the police department, adding a humanizing dimension to the people halves of their teams. They get the attention of bad guys, too. Criminals who wouldn't think twice about challenging a human officer wouldn't think at all of challenging a canine one. Many K-9s have literally saved the lives of their handlers; regrettably, many have given their own lives in the effort. Despite the risks, the life of a K-9 is good. These dogs get to work with their special people, part of a team on the lookout for adventure.

Most police dogs are trained for drug detection, and some are also trained for explosives detection. Many are specialists used exclusively for bomb detection at airports or for drug detection in building and automobile searches. The Federal Aviation Association makes extensive use of dogs, including German Shepherds. No machine has ever been found that can compete with a dog's sense of smell, and studies have shown the GSD to be among the best scenters. Dogs have been used to find all sorts of contraband: termites and other insect pests, gas leaks, and even cows in estrus — if it can be smelled, a German Shepherd can smell it.

Nonetheless, only special dogs with special training make the grade, and few, if any, police or contraband detection dogs come from the ranks of hobby breeders. Instead, most come from kennels with intensive breeding and training operations.

Guarding the People They Love

Dogs have a natural tendency to protect their own territory, and in guard dogs this tendency is encouraged. German Shepherds are naturally protective and courageous and have long been a favorite breed for guard duty. They may accompany their handlers on patrol, run loose within the confines of a secured area, or even perform their guard duties from the foot of a bed at night. A GSD's superior senses of smell and hearing, as well as his night vision, make him adept at detecting the creepiest of creeps.

Even without training, most German Shepherds will deter intruders simply by barking. Trained dogs, and even some untrained ones, will detain an intruder by barking and grasping the person if the person tries to escape. As a general rule, it's unwise to have a guard dog trained to attack an intruder because of the possibility of "innocent" intruders, such as children or mentally unsound people.

Part of the purpose of Schutzhund training (see Chapter 16) is to produce a reliable protection dog. Training a dog to protect you is not something you should undertake halfheartedly or on your own. A German Shepherd is a dangerous weapon; one who is poorly trained in protection is a dangerous weapon that may be out of control. Good protection dogs are built on a foundation of love, trust, and basic obedience.

Working titles

The SV gives GSDs with working abilities the following titles:

- ✔ **BIL:** Guide dog for the blind
- ✔ **DH:** Service dog
- ✔ **DPH:** Police service dog
- ✔ **FH:** Tracking dog
- ✔ **HGH:** Herding dog
- ✔ **PFP:** Police tracking dog
- ✔ **PH:** Police dog
- ✔ **ZH:** Customs service dog

Part VI
The Part of Tens

The 5th Wave   By Rich Tennant

@RICHTENNANT

Peterson's
PUMPKIN PATCH

CLOSED

DANGER
GOURD DOG
ON DUTY

Chapter 18

Ten Tips for Traveling with Your Dog

. . . .

In This Chapter

▶ Traveling the right way by land and by air

▶ Considering stay-at-home options

. . . .

*H*itting the road with your German Shepherd pal may seem like a good idea, but taking your dog on a trip without forethought can lead to a miserable time — and maybe even a dangerous time — for both of you. With some planning, though, you may find your Shepherd to be a wonderful traveling companion. After all, dogs seldom argue about which radio station to listen to in the car! This chapter gives you ten tips for making travel adventures with your GSD as safe and enjoyable as possible.

Plan Ahead

With proper planning, a German Shepherd copilot can steer you to destinations you might otherwise have passed. Without proper planning, sharing your trip with any dog can be a nightmare as you are turned away from motels, parks, attractions, and beaches. Before taking your GSD with you on vacation, consider these questions:

✔ **Will you be traveling by car or by plane?** Airline travel can mean extra hassle for you and extra trauma for your dog, so think carefully before taking your dog on a trip that involves flying. (See the section "Play It Safe with Air Travel," later in this chapter, for more information.)

✔ **What will the weather be like where you're going?** Taking a trip in hot weather means taking extra precautions for your dog's safety and comfort. How will you run into the bathroom at a rest stop when it's too hot to leave your dog in the car for even a couple of minutes? Hot weather means skipping all the inviting shops and eating from drive-thru windows. It also means that many airlines will refuse to take dogs at all.

- ✔ **Will you be traveling alone?** Having your dog with you can provide you with a little extra protection — and that can make a big difference in today's not-always-safe world. However, if you're traveling alone with your dog, you alone will have to attend to him at all times.

- ✔ **How healthy is your dog?** Travel can put a great deal of stress on a dog, so if your dog isn't in good health, don't bring him with you on a trip.

- ✔ **Where will you be staying?** Not all accommodations — whether it's a fancy hotel or your grandmother's house — welcome dogs, and not all places are safe for dogs.

- ✔ **How does your dog react when locked in a strange place?** If your GSD is prone to panic attacks, he probably won't be a good traveler unless he can be with you at all times.

- ✔ **Is your dog crate-trained?** A cage can be a wonderful asset when you travel because it allows your dog to have a place of his own that is familiar and comforting. Don't wait until the trip to acclimate your dog to a cage.

- ✔ **What do you really want to do on your vacation?** If you're planning to hike outdoors in parks that are dog-friendly, great. If you'd like to visit museums, eat in fancy restaurants, and so on, leave Shep at home.

- ✔ **What are your alternatives to taking your dog?** You may have no choice but to take your dog with you when you travel. If you have friends who are willing to dog-sit, or if you can afford to leave your dog with a trustworthy kennel, those options might prove better for your sanity and your dog's.

Several available books list establishments that accept pets; make sure to find places that will welcome you and your dog *before* you hit the road.

Be Realistic about What You Can and Can't Do

If the weather is warm, plan on driving past all the great attractions. They cost too much anyway — see how your dog is saving you money? If you must play tourist, call ahead to attractions to see whether they have safe boarding arrangements for pets. Safe means a secure, locked kennel run, not a chain next to the parking lot. Plan on driving past all those great shopping places, too. See how your dog is saving you even more money? With all the money you save, you may even be able to take another vacation — this time without your dog, so you can actually do something.

Of course, many vacations are great for dogs *and* people! Most campgrounds allow dogs, as do many state and national parks and forests. Camping and hiking with your dog can be a perfect vacation (but you still must take precautions to prevent your dog from getting injured or being a nuisance to wildlife). Some beaches allow dogs during the off-season. Even a driving vacation during cool weather can be a good doggy vacation. Some doggy bed and breakfasts and camps are even springing up to accommodate people who want to share their vacations with their best friends.

If You Take Your Dog with You, Take Him with You

If you're going to travel with your dog, make sure that the dog has a reason to be there. If you aren't planning to spend time with your dog while you're away, don't bring him along! You'll be frustrated that you can't go off and do what you want without worrying about your dog, and your dog will be frightened in his new surrounding and probably will "misbehave" in an attempt to show you how miserable he is.

While you're traveling, you may be tempted to leave your dog in your car with the windows down. If your dog is sufficiently protective and tough-looking, this approach might work, but even the toughest dog can be a target for dognappers or weirdoes. If you have a cage, you can place your dog in it, padlock the cage door, and padlock the cage to the car for security.

Never leave your dog tied in or to your car. Many a dead dog has been found hanging out the car window after being tied inside.

If you're crazy with the urge to spend money on local color and the conditions are unsafe for leaving your dog in your car, one possible compromise exists: a local boarding kennel. Call around and see whether you can arrange doggy daycare at a safe facility.

You may also be tempted to leave your dog in your motel room during the day. Do so only if you can afford to have the room redone after your dog redecorates it. The dog will perceive that you have left him in a strange place and forgotten him; he will either bark or try to dig his way out through the doors and windows in an effort to find you, or become upset and relieve himself on the carpet.

Bring sheets from home to place on the carpet or bed if you allow your Shepherd loose in a motel room.

Ask Beforehand Whether You Can Bring Your Dog

If you plan to stay with friends, ask beforehand whether you may bring your German Shepherd. After all, a GSD is no toy dog, and although your friends certainly will enjoy your company, they may not be dog people.

If you do get the okay to bring your dog along, make sure that your dog is clean and parasite free. Bring your dog's own clean blanket or bed or, better yet, his cage. Your dog will appreciate the familiar place to sleep, and your friends will breathe sighs of relief. Do not allow your dog to run helter-skelter through their home, either. Even though your dog may be accustomed to sleeping on furniture at home, a proper canine guest stays off the furniture when visiting. If your hosts have pets of their own, be sure that your dog does not chase or fight with them.

Walk and walk your dog (and clean up after him) to make sure that no accidents occur inside. If they do, clean them up immediately. Don't leave any surprises for your hosts! Changes in water or food, or simply stress, often result in diarrhea, so be particularly attentive to taking your dog out often.

Pack Wisely

You may think that packing for your dog will be a cinch — after all, your Shepherd is wearing his entire wardrobe on its back! But unlike you, your dog needs almost all of his food packed, as well as a lot of other things that you won't want to have to hunt down in a strange place. Most of all, you need to pack with your dog's health and safety in mind. Consider packing the following items:

- Food and water bowls, food, and dog biscuits
- Bottled water or water from home — many dogs are very sensitive to changes in water and can develop diarrhea
- Chewies and toys
- Medications, especially antidiarrhea medicine and heartworm preventive
- Flea comb and brush
- Bug spray or flea spray
- Moist towelettes, paper towels, and self-rinse shampoo
- Cage and bedding
- Short and long leashes
- Flashlight for night walks

✔ Plastic baggies or other poop-disposal means

✔ Health and rabies certificates

✔ Recent color photo in case your dog gets lost

Place all of your dog's belongings in a separate bag. Doing so makes his things easier to locate and keeps your own stuff from being covered with dog stuff.

Buckle Up in the Car

Bliss for a dog is a ride in the car as he hangs his head out the windows with the wind in his fur and bugs in his teeth. Sure, that seems fun, but your dog could be thrown from the car, get his nose stung by a bee, or get his eye put out by a rock.

Your dog has a higher center of gravity than you do when riding in the car, and far less ability to grab onto something. It doesn't take much to send your German Shepherd flying into the dash, windshield, or you — or out of the vehicle altogether. Dogs have been killed, and people have been killed by their flying dogs, as a result of relatively small accidents. Dogs have been killed by airbags. Dogs have been killed by being run over after being thrown from vehicles. Dogs have also caused deadly accidents by getting a leg caught in the steering wheel, bumping the car out of gear, or jumping into the driver's lap.

You can't exactly teach your Shepherd to buckle up for safety, but you can use a doggie seatbelt and buckle up your dog for his own safety. These seatbelts are available at pet stores and through pet catalogs, and many GSDs have learned to wear them.

Don't think that tying your dog in place by his collar will do just as well — that's a good way for your dog to get a broken neck. You can improvise by fitting your dog with a harness and attaching that to the seatbelt. The back seat is safer than the front; the front seat is absolutely off-limits if your car has passenger-side airbags.

You can also keep a sturdy cage in your car, which has saved many a dog's life. Cages can go flying, too, so remember that the cage should be securely fastened to the car for human as well as canine safety. On the cage should be a sticker or tag that reads "In case of an accident, take this dog to a veterinarian, and then contact the following persons (list names and phone numbers), who have guaranteed payment of all expenses incurred." Remember that you may not be able to speak for your dog in the event of a serious accident.

There's a time and place for your German Shepherd to run amok and be a free spirit. A ride in the car is not one of them. The truck in Figure 18-1 should not take off before the dogs in the back are secured.

Figure 18-1:
German
Shepherds
love to go
for rides, but
you must
secure them
in moving
vehicles.

Play It Safe with Air Travel

Air travel is fairly safe for dogs but should not be undertaken frivolously. Here are some tips for making air travel as safe and comfortable for your dog as possible:

✔ When you make your airline reservations, mention that you're flying with a dog. Doing so costs extra money, but more important, most flights restrict the number of dogs they can carry because they have limited room. Show up early for the flight.

✔ Chances are your German Shepherd won't fit under the seat, so unless he's a service dog, he will ride in the baggage compartment. It's best if your dog can fly as excess baggage rather than as air freight. Air freight usually requires the dog to be at the airport earlier, often in a different terminal. In addition, excess baggage involves a flat fee, whereas air freight is based on size and is a lot more expensive for a large dog.

✔ Although baggage compartments are heated, they're not air-conditioned, and in hot weather dogs have been known to overheat while the plane was still on the runway. Never ship a dog in the heat of day or the middle of the summer. If the airline says that it's too hot, believe them. If they say that it's not too hot, doubt them.

✔ Don't ship air freight on Fridays or the day before holidays. Dogs do occasionally get misrouted and have been found on Mondays after spending a weekend alone in a closed freight office.

✔ Buy an airline-approved cage, which meets specifications for size, strength, and ventilation. If your dog is not crate-trained, set it up in your house and get your dog used to eating and sleeping in it. Ready the cage for the trip by securing its fasteners super-tight, adding bedding that can be thrown away at your destination if necessary, and finding a water bowl or bucket that won't spill and in which your dog's head can't get caught. (You can hang a bucket from the cage door with an eyebolt snap.) Plaster your name and address and the words "LIVE ANIMAL" all over the outside.

✔ The night before the trip, fill the water bowl with water and freeze it. Take it out of the cooler just before the flight and attach it to the inside of the cage. As it melts during the flight, the dog will have water that otherwise might have spilled out during the loading process.

✔ Don't feed your dog before an airplane trip. There's no place for a dog to answer nature's call 10,000 feet up.

✔ Show up early for the flight. Be sure to walk your dog one last time, and stay with him as long as possible before loading.

✔ Once you're on the plane, request that the flight attendant check to make sure the dog has been loaded before you take off. If the weather is hot and you sit on the runway, make your concerns known. Then sit back and anticipate a joyous reunion when you get to your destination!

Keep the Dog on Lead

Always walk your German Shepherd on lead when you're away from home. If frightened or distracted while off lead, your dog could become disoriented and lost. A long, retractable lead (see Chapter 5) is perfect for traveling because it gives your dog some freedom to investigate without the risk of becoming lost or hurt.

If you're staying at a campground, keep your dog on a leash or in an X-pen at all times. Other campers may have tiny dogs that your dog might chase, and many campgrounds have wildlife wandering through that could prove too tempting for your GSD. Walk your dog away from campsites, and always clean up after him.

Whenever you leave home with your dog, your dog should be wearing a collar with license tags, including a tag indicating where you can be reached while on your trip or the address of someone you know will be at home.

Leave Your Shepherd at Home or at a Kennel Instead

Both you and your dog may be better off if you take your trip with human companions only. Should you hire a dog sitter or use a boarding kennel?

Your dog will no doubt be more comfortable in his own home, so you can arrange for a pet-sitter to visit twice a day if you're planning a longer trip. Again, this approach works best if your home is equipped with a dog door and a secure fence. You also need to have a dog who will accept a stranger into the home.

Good pet-sitters will want to make friends with the dog before you leave home. Hire a bonded, professional pet-sitter; the kid next door is seldom a good choice for this important responsibility. It's too easy for the dog to slip out the door, or for signs of illness to go unnoticed, if the sitter is not an experienced dog person. The life of your dog is a heavy responsibility for a child. You can find pet sitters through Pet Sitters International at 800-268-SITS or on the Web at www.petsit.com.

Your dog may be safer (if not quite as contented) if you board him at a kennel. Here are the characteristics of the ideal kennel:

✔ It is approved by the American Boarding Kennel Association.

✔ It has climate-controlled accommodations and keeps the dogs either indoors or in a combination indoor/outdoor run. The run should be covered so that a climbing or jumping dog cannot escape, and an extra security fence should surround the entire kennel area.

✔ Someone is on the grounds 24 hours a day.

✔ The runs are clean and the odor is not overwhelming (although you can't expect spotlessness and a perfumed atmosphere). Make an unannounced visit to the kennel and ask to see the facilities.

✔ All dogs have clean water and have bedding or a raised area for sleeping.

✔ A solid divider prevents dogs in adjoining runs from direct contact with one another. With the exception of dogs that are housemates, dogs should never be housed or run with other dogs they do not know.

✔ The kennel requires proof of immunizations and performs an incoming check for fleas. They should demand to bathe your dog (for a fee) if he has fleas and offer to bathe him again (again for a fee) before you pick him up. (Most dogs smell pretty doggy after staying in a kennel.)

✔ The kennel will allow you to bring toys and bedding and will administer prescribed medication.

✔ The kennel has made arrangements for emergency veterinary care.

Whatever means you choose, always leave your dog's caretaker with emergency numbers and your veterinarian's name. Make arrangements with your vet to treat your dog for any problems that may arise. This means leaving a written agreement stating that you give permission for treatment and accept responsibility for charges.

Chapter 19

Ten Fun Games You Can Play with Your Shepherd

Sometimes it sounds like having a dog is nothing but work, but nothing could be further from the truth. Dogs provide comfort, companionship, protection, and, most of all, lots of fun! You will no doubt come up with your own set of custom games that only you and your dog share. To get you started, though, here are a few that you may not have thought of.

Finding Hidden Treasure

Shepherds have always been prized for their scent-finding abilities — they love to use their noses to sniff out all kinds of treasure. You can even play this game indoors on rainy days.

To start, let your dog watch you hide a treat. Start with a simple hiding place, such as under a chair or in tall grass. Then say, "Find it!" and let him go find the treat right away. Of course he gets to eat what he finds! Practice this until he knows what the game is about. Up the ante by asking him to sit and stay, and don't let him see you hide the treat. This time, he has to search for it with his nose. You can give him a few hints at first, but in no time he should be using his nose to ferret out the goodies. Keep hiding treats in harder and harder places; your dog will enjoy the challenge — and the rewards!

Testing Your Dog's Memory

Here's another rainy-day game that can entertain your dog. In this game, you let your dog watch you hide a treat in a sealed plastic bag (to prevent — to some extent — your dog from finding it by nose). At first, make him wait only about 30 seconds before saying, "Where was it?" Gradually stretch out the time and add distractions. For example, you can train your dog to sit or catch for ten minutes before you let him go find the hidden treat. Feed your Shepherd the treat from the bag so that he doesn't eat the plastic by mistake.

Retrieving the Right Object

Have you ever wished that your dog could find your car keys? Although that may be pushing it, you can teach your Shepherd to find and retrieve items that you've handled. This fun game might come in handy one day.

Some dogs are naturals at this game. If you throw a rock onto a pile of rocks, they'll come up with the right one every time. All you have to do is teach them a command word such as "Find mine!" and practice.

Other dogs need some work to understand what you want. You can train them by using several identical items that you handle with tongs and tie down to a piece of pegboard. Start by teaching your dog to retrieve your item (which you've scented by rubbing in your hands) when it's the only one to choose. When he gets the idea, throw it in the middle of the other items, which are tacked down to the pegboard. If he tries to pick them up, they won't budge. He'll soon learn that the only one he can retrieve is the one with your scent.

Now comes the fun part — testing him with all sorts of items in all sorts of places. Always be careful to keep your scent off the other items, and give your dog lots of praise and treats for his hard work.

Following Your Trail

If you've ever wanted a trailer, here's your chance: You can train your Shepherd the same way Bloodhounds are trained. One way to teach your dog to trail you is to show him that he can find treats along your scent trail.

You need a large field that doesn't have your scent in it. Take careful note of where you step, because you will be asking your dog to follow your scent trail. It's easier for dogs to follow your trail on moist, grassy surfaces, and also easier at night or first thing in the morning.

Have a helper hold your dog back while you walk about 20 feet away, dropping small dog treats every few feet. Retrace your steps exactly, and when you get to your dog, tell him, "Track!" Practice this many times, gradually making longer trails with longer intervals between treats.

Once your dog appears to be using his nose to trace your path from treat to treat, place a right-angle turn about midway in the trail. (Place a marker there so that you can remember the spot.) Eventually, your dog will master that turn, and then you're home free! Now you can add more turns and take the track across various surfaces.

Dancing with Your Dog

Does your dog have a talent for obedience, and especially for heeling? Do you like to dance? Have you ever dreamed of being in the limelight? Then why not teach your dog to be your dance partner?

Musical freestyle is the latest craze to hit the dog world. No more boring heeling in a square and sitting! In freestyle, dogs heel on both sides; weave in and out between the person's legs; go forward, backward, sideways, and in circles; jump, spin, and take bows — all to the tune of music. Dances can be elegant or lively, and in competition, handlers (and sometimes dogs) dress in costume to enhance their numbers.

You can get started in your own home by teaching your dog some basic commands, such as Heel Right, Heel Left, Back, Forward, Around, Spin, and Weave. Then pick a tune, choreograph your number, and get dancing! For more information, contact the World Canine Freestyle Association at P.O. Box 350122, Brooklyn, NY 11235; 718-332-8336; or on the Web at www.woofs.org/wcfo/.

Playing a Game of Catch

You can teach your Shepherd to catch treats, balls, toys, and Frisbees, all using the same basic concept. Catching treats is the easiest to teach. Start by tossing a treat in an arc over your dog's head. Aim so that it would land on the top of the muzzle about midway down. If your dog misses, grab the treat off the ground before your dog can reach it. Don't try this with a possessive dog that might become protective of the treat, however. You don't want to risk getting a dog bite!

Most dogs will figure out that the best way to get the object of their desire is to snatch it out of the air before it hits the ground. After they do so a few times, they seem to enjoy the challenge of catching, and they're better prepared to start catching inedible items.

If your dog has a favorite stuffed toy, it's a good choice for a second catch item. Not only is such a toy easy to catch, but the dog isn't intimidated by it hurting when it hits him on the head. Use the same method you used with the treat: Throw the toy so that it arcs down toward your dog's muzzle, just behind the snout. Once your dog has the knack of catching a toy, you can back away and practice throwing it higher and from greater distances.

A ball is the next challenge. Use a tennis ball or a soft rubber ball. Start close again and use the same technique as before. When your dog gets adept at catching the ball, add variations, such as bounces.

Frisbee catching is the most difficult to teach. Start with a soft flying disc that won't hurt your Shepherd when he catches it. Let your dog get the feel of the Frisbee by holding it and catching it when you roll it on its side. Then start from only a few inches away and encourage him to grab it by the edge. Next, back up and throw it from a few feet away. Continue to increase the distance. The transition from facing you in order to catch the Frisbee to running after and jumping for the Frisbee will take time and a dog who is naturally enthusiastic. If your dog is a Frisbee addict, start practicing your throws! If not, there are plenty of other ways to have fun.

Teaching Your Dog Tricks

Dog tricks, another rainy-day activity, are a fun challenge for you and your dog. All these tricks are easy to teach with the help of the obedience concepts outlined in Chapter 8.

- ✔ **Play Dead:** Teach Play Dead by teaching your dog to lie down from a standing position. You do so by guiding him with a treat. Require him to drop quickly in order to get the reward. Then lure him over onto his side, requiring him to stay down for longer periods before getting the reward. Getting his head down is the hard part. You can try placing the reward on the floor and not giving it unless the dog puts his head down, but you may have to use your hand for a little extra guidance.

- ✔ **Roll Over:** Teach your dog to roll over by telling him to lie down, saying, "Roll over," and then luring him over onto his side with a treat. Once the dog is reliably rolling onto his side, use a treat to guide him onto his back. Then guide him the rest of the way, eventually giving a treat only when the dog rolls all the way over.

- ✔ **Shake:** Teach your dog to shake by having him sit. Say, "Shake," and hold a treat in your closed hand in front of your dog. Many dogs will pick up a foot to paw at your hand. These dogs are the naturals! With others, you have to nudge the leg to get it up or lure the dog's head way to one side so that he has to lift his leg on the opposite side. As soon as the paw leaves the ground, reward. Then require the dog to lift his paw higher and for longer.

✔ **Speak:** Teach Speak by saying, "Speak," when it appears that your dog is about to bark. Then reward. Don't reward barking unless you've first said, "Speak."

✔ **Count:** This is a fun trick you can use to convince your friends that your dog is really gifted. Once your dog knows how to speak, change your command to an imperceptible tap of your foot, a nod of your head, or a twitch of your finger. To do so, you have to start with a more noticeable movement, of course. Now you want this movement to tell your dog that you are about to command, "Speak." Each time you make the movement command, follow it immediately with the verbal command. Eventually, your dog will realize that the gesture is also a Speak command. Then you can reduce how noticeable the gesture is. Finally, teach your dog to bark each time you make the gesture. Your dog should continue to bark until you stop, so you can get your dog to bark however many times you want.

If your dog can do something physically, you can teach your dog *when* to do it. Just use your imagination. Rin Tin Tin, look out!

Conquering a Backyard Obstacle Course

You don't have to have a military dog or even an agility dog to appreciate the challenge of an obstacle course. Nor do you have to have fancy equipment. Here are some fun obstacles you can make or buy fairly inexpensively.

Square hay bales make the best and most versatile dog obstacles. You can stack and restack them in all sorts of configurations, making pyramids, steps, high jumps, broad jumps, narrow runways, and even tunnels with twists and turns. You can hide in them and behind them. You can teach your dog to weave in and out of them. Use your imagination, make sure that they are securely in place, and then have fun.

You can also make a hoop jump with an old tire. Tie it between two trees or posts so that it is secured on four sides. Then teach your dog to jump through it.

You can find a lot of neat dog obstacles at large toy stores for children. Admittedly spoiled dogs often appreciate children's tunnels, sand boxes, and even playhouses. And don't forget the number-one accessory: a children's wading pool. It's perfect for both of you to cool off in after playing on your obstacle course.

Chasing a Pole-Lure

Not all dogs like this game, but many dogs who enjoy running and chasing will take right to it. The pole-lure is the same way many racing Greyhounds are introduced to racing. It's a great way to give your GSD a workout, but don't overdo it.

You need a pole about 4 to 8 feet long with a 4- to 6-foot string tied to the end of it. (A horse-lunging whip works great.) Tie a rag, plastic bag, rabbit skin, or toy to the end of the string as a lure. Then run around the yard and let your dog chase the lure. The longer your pole and string, the faster it will go.

It's easy to overdo it with this game. Be careful not to make your dog make turns that are too sharp, and also be careful not to inadvertently lure your dog into hitting a tree or other obstacle. Also, don't encourage your dog to leap too high. Most of all, don't let your neighbors see you. They'll be sure that you've lost your mind.

Playing Tag

Sometimes the basics are the most fun. All you need is a big yard and a lot of energy. Most dogs love a game of keep-away, tearing around you in gleeful circles as they stay just out of reach.

A word of warning: Your dog should know that it's just a game. You don't want him to get the idea that he can run away and ignore you whenever he feels like it, so once in a while, add a serious Come command and make sure that he obeys it. Then release him and get back to playing.

While you're at it, don't forget the other basics: throwing a ball, splashing in the water, taking a walk, and sharing a sunrise. You don't need fancy games to have a good time with your dog — you just need each other.

Appendix A

Glossary

Alsatian: The name for German Shepherd Dogs during World War II; still in use in England.

American-Canadian White Shepherd: The name for a White German Shepherd in Europe.

angulation: Angles between the proximal bones of the fore and hind limbs, typically between the shoulder blade and upper arm (called *shoulder angulation*) and between the upper and lower thigh and the hock (called *rear angulation*).

aspergillus: A fungal infection, either of the nose or entire body, to which German Shepherds seem to be predisposed.

autoimmune disease: A defect of the body's immune system in which the immune system reacts to components of its own body as though they were foreign invaders. Both dogs and humans can acquire autoimmune dysfunctions.

backyard breeder: An uninformed person who breeds dogs irresponsibly.

BARF: Bones and raw food diet (see Chapter 7).

bitch: A female canine.

bite: Occlusion, or the way the teeth interdigitate. Also refers to how hard a dog bites in protection work.

bloat: See gastric dilatation volvulus.

breed warden: The local representative of the SV who evaluates prospective breedings and inspects litters.

Bundesleistungshueten: The German national herding trial.

castration: Removal of the testicles to render a dog unable to breed. Also known as *neutering*.

cauda equina syndrome: A group of neurological signs resulting from compression of spinal nerves (known as the *cauda equina*) as a result of narrowing of the lumbosacral vertebral canal. The condition is most common in large dogs, and especially in German Shepherds.

CBC (complete blood count): A test that counts or estimates the cells making up a blood sample, including red blood cells, white blood cells, and platelets.

chem panel: A test that measures various chemical elements in the blood. Formally known as a *blood chemistry panel.*

coarse: A term used by a dog show judge or in a breed survey to describe a dog who is large-boned and lacking in refinement.

conformation: The structure of a dog. Conformation shows evaluate how well a dog conforms to the breed standard.

Cushing's syndrome: Hyperadrenocorticism, a hormonal imbalance seen mostly in older dogs. It results from overproduction of cortisol by the cortex of the adrenal gland. Most cases are caused by enlargement of the cortex, which in turn most often occurs because of an adrenal or pituitary tumor.

dam: The mother of a puppy or litter.

degenerative myelopathy: A progressive disease in which a dog gradually loses control of his hind limbs and then his forelimbs.

demodicosis: Demodectic mange, also called *red mange.* Although most dogs have the demodex canis mite as a normal inhabitant of their hair follicles, for unknown reasons in some dogs the mites proliferate to the extent that hair is lost. These dogs may have localized or generalized demodicosis.

Deutsche Schaferhunde: German for German Shepherd Dog.

disqualification: A trait that renders a dog ineligible to compete in AKC, CKC, or SV conformation shows, and in some venues ineligible for breeding.

distemper: An extremely contagious and serious viral disease against which all dogs should be immunized.

dominance aggression: Aggressive behavior aimed at being top dog, even over the owner.

double-handling: Having a second person attract a dog's attention from outside the show ring so that the dog will look alert. Also known as *doubling.*

drive: When analyzing movement, this term refers to a strong thrust from the hindquarters. When analyzing behavior, it refers to a strong motivation, most often (but not exclusively) in reference to chase, protection, or play.

elbow dysplasia: Malformation of the elbow joint, often resulting in lameness.

ehrlichiosis: A tick-borne disease that can result in a number of diffuse symptoms, including intermittent fever and decreased production of red blood cells, platelets, and white blood cells.

exocrine pancreatic insufficiency: A disease of the pancreas characterized by a reduction in the normal digestive enzymes secreted by the pancreas into the small intestine, resulting in diarrhea, weight loss, and poor nutrition. It is diagnosed most often in German Shepherds.

flea allergy dermatitis (FAD): An allergic reaction to a flea bite.

flooding: A misguided attempt to cure a dog's fear by overwhelming him with the stimuli that he fears.

flying trot: A trot in which all four feet are suspended off the ground at full extension. The correct movement of a GSD is the flying trot.

furunculosis: See perianal fistula.

gastric dilatation volvulus: A life-threatening condition in which gases become trapped in the stomach, often as a result of the stomach twisting. Large, deep-chested breeds are more susceptible.

gastric torsion: See gastric dilatation volvulus.

Grand Victor (GV): The best of breed male at the GSDCA or GSDCC annual national specialty show.

Grand Victrix (GV): The best of breed female at the GSDCA or GSDCC annual national specialty show.

guard hairs: The longer, smoother, and stiffer hairs that grow through a GSD's undercoat.

GSD pyoderma: A skin infection to which German Shepherds are predisposed.

heartworm: A potentially deadly parasite that lives in the heart and is spread by mosquitoes.

hemophilia: Deficiency in a specific blood-clotting factor. Two types of hemophilia exist: A and B.

Herdengebrauchshund: A herding utility dog title recognized by the SV.

hip dysplasia: Abnormal development of the hip joint in which the ball and socket do not make a snug fit, often resulting in debilitating lameness due to arthritic changes. The condition is found mostly in giant and large breeds, including GSDs.

hot spot (pyotraumatic dermatitis): A moist, reddened area caused by a dog chewing on himself, often in response to an allergic reaction.

hypothyroidism: Decreased production of thyroid hormone, resulting in a wide spectrum of symptoms.

kennel cough: A highly infectious respiratory disease. Formally known as *tracheobronchitis.*

Koerung: The survey system of the SV that recommends whether a dog should be bred.

occlusion: The way the teeth and jaws interlock, often called the *bite.* Normal and desired occlusion in GSDs is a *scissors bite,* in which the upper incisors slide just over the front surface of the lower incisors when the mouth is closed.

OFA (Orthopedic Foundation for Animals): A not-for-profit organization established in 1966 to assist breeders in addressing hip dysplasia. It serves as a registry of dogs for hip and elbow dysplasia, among other disorders. Every dog registered receives an OFA number that records the dog's rating or whether he passed, depending on the condition being tested. A passing OFA rating is highly desirable for breeding stock and may be required by some organizations.

osteochondrosis dissecans: Disruption of normal cartilage growth around some limb joints; loose flaps of cartilage break away and irritate the affected joint, resulting in pain. Lameness is usually evident by the time an affected dog is 1 year old.

osteosarcoma: Malignant bone cancer.

overshot: Occlusion (bite) in which the top incisors are in front of the bottom incisors, with a gap between them. In severe cases, the upper canine teeth may be positioned in front of the lower canine teeth.

pannus: An autoimmune problem in which the cornea of the eye becomes opaque.

panosteitis: An intermittent and transitory inflammation that affects a dog's long bones, resulting in pain, lameness, and sometimes fever. The cause is unknown, but the condition is diagnosed most often in German Shepherds.

parvovirus: An extremely contagious gastrointestinal disease that causes smelly diarrhea, vomiting, and dehydration in puppies. It is an airborne and fecal-borne disease resulting from a virus and can be fatal.

patent ductus arteriosis: The second most commonly diagnosed congenital heart defect in dogs, resulting from the failure of a blood vessel that connects the aorta and the pulmonary artery in fetal dogs to close at birth as it should. The condition causes insufficient blood circulation and often ultimately results in congestive heart failure and death. Surgery to close up the connection is over 90 percent effective.

perianal fistula: A draining tract in the area around the anus.

pink papers: SV registration papers designating that both parents are recommended for breeding.

pituitary dwarfism: A type of hereditary dwarfism in German Shepherds that's caused by lack of growth hormone.

puppy mill: A large-scale breeding operation dealing in many different breeds, usually in substandard conditions.

reach: Length of a dog's forward stride.

rescue: A person or group that rescues animals from bad situations and attempts to place them in new homes. Also, any such rescued animal.

roach: An arched or convex spine with curvature rising from the withers and up over the loins; a camel back.

sable: Black-tipped outer hair in which the base of the hair is lighter in color; the undercoat is usually lighter as well.

saddle: A dark patch over the back.

set up: To pose a dog by hand in the show ring.

Schutzhund: A sport involving a multifaceted approach of tracking, obedience, and protection tests. It was originally designed as one of several ways to test for breed suitability but has rapidly developed into a competitive sport for many enthusiasts. *Schutzhund* is German for "protection."

scissors bite: A bite in which the incisors of the upper jaw overlap and fit snugly against the teeth of the lower jaw.

Seiger: The best male at the annual SV show.

Seigerin: The best female at the annual SV show.

separation anxiety: Abnormal stress in response to an owner's absence.

spay: To surgically remove a bitch's reproductive organs to render her unable to breed; the technical term is *ovariohysterectomy.*

specialty: A prestigious show in which only one breed is shown.

sound: A dog who is healthy in mind and body. When referring to conformation, soundness means that a dog is built and moves correctly, particularly referring to movement as viewed from the front and rear. When referring to temperament, soundness means that a dog is stable and dependable.

stop: As viewed in profile, the depression or "step" denoting the transition point from muzzle to forehead, located roughly between the eyes.

subvalvular aortic stenosis: A congenital heart defect in which the opening between the heart's left ventricle and aorta is abnormally narrow, obstructing the blood flow. The condition can lead to early death.

type: Essential characteristics of the breed.

undershot: A bite in which the top incisors are behind the bottom incisors.

Verein fur Deutsche Schaferhunde (SV): The German club for German Shepherds, and the largest breed club in the world.

veteran: An older dog, usually over 7 years of age.

von Willebrand's disease: A hereditary deficiency in one of the clotting factors (factor VIII) that can result in excessive bleeding. The degree of deficiency varies greatly among affected dogs and can be exacerbated if a dog also has hypothyroidism.

weedy: Lacking sufficient bone and musculature.

withers: The highest point of the shoulders, where a dog's height is normally measured.

WUSV: The World Union of SV clubs. This organization provides a governing function overseeing the breed throughout much of the world.

X-pen: A small, portable enclosure that is made of wire or (occasionally) PVC. It is useful for keeping dogs within a small area when traveling and can also function as a "playpen" for puppies.

Appendix B

Resources

∙ ∙

*H*ere's your one-stop source for all things GSD. Check out the organizations to find out more about registering or competing with your dog. Subscribe to some magazines to keep yourself abreast of current happenings in the dog world. If you want to delve deeper into German Shepherd pedigrees and history, try some of the books gathered here. Finally, for a round-up of some of the best GSD and dog sites on the Web, surf the sites suggested in this appendix.

Organizations

Agility Association of Canada (AAC)
RR#2, Lucan
Ontario N0N 2J0
Canada
519-657-7636

American Kennel Club (AKC)
5580 Centerview Drive
Raleigh, NC 27606-3390
919-233-9767
www.akc.org

American White Shepherd Association
http://onewaits.com/awsaclub

Assistance Dogs International
c/o Canine Partners For Life
334 Faggs Manor Road
Cochranville, PA 19330
610-869-4902
www.assistance-dogs-intl.org

Canine Companions for Independence
(Service, signal, social, and therapy dogs)
P.O. Box 446
Santa Rosa, CA 95402-0446
800-572-2275 (V/TDD)
www.caninecompanions.org

Canine Performance Events (CPE)
P.O. Box 445
Walled Lake, MI 48390
E-mail: cpe-agility@juno.com

Delta Society National Service Dog Center
289 Perimeter Road East
Renton, WA 98055-1329
800-869-6898
http://deltasociety.org/dsb000.htm

Deutscher Verband der Gebrauchshundsportvereine (DVG)
5718 Watson Circle
Dallas, TX 75225
214-361-0183
webusers.anet-stl.com/~dvgamer/

German Shepherd Dog Club of America
4120 Douglas Blvd. #306-102
Granite Bay, CA 95746-9437
916-791-5642
www.gsdca.org

**German Shepherd Dog Club of America:
Working Dog Association**
c/o Martylou Plinski
5649 Sweigert Road
San Jose, CA 95132-3402
408-262-8064
www.gsdca-wda.org

German Shepherd Dog Club of Canada
RR 3
Fergus, ON N1M 2W4
Canada
http://juliet.albedo.net/~gsdcc/

German Shepherd Rescue
417 North Moss Street
Burbank, CA 91502
818-558-7560
www.GSRescue.org

The Kennel Club
1-5 Clarges Street
Picadilly
London W1Y 8AB
www.the-kennel-club.org.uk

**North American Dog Agility Council
(NADAC)**
HCR 2 Box 277
St. Maries, ID 83861
208-689-3803
www.nadac.com

**North American Police Work Dog
Association**
4222 Manchester Avenue
Perry, OH 44081
888-4CANINE
www.napwda.com

**North American Ring Association
(French Ring Sport)**
618 Laurel Avenue SE
Grand Rapids, MI 49506
www.cybertours.com/~pettrain/
narahome.htm

Orthopedic Foundation for Animals
2300 East Nifong Boulevard
Columbia, MO 65201
573-442-0418
www.offa.org

Paws with a Cause
4646 South Division
Wayland, MI 49348
616-877-PAWS (TDD/voice)
800-253-PAWS (TDD/voice)
www.ismi.net/paws/

PennHip
271 Great Valley Parkway
Malvern, PA 19355
800-248-8099
www.vet.upenn.edu/pennhip/

Rin Tin Tin Canine Ambassador Club
P.O. Box 1505
Rosenberg, TX 77471
281-239-7106
www.rintintin.org/ambassador

United Kennel Club (UKC)
100 East Kilgore Road
Kalamazoo, MI 49002-5584
616-343-9020
www.ukcdogs.com

**United Schutzhund Clubs of America
(USA)**
3810 Paule Avenue
St. Louis, MO 63125-1718
314-638-9686
www.germanshepherddog.com

**United States Dog Agility Association
(USDAA)**
109 South Kirby Street
Richardson, TX 75085-0955
972-231-9700
www.usdaa.com

Verein fur Deutsche Schaferhunde (SV)
Steinerne Furt 71/71a
D-86167 Augsburg
Germany
www.schaeferhund.de

**White German Shepherd Dog Club
International, Inc.**
P.O. Box 70222
Salt Lake City, UT 84170-0222
www2.aros.net/~wgsdcii

Magazines

AKC Gazette
Official Publication of the
American Kennel Club
260 Madison Avenue
New York, NY 10016
800-533-7323
919-233-9767
www.akc.org

Canadian GSD Gazette
Available through the GSD Club of Canada

Clean Run (Agility)
35 Walnut Street
Turners Falls, MA 01376
800-311-6503
www.cleanrun.com

Dog Fancy
3 Burroughs
Irvine, CA 92618
949-855-8822
www.dogfancy.com

Dog Sports magazine (Covers protection,
Schutzhund, and search and rescue)
231 Orin Way
Douglas, WY 82633-9232
307-358-3487
www.cyberpet.com/cyberdog/
products/pubmag/dgsptmag.htm

Dog World Magazine
P.O. Box 56240
Boulder, CO 80322-6240
800-361-8506
www.dogworldmag.com

DVG America
Available through Deutscher Verband der
Gebrauchshundsportvereine (DVG)

German Shepherd Dog Quarterly
Hoflin Publishing
4401 Zephyr St.
Wheat Ridge, CO 80033
303-420-2222
web.hoflin.com/Magazines/
The%20German%20Shepherd%20Qrtly.
html

German Shepherd Dog Review
Editor: Gail Sprock
190C North Abrego
Green Valley, AZ 85614
E-mail: gsreview@azstarnet.com

Schutzhund USA
Available through United Schutzhund
Clubs of America

The Shepherd's Din (White GSDs)
Available through White German Shepherd
Dog Club International, Inc.

Web Sites

Conformation Showing *Auf Deutshe!* (Describes the SV conformation show system):
www.ultranet.com/~reiher/conformat.html

Conformation showing AKC/CKC (Site and e-mail list for people interested in conformation competition in the American or Canadian system):
www.userhome.com/showgsd

Dog Agility Page (A comprehensive site about the sport of dog agility):
www.dogpatch.org/agility/

German Shepherds in herding (Describes the varied ways in which GSDs participate in herding): www.geocities.com/Heartland/Ranch/5093/

GSD Infoline (Extensive site for various aspects of GSD information, in English and German): www.gsd-infoline.com/index-e.htm

GSD Ring of GSD sites on the Web (Go to a new GSD site with every click!): dbirtwis.interspeed.net/gsdring.html

Information about responsible breeding: www.dog-play.com/ethics.html

List of GSD e-mail discussion lists (Some of the best Internet GSD lists; find one that interests you): dbirtwis.interspeed.net/lists.html

List of local GSD clubs (The most complete and up-to-date listing of GSD organizations near you): www.cheta.net/connect/canine/Clubs/germshep.htm

National Animal Poison Control Center (The site to visit if you think that your dog has ingested poison; bookmark it!): www.napcc.aspca.org/

National Association for Search and Rescue (NASAR) dog/handler guidelines (Gives you all the details on training for search and rescue): www.nasar.org/prod/members/canine/caninegd.htm

Obedience Home Page for the sport of dog obedience (A comprehensive site for those interested in competing in obedience trials): www.princeton.edu/~nadelman/obed/obed.html

Rainbow Bridge Tribute Page dealing with the loss of a pet: rainbowbridge.tierranet.com/bridge.htm

The Tracking Page (Site for people interested in training or competing in tracking): personal.cfw.com/~dtratnac/

VetMedCenter (The most comprehensive veterinary information center on the Web): www.vetmedcenter.com

Working Dogs (Extensive links dealing with GSD performance and work): workingdogs.com/doc0007.htm

Working Dogs International Cyberzine (An online magazine about GSD sports): www.workingdogs.com/

WUSV GSD breed standard: sentex.net/~sirius/breed_standard.htm

WUSV information: www.tp-hundeguide.dk/index/wusv/index.htm

Videos

The AKC German Shepherd Standard
Video #VVT 812
AKC
Attn: Video fulfillment
5580 Centerview Drive
Raleigh, NC 27606-3390
919-233-9767

Complete line of GSD training videos and equipment, including obedience, tracking, Schutzhund, and police work:

Leerburg Video
P.O. Box 218
Menomonie, WI 54751
715-235-6502
leerburg.com/table.htm

German Shepherd: Structure
German Shepherd: Gait
German Shepherd: Handling
All three videos produced by Canine Training Center, 1998
www.dogandcatbooks.com

Appendix C

The Official AKC Breed Standard for the German Shepherd Dog

Temperament — The breed has a distinct personality marked by direct and fearless, but not hostile, expression, self-confidence and a certain aloofness that does not lend itself to immediate and indiscriminate friendships. The dog must be approachable, quietly standing its ground and showing confidence and willingness to meet overtures without itself making them. It is poised, but when the occasion demands, eager and alert; both fit and willing to serve in its capacity as companion, watchdog, blind leader, herding dog or guardian, whichever the circumstances may demand. The dog must not be timid, shrinking behind its master or handler; it should not be nervous, looking about or upward with anxious expression or showing nervous reactions, such as tucking of tail, to strange sounds or sights. Lack of confidence under any surroundings is not typical of good character. Any of the above deficiencies in character which indicate shyness must be penalized as very *serious faults* and any dog exhibiting pronounced indications of these must be excused from the ring. It must be possible for the judge to observe the teeth and to determine that both testicles are descended. Any dog that attempts to bite the judge must be *disqualified.* The ideal dog is a working animal with an incorruptible character combined with body and gait suitable for the arduous work that constitutes its primary purpose.

General Appearance — The first impression of a good German Shepherd Dog is that of a strong, agile, well muscled animal, alert and full of life. It is well balanced, with harmonious development of the forequarter and hindquarter. The dog is longer than tall, deep-bodied, and presents an outline of smooth curves rather than angles. It looks substantial and not spindly, giving the impression, both at rest and in motion, of muscular fitness and nimbleness without any look of clumsiness or soft living. The ideal dog is stamped with a look of quality and nobility — difficult to define, but unmistakable when present. Secondary sex characteristics are strongly marked, and every animal gives a definite impression of masculinity or femininity, according to its sex.

Size, Proportion, Substance — The desired *height* for males at the top of the highest point of the shoulder blade is 24 to 26 inches; and for bitches, 22 to 24 inches.

The German Shepherd Dog is longer than tall, with the most desirable *proportion* as 10 to 8½. The length is measured from the point of the prosternum or breastbone to the rear edge of the pelvis, the ischial tuberosity. The desirable long proportion is not derived from a long back, but from overall length with relation to height, which is achieved by length of forequarter and length of withers and hindquarter, viewed from the side.

Head — The *head* is noble, cleanly chiseled, strong without coarseness, but above all not fine, and in proportion to the body. The head of the male is distinctly masculine, and that of the bitch distinctly feminine.

The *expression* keen, intelligent and composed. *Eyes* of medium size, almond shaped, set a little obliquely and not protruding. The color is as dark as possible. *Ears* are moderately pointed, in proportion to the skull, open toward the front, and carried erect when at attention, the ideal carriage being one in which the center lines of the ears, viewed from the front, are parallel to each other and perpendicular to the ground. A dog with cropped or hanging ears must be *disqualified.*

Seen from the front the forehead is only moderately arched, and the *skull* slopes into the long, wedge-shaped muzzle without abrupt stop. The *muzzle* is long and strong, and its topline is parallel to the topline of the skull. *Nose* black. A dog with a nose that is not predominantly black must be *disqualified.* The lips are firmly fitted. Jaws are strongly developed. *Teeth* — 42 in number — 20 upper and 22 lower — are strongly developed and meet in a scissors bite in which part of the inner surface of the upper incisors meet and engage part of the outer surface of the lower incisors. An overshot jaw or a level bite is undesirable. An undershot jaw is a *disqualifying fault.* Complete dentition is to be preferred. Any missing teeth other than first premolars is a *serious fault.*

Neck, Topline, Body — The *neck* is strong and muscular, clean-cut and relatively long, proportionate in size to the head and without loose folds of skin. When the dog is at attention or excited, the head is raised and the neck carried high; otherwise typical carriage of the head is forward rather than up and but little higher than the top of the shoulders, particularly in motion.

Topline — The *withers* are higher than and sloping into the level back. The *back* is straight, very strongly developed without sag or roach, and relatively short.

The whole structure of the *body* gives an impression of depth and solidity without bulkiness.

Chest — Commencing at the prosternum, it is well filled and carried well down between the legs. It is deep and capacious, never shallow, with ample room for lungs and heart, carried well forward, with the prosternum showing ahead of the shoulder in profile. *Ribs* well sprung and long, neither barrel-shaped nor too flat, and carried down to a sternum which reaches to the elbows. Correct ribbing allows the elbows to move back freely when the dog is at a trot. Too round causes interference and throws the elbows out; too flat or short causes pinched elbows. Ribbing is carried well back so that the loin is relatively short. *Abdomen* firmly held and not paunchy. The bottom line is only moderately tucked up in the loin.

Loin — Viewed from the top, broad and strong. Undue length between the last rib and the thigh, when viewed from the side, is undesirable. *Croup* long and gradually sloping.

Tail bushy, with the last vertebra extended at least to the hock joint. It is set smoothly into the croup and low rather than high. At rest, the tail hangs in a slight curve like a saber. A slight hook — sometimes carried to one side — is faulty only to the extent that it mars general appearance. When the dog is excited or in motion, the curve is accentuated and the tail raised, but it should never be curled forward beyond a vertical line. Tails too short, or with clumpy ends due to ankylosis, are *serious faults*. A dog with a docked tail must be *disqualified*.

Forequarters — The shoulder blades are long and obliquely angled, laid on flat and not placed forward. The upper arm joins the shoulder blade at about a right angle. Both the upper arm and the shoulder blade are well muscled. The forelegs, viewed from all sides, are straight and the bone oval rather than round. The pasterns are strong and springy and angulated at approximately a 25-degree angle from the vertical. Dewclaws on the forelegs may be removed but are normally left on.

The *feet* are short, compact with toes well arched, pads thick and firm, nails short and dark.

Hindquarters — The whole assembly of the thigh, viewed from the side, is broad, with both upper and lower thigh well muscled, forming as nearly as possible a right angle. The upper thigh bone parallels the shoulder blade while the lower thigh bone parallels the upper arm. The metatarsus (the unit between the hock joint and the foot) is short, strong and tightly articulated. The dewclaws, if any, should be removed from the hind legs. Feet as in front.

Coat — The ideal dog has a double coat of medium length. The outer coat should be as dense as possible, hair straight, harsh and lying close to the body. A slightly wavy outer coat, often of wiry texture, is permissible. The head, including the inner ear and foreface, and the legs and paws are covered with short hair, and the neck with longer and thicker hair. The rear of the forelegs and hind legs has somewhat longer hair extending to the pastern and hock, respectively. *Faults* in coat include soft, silky, too long outer coat, woolly, curly, and open coat.

Color — The German Shepherd Dog varies in color, and most colors are permissible. Strong rich colors are preferred. Pale, washed-out colors and blues or livers are *serious faults*. A white dog must be *disqualified*.

Gait — The German Shepherd Dog is a trotting dog, and its structure has been developed to meet the requirements of its work. *General Impression* — The gait is outreaching, elastic, seemingly without effort, smooth and rhythmic, covering the maximum amount of ground with the minimum number of steps. At a walk it covers a great deal of ground, with long stride of both hind legs and forelegs. At a trot the dog covers still more ground with even longer stride, and moves powerfully but easily, with coordination and balance so that the gait appears to be the steady motion of a well-lubricated machine. The feet travel close to the ground on both forward reach and backward push. In order to achieve ideal movement of this kind, there must be good muscular development and ligamentation. The hindquarters deliver, through the back, a powerful forward thrust which slightly lifts the whole animal and drives the body forward. Reaching far under, and passing the imprint left by the front foot, the hind foot takes hold of the ground; then hock, stifle and upper thigh come into play and sweep back, the stroke of the hind leg finishing with the foot still close to the ground in a smooth follow-through. The overreach of the hindquarter usually necessitates one hind foot passing outside and the other hind foot passing inside the track of the forefeet, and such action is not faulty unless the locomotion is crabwise with the dog's body sideways out of the normal straight line.

Transmission — The typical smooth, flowing gait is maintained with great strength and firmness of back. The whole effort of the hindquarter is transmitted to the forequarter through the loin, back and withers. At full trot, the back must remain firm and level without sway, roll, whip or roach. Unlevel topline with withers lower than the hip is a *fault*. To compensate for the forward motion imparted by the hindquarters, the shoulder should open to its full extent. The forelegs should reach out close to the ground in a long stride in harmony with that of the hindquarters. The dog does not track on widely separated parallel lines, but brings the feet inward toward the middle line of the body when trotting, in order to maintain balance. The feet track closely but do not strike or cross over. Viewed from the front, the front legs function from the shoulder joint to the pad in a straight line. Viewed from the rear, the hind legs function from the hip joint to the pad in a straight line. Faults of gait, whether from front, rear or side, are to be considered very *serious faults*.

Disqualifications

Cropped or hanging ears.

Dogs with noses not predominantly black.

Undershot jaw.

Docked tail.

White dogs.

Any dog that attempts to bite the judge.

GSD Abbreviations

· ·

*T*he number of titles awarded by various organizations is growing constantly. You can find the latest updates at `www.redstonegroup.org/GSD/` under Titles.

Organizations

AKC: American Kennel Club

CKC: Canadian Kennel Club

CKC: Continental Kennel Club (not to be confused with the Canadian KC)

DHV: *Deutscher Hundesport Verein* (German Dog Sport Club)

DVG: *Deutscher Verband der Gebrauchshundsport Vereine e.V.* (German member of DHV)

DVG America: American DVG region

FCI: *Fédération Cynologique Internationale* (World Dog Club)

GSDCA: German Shepherd Dog Club of America

GSDCA-WDA: German Shepherd Dog Club of America — Working Dog Association

GSDCC: German Shepherd Dog Club of Canada

GSSCC: German Shepherd Schutzhund Club of Canada

KC: Kennel Club (Great Britain)

SV: *Verein für Deutsche Schäferhunde* (German Shepherd Dog Club)

UKC: United Kennel Club

USA: United Schutzhund Clubs of America

VDH: *Verein für Deutsche Hundeswesen* (German member of FCI)

WUSV: World Union of Schäferhunde Vereins (World Union of GSD clubs)

Conformation Awards

North American All-Breed and German Shepherd Kennel Club Awards

AOE: Award of Excellence (GSDCA: Dog must have OFA-certified hips and elbows, have a recognized working title, and be temperament certified by the GSDCA)

AOM: Award of Merit (AKC: Awarded by judges at special events denoting that the dog was in serious contention for Best of Breed)

BIF: Best in Futurity (an annual GSDCC/GSDCA competition for young dogs)

BIM: Best in Maturity (an annual GSDCC/GSDCA competition for dogs who were eligible for Futurity competition the preceding year)

BIS: Best in Show (all-breed show award, awarded to the best of the seven Group Winners)

BISS: Best in Sweepstakes or Best in Specialty Show (Canada)

BOB: Best of Breed

BOF: Best of Opposite Sex in Futurity

BOG: Best of Group

BOM: Best of Opposite Sex in Maturity

BOS: Best of Opposite Sex (awarded to the best dog of the opposite sex to the Best of Breed winner)

BOW: Best of Winners (awarded to the best dog, between Winners Dog and Winners Bitch)

BP: Best Puppy (of breed)

BPIS: Best Puppy in Show (best puppy of all breeds at an all-breed show)

BOP: Best of Opposite Sex Puppy (opposite sex to BP)

CH: Champion

FV: Futurity Victor (BIF/BOF male at GSDCA National Futurity Finals)

FVX: Futurity Victrix (BIF/BOF female at GSDCA National Futurity Finals)

Group I (or II, III, and IV): Ranking in Herding Group competition at all-breed shows

GV: Grand Victor (BOB/BOS male at GSDCA/GSDCC national)

GVX: Grand Victrix (BOB/BOS female at GSDCA/GSDCC national)

MV: Maturity Victor (BIM/BOM male at GSDCA National Maturity Finals)

MVX: Maturity Victrix (BIM/BOM female at GSDCA National Maturity Finals)

ROM: Register of Merit (GSDCA: A dog or bitch achieves this designation through the conformation and performance accomplishments of his or her progeny)

ROMC: Register of Merit (GSDCC)

RWB: Reserve Winners Bitch (runner-up to Winners Bitch)

RWD: Reserve Winners Dog (runner-up to Winners Dog)

SEL: Select (GSDCA: Awarded by judges who may find that although a dog is not the best dog of the day at the National Specialty Show, he was seriously considered for BOB)

WB: Winners Bitch (best bitch shown in the regular classes; awarded points toward her championship)

WD: Winners Dog (best dog shown in regular classes; awarded points toward his championship)

International (FCI) Awards

CACIB: *Certificat d'Aptitude au Championat International de Beauté,* European International Champion

SV Awards

A: *Ausreichend* (sufficient show or performance rating)

G: *Gut* (good show or performance rating)

KKLI: *Körklasse* 1 (rated especially recommended for breeding by the SV)

KKLII: *Körklasse* 2 (rated suitable for breeding by the SV)

Körung (Breed Survey)

Lbz.: *Lebenszeit* (breed surveyed for life)

M: *Mangelhaft* (faulty show or performance rating)

SG: *Sehr Gut* (very good show or performance rating)

Sieger: Grand Victor at the National Sieger show (VA-1)

Siegerin: Grand Victrix at the National Sieger show (VA-1)

U: *Ungenugend* (insufficient show or performance rating)

V: *Vorzüglich* (excellent show or performance rating)

VA: *Vorzüglich-Auslese* (Excellent Select show rating given only at Sieger show)

VH: *Vorhanden* (sufficient show or performance rating)

Agility Titles

Agility Association of Canada

ADC/SADC/VADC: Agility/Special Agility/Veteran Agility Dog of Canada (first level AAC title requiring three legs under two different judges)

AADC/SAADC/VAADC: Advanced/Special Advanced/Veteran Advanced Agility Dog of Canada (second level AAC title requiring three legs under two different judges)

MADC/SMADC/VMADC: Master/Special Master/Veteran Master Agility Dog of Canada (third level AAC title requiring seven legs — three started, four advanced)

MGDC/SMGDC/VMGDC: Masters/Special Masters/Veteran Masters Gamblers Dog of Canada (requiring three legs)

MJDC/SMJDC/VMJDC: Masters/Special Masters/Veteran Masters Jumpers Dog of Canada (requiring three legs)

MSDC/SMSDC/VMSDC: Masters/Special Masters/Veteran Masters Snooker Dog of Canada (requiring three legs)

MTRDC/SMTRDC/VMTRDC: Masters/Special Masters/Veteran Masters Team Relay Dog of Canada (requiring three legs)

ATChC/SATChC/VATChC: Agility/Special Agility/Veteran Agility Trial Champion of Canada (requiring MADC/SMADC/VMADC + MSDC/SMSDC/VMSDC + MGDC/SMGDC/VMGDC + MTRDC/SMTRDC/VMTRDC + MJDC/SMJDC/VMJDC)

American Kennel Club

NA: Novice Agility (first level AKC agility title requiring three legs under two different judges)

OA: Open Agility (second level AKC agility title requiring three legs under two different judges)

AX: Agility Excellent (third level AKC agility title requiring three legs under two different judges)

MX: Master Agility Excellent (fourth level AKC agility title requiring ten legs)

NAJ: Novice Jumpers With Weaves (first level AKC agility title requiring three legs under two different judges)

OAJ: Open Jumpers With Weaves (second level AKC agility title requiring three legs under two different judges)

AXJ: Excellent Jumpers With Weaves (third level AKC agility title requiring three legs under two different judges)

MXJ: Master Excellent Jumpers With Weaves (fourth level AKC agility title requiring ten legs)

MACH: Master Agility Champion (requiring 750 championship points and 20 double qualifying runs)

United Kennel Club

U-AgI-II: Agility Level 1–2 (each level requiring three qualifying scores at three different UKC events)

U-ACH: Agility Champion (requiring the accumulation of 100 points, at least 40 of which must be obtained from the Agility II Class)

U-ACHX: Agility Champion Excellent (U-ACH + receiving five qualifying scores at five different UKC events)

United States Dog Agility Association

AD/VAD: Agility/Veteran Agility Dog (requiring three clear rounds under two different judges)

AAD/AVAD: Advanced/Veteran Advanced Agility Dog (requiring three clear rounds under two different judges)

MAD/MVAD: Master/Veteran Master Agility Dog (requiring nine clear rounds under five different judges plus a qualifying score at the masters in each of the following from at least two different judges: Gamblers Competition, Pairs or Team Relay, Jumping Class, Snooker Competition)

GM/VG: Gambler Master (requiring five clear rounds under at least two different judges)

JM/VJ: Jumpers Master (requiring five clear rounds under at least two different judges)

RM: Relay Master (requiring five clear rounds under at least two different judges)

SM/VS: Snooker Master (requiring five clear rounds under at least two different judges)

VPD: Veteran Performance Dog (requiring MVAD +VG + VJ + VS)

ADCH: Agility Dog Champion (requiring MAD + GM + JM + RM + SM)

PDI: Performance Dog I (requiring three clear rounds under two different judges)

PDII: Performance Dog II (requiring three clear rounds under two different judges)

PDIII: Performance Dog III (requiring three clear rounds under two different judges)

PG: Performance Gambler (requiring five clear rounds under at least two different judges)

PJ: Performance Jumper (requiring five clear rounds under at least two different judges)

PS: Performance Snooker (requiring five clear rounds under at least two different judges)

APD: Advanced Performance Dog (requiring PDIII + PG + PJ + PS + four additional qualifying scores)

Herding Titles

Australian Shepherd Club of America

Trial titles are stock specific — d = ducks, s = sheep, c = cattle.

STD (class of stock): Started Trial Dog(class of stock) (requiring two qualifying scores under two different judges)

OTD (class of stock): Open Trial Dog(class of stock) (requiring two qualifying scores under two different judges)

ATD (class of stock): Advanced Trial Dog(class of stock) (requiring two qualifying scores under two different judges)

PATD (class of stock): Post-Advanced Trial Dog(class of stock) (requiring two qualifying scores under two different judges)

RTD (class of stock): Ranch Trial Dog(class of stock) (requiring one qualifying score)

RD: Ranch Dog (awarded by individual certification by judges on the dog's home ranch doing everyday tasks)

WTCh: Working Trial Championship (requiring an ATD on all three types of stock)

American Herding Breed Association

Trial titles are stock specific — d = ducks, s = sheep, c = cattle.

HCT: Herding Capability Tested (requiring two qualifying legs under two different judges)

JHD: Junior Herding Dog (requiring two qualifying legs under two different judges)

HTD I–III (class of stock): Herding Trial Dog 1–3(class of stock) (requiring two qualifying legs under two different judges)

HRD I–III (class of stock): Herding Ranch Dog 1–3(class of stock) (requiring two qualifying legs under two different judges)

HTCh: Herding Trial Champion (requiring ten points under three different judges, with no more than three points on ducks or geese)

American Kennel Club

Test/trial titles are stock specific — d = ducks, s = sheep, c = cattle; and trial titles are course specific — A = A course, B = B course, C = C course.

HT(class of stock): Herding Tested(class of stock) (requiring two legs under two different judges)

PT(class of stock): Pre-trial Tested(class of stock) (requiring two legs under two different judges)

HS(course)(class of stock): Herding Started(course)(class of stock) (requiring three legs under three different judges)

HI(course)(class of stock): Herding Intermediate(course)(class of stock) (requiring three legs under three different judges)

HX(course)(class of stock): Herding Excellent(course)(class of stock) (requiring three legs under three different judges)

HC/HCH: Herding Champion (requiring HX plus 15 championship points and at least two first-place finishes)

HIT: High in Trial

RHIT: Reserve High in Trial

Canadian Kennel Club

HT: Herding Tested (requires two legs under two different judges)

HS: Herding Started (requires three qualifying scores under at least two different judges)

HI: Herding Intermediate (requires three qualifying scores under at least two different judges)

HA: Herding Advanced (requires three qualifying scores under at least two different judges)

SV

HGH: *Herdengebrauchshund* (Herding Utility Dog)

Hutesieger: Champion Herding Dog

Various clubs

HIC: Herding Instinct Certified

Obedience Titles

AKC and CKC — North American Kennel Clubs

CD: Companion Dog (requires three qualifying scores under three different judges)

CDX: Companion Dog Excellent (requires three qualifying scores under three different judges)

UD: Utility Dog (requires three qualifying scores under three different judges)

UDX: Utility Dog Excellent (requires ten qualifying scores)

UDTD/UDT: Utility Dog Tracker (UD + TD)

UDTDX/UDTX: Utility Dog Tracker Excellent (UD + TDX)

UDXTD: Utility Dog Excellent Tracking Dog (UDX + TD)

UDXTDX: Utility Dog Excellent Tracking Dog Excellent (UDX + TDX)

UDVST: Utility Dog Variable Surface Tracking (UD + VST)

UDXVST: Utility Dog Excellent Variable Surface Tracking (UDX + VST)

OTCh: Obedience Trial Champion (requiring 100 points plus three first-place finishes under three different judges)

NOC: National Obedience Champion (winner of the National Obedience Championship)

HC: High Combined (High combined score from the Open B and Utility B classes at the same show)

HIT: High in Trial

RHIT: Reserve High in Trial

United Kennel Club

U-CD: Companion Dog (requires three qualifying scores under two different judges)

U-CDX: Companion Dog Excellence (requires three qualifying scores under two different judges)

U-UD: Utility Dog (requires three qualifying scores under two different judges)

U-OCH: Obedience Champion (requires 100 championship points plus a qualifying score in the Open B and Utility B classes at the same trial, with a combined score of 370 or above at five trials)

SV (and SV-recognized titles)

AD: *Ausdauerpruefung* (SV endurance title)

BlH: *Blindenhund* (Guide Dog for the Blind)

BPA: *Bundessiegerprüfung* (German National Working Show)

BpDH I–II: *Bahnpolizeidiensthund* (Railroad Police Service Dog)

Bundesleistungssieger (German National Working Dog Champion)

Bundeszuchtsieger (Conformation winner at the German National All-Breed show)

DH: *Diensthund* (Service Dog)

DPH: *Dienstpolizeihund* (Service Police Dog)

GrH: *Grenzenhund* (Border Patrol Dog)

IPO I–III: *Internationale Prüfungs-Ordnung* level 1–3 (international version of Schutzhund titles)

Junghundsieger [winner of the young class (12–18) at the Sieger show]

KNPV: Ring work

Landessieger (winner at the Regional SchH III competition)

LawH: *Lawinen Hund* (Avalance Rescue Dog)

PFP I–II: *Polizeifahrtenhund* (Police Tracking Dog)

PH: *Polizeihund* (Police Dog)

PSP I–II: *Polizeischutzhundprüfung* (Police Protection Dog)

SchHA: *Schutzhundprüfung* A (Novice Schutzhund obedience and protection)

Sch I–III: *Schutzhundprüfung* 1 (novice) – 3 (master level)

WH: Schutzhund title related to protection work

ZH I–II: *Zollhund* (Customs Dog)

Temperament Certifications

CGC: Canine Good Citizen (AKC)

TDI: Therapy Dog International Certification (TDI)

BH: German Companion Dog (SV)

TT: Temperament Tested (awarded by the American Temperament Test Society)

TC: Temperament Certificate (awarded by the GSDCA)

Tracking Titles

American Kennel Club
TD: Tracking Dog (requires one passing track)

TDX: Tracking Dog Excellent (requires one passing track)

VST: Variable Surface Tracker (requires one passing track)

UDTD/UDT: Utility Dog Tracker (UD + TD)

UDTDX/UDTX: Utility Dog Tracker Excellent (UD + TDX)

UDXTD: Utility Dog Excellent Tracking Dog (UDX + TD)

UDXTDX: Utility Dog Excellent Tracking Dog Excellent (UDX + TDX)

UDVST: Utility Dog Variable Surface Tracking (UD + VST)

UDXVST: Utility Dog Excellent Variable Surface Tracking (UDX + VST)

CT: Champion Tracker (TD + TDX + VST)

Canadian Kennel Club

TD: Tracking Dog

TDX: Tracking Dog Excellent

UDT: Utility Dog Tracker (UD + TD)

UDTX: Utility Dog Tracker Excellent (UD + TDX)

CT: Champion Tracker

SV

FH I–III: *Fahrtenhund* level 1–3

Versatile Companion Dog

American Kennel Club

VCD1: Versatile Companion Dog 1 (CD + NA + NAJ + TD)

VCD2: Versatile Companion Dog 2 (CDX + OA + OAJ + TDX)

VCD3: Versatile Companion Dog 3 (UD + AX + AJX + TDX)

VCD4: Versatile Companion Dog 4 (UDX + MX + MXJ + VST)

VCCH: Versatile Companion Champion (OTCH + MACH + CT)

Index

From the pet experts at Howell Book House, titles of interest to German Shepherd enthusiasts:

Books on German Shepherds:

The German Shepherd Today
By Winifred Gibson Strickland and
James A. Moses
ISBN 0-87605-154-9
$29.95

The Ultimate German Shepherd Dog
By Sheila Rankin
ISBN 0-87605-035-6
$34.95

Training guides:

Dog Behavior: An Owner's Guide to a Happy, Healthy Pet
By Ian Dunbar
ISBN 0-87605-236-7
$12.95

Dog-Friendly Dog Training
By Andrea Arden
ISBN 1-58245-009-9
$17.95

DogPerfect: The User-Friendly Guide to a Well-Behaved Dog
By Sarah Hodgson
ISBN 0-87605-534-X
$12.95

Dog Training in 10 Minutes
By Carol Lea Benjamin
ISBN 0-87605-471-8
$14.95

Activities/General:

All About Agility
By Jacqueline O'Neil
ISBN 1-58245-123-0
$12.95

Canine Good Citizen: Every Dog Can Be One
By Jack and Wendy Volhard
ISBN 0-87605-452-1
$14.95

The Complete Dog Book, 19th Edition, Revised
By The American Kennel Club
ISBN 0-87605-047-X
$32.95

Flyball Racing: The Dog Sport for Everyone
By Lonnie Olson
ISBN 0-87605-630-3
$14.95

Schutzhund: Theory and Training Methods
By Susan Barwig and Stewart Hilliard
ISBN 0-87605-731-8
$24.95

Search and Rescue Dogs Training Methods
By American Rescue Dog Association
ISBN 0-87605-733-4
$24.95